Using Microsoft® Word 4

Macintosh® Version

Bryan Pfaffenberger

QUE™
CORPORATION
LEADING COMPUTER KNOWLEDGE

Using Microsoft® Word 4

Macintosh® Version

Copyright © 1989 by Que® Corporation

Library of Congress Catalog No.: 89-60843

ISBN 0-88022-451-7

92 91 90 89   8 7 6 5 4 3 2

Interpretation of the printing code: the rightmost double-digit number is the year of the book's printing; the rightmost single-digit number, the number of the book's printing. For example, a printing code of 89-1 shows that the first printing of the book occurred in 1989.

Using Microsoft Word 4: Macintosh Version is based on Microsoft Word 4 for the Macintosh, Versions 3 and 4.

DEDICATION

To Suzanne

Publishing Manager

Lloyd J. Short

Production Editors

Jeannine Freudenberger
Gregory Robertson

Editors

Sara Allaei
Jo Anna Arnott
Sandra Blackthorn
Fran Blauw
Kelly D. Dobbs
Alice Martina Smith

Technical Editor

Christopher Mascis

Editorial Assistant

Stacie Lamborne

Indexer

Brown Editorial Service

Book Design and Production

Dan Armstrong
Brad Chinn
David Kline
Lori A. Lyons
Jennifer Matthews
Mitzi Parsons
Cindy L. Phipps
Joe Ramon
Dennis Sheehan
Louise Shinault

Composed in Times Roman and Excellent No. 47
by Que Corporation

ABOUT THE AUTHOR

Bryan Pfaffenberger

A nationally known writer on computer-related topics, Bryan Pfaffenberger, Ph.D., teaches in the School of Engineering and Applied Science at the University of Virginia, where he is Assistant Professor of Humanities. He is contributing editor of the *Research in Word Processing Newsletter* and the author of more than a dozen books, including *Microsoft Word Techniques and Applications*; *Microsoft Word Tips, Tricks, and Traps*, 2nd Edition; *Using Microsoft Word 5: IBM Version*; and *Using Sprint*, all published by Que Corporation; and *Microcomputer Applications in Qualitative Research*, published by Sage. Dr. Pfaffenberger's interests include the social history and sociology of technology, international studies (he is the Associate Director of the University of Virginia's Center for South Asian Studies), and the anthropology of science and engineering. Dr. Pfaffenberger also enjoys spending time with his children. He lives in Charlottesville, Virginia.

Contents at a Glance

TABLE OF CONTENTS ⑭

I   Getting Started with Word 4

II   Word 4 Fundamentals

III   Word 4's Features and Applications

ACKNOWLEDGMENTS

A project like this one requires help from many people, and even though I alone take responsibility for this book's shortcomings, I would like to thank Lloyd Short, publishing manager; Jeannine Freudenberger and Greg Robertson, production editors; Christopher Mascis, technical editor; and the other editors and production personnel.

TRADEMARK ACKNOWLEDGMENTS

Que Corporation has made every effort to supply trademark information about company names, products, and services mentioned in this book. Trademarks indicated below were derived from various sources. Que Corporation cannot attest to the accuracy of this information.

Apple, AppleTalk, ImageWriter, LaserWriter, MacDraw, Macintosh, MacPaint, and MacWrite are registered trademarks and Finder and MultiFinder are trademarks of Apple Computer, Inc.

COMPAQ is a registered trademark of COMPAQ Computer Corporation.

Cricket Draw is a trademark of Cricket Software, Inc.

IBM is a registered trademark of International Business Machines Corporation.

PostScript is a registered trademark and Illustrator is a trademark of Adobe Systems Incorporated.

Microsoft and MS-DOS are registered trademarks of Microsoft Corporation.

PageMaker is a registered trademark of Aldus Corporation.

SuperPaint is a trademark of Silicon Beach Software, Inc.

Word Finder is a trademark of Microlytics, Inc.

WordPerfect is a registered trademark of WordPerfect Corporation.

CONVENTIONS USED IN THIS BOOK

The conventions used in this book have been established to help you learn to use the program quickly and easily. As much as possible, the conventions correspond with those used in the Microsoft Word 4 documentation.

Material that you are to type is in *italic*. Messages that appear on-screen are in a `special typeface`. Menu options, dialog box names, and commands are in upper- and lowercase (the Paragraph Borders dialog box).

Introduction

Once regarded in straight-laced business circles as an odd and rather laughable development of the counter-culture, the Macintosh has come into its own in offices throughout the world. And the reason, very simply, is the Macintosh's technological superiority.

While the MS-DOS world still struggles with 640K barriers and a new operating system that's slow to find acceptance, the Macintosh has already brought to life the promises of personal computing: an operating system that can run several programs at once, a display that can show text and graphics simultaneously, and a working environment noted for its ease of use and design elegance. All these components came together in the Macintosh environment, and it happened at least two years before the same coalescence of trends will occur in the world of MS-DOS computing—if it ever does. And for that reason, the Macintosh SE and Macintosh II are pushing COMPAQs and IBM Personal Computers off the desktops of growing numbers of business and professional workers.

Version 4 of Microsoft Word, the astonishing new version of this already impressive program, does for Macintosh word processing what the Macintosh II and MultiFinder did for the Macintosh in general: Word 4 is making clear that the Macintosh is the environment of choice for business and professional writing. You can see precisely the same trend at work in software as well as hardware. Just as MS-DOS computer users once sneered at the Macintosh, so too did users of MS-DOS power packages like WordPerfect tend to look at Macintosh word processing programs as amusing toys. But in the meantime, Microsoft Word has grown up. And just as everything came together for the Macintosh before it did for MS-DOS computing, the two separate strands of word processing technology (text editing and page design) have come together in Version 4 of Microsoft Word. And the result is astonishing. If you have been working with even the best MS-DOS packages, a little familiarity with Word 4 will convince you that the future is already here.

Attempts have been made before, to be sure, to blend text editing and page design features into a single package—and for good reason. To create text effectively, writers need features that help them organize, expand, edit, restructure, and proofread the text they have written. That's what a good text editor is for. To express the text on paper with a design that's appropriate to its content, moreover, writers also need page design software—software that presents an on-screen simulation of page design elements, such as fonts, font sizes, headers, footers, page numbers, graphics, borders, columns, and footnotes. To achieve the highest rates of productivity and ensure that their work meets the highest standards of professionalism and esthetics, business writers need an excellent text editor and good page design features.

Until Version 4 of Word, getting a good text editor and good page design features meant buying two expensive programs (such as Word and a desktop publishing program like PageMaker) or settling for a memory-hungry, sluggish behemoth of a program that tried to do everything (and wound up doing little of it well). In Version 4 of Word, text editing and page design come together in a package that's truly astonishing for its speed and elegance. To be sure, in previous versions, Word has been an outstanding program for text creation, editing, and formatting; and two of its most remarkable features have been improved and expanded in Version 4:

❏ *Outlining* permits you to construct (and edit) a view of your document that shows its overall structure. In Version 4, new features make restructuring outlines with the mouse much easier.

❏ *Style sheets*, a unique Word feature, give you a way to enter several formats at once (instead of choosing them one by one). Version 4 enhancements make it easier to choose styles (and to remove them once you have applied them).

These features complement an impressive armada of word processing features that rival any of the popular MS-DOS packages. Some of these features are automatic footnote numbering and placement, automatic generation of form letters, automatic generation of tables of contents and indexes, spell checking, and many more.

The big news about Version 4, however, is the program's new page design features, which would do credit to a world-class desktop publishing program:

❏ *New table formatting commands* set up a spreadsheetlike matrix of rows and columns, simplifying the tasks of creating and editing text in tables—and all without setting tabs!

❏ *Dynamic page breaks* show you precisely where Word will end one page and start another, even as you insert and delete text on the screen.

❑ *Anchored text and graphics*, which you can size and position on the page so that text "floats" around them. With this feature, you can create handsome newsletters, brochures, price lists, fliers, and forms.

❑ *A dynamic Page View mode*, in which virtually all document formats—including columns, headers, footnotes, graphics, and page numbers—can be edited on-screen, even as you view these formats the way they will print. You can experiment with design features right on the screen until you're sure that you have achieved the best possible results.

As if these new features weren't enough to establish Word's credentials, Microsoft is shipping the software with free specially enhanced versions of SuperPaint (a graphics program), AutoMac III (a macro program that records and plays back sequences of commands), and WordFinder (an outstanding electronic thesaurus). All three are specially designed to work seamlessly with Word, so they're only a click of the mouse away while you're running Word. You will be hard pressed to think of a word processing program feature that's not available somewhere in this remarkable package.

Why a Book about Word 4?

The Macintosh was designed to be easy to use, and it is. For this reason, you can use Word at an elementary level, ignoring the complexity that lies beneath the surface of this program. If you choose Short Menus from the Edit menu within Word, you get assistance from Word itself in hiding its own complexity: the Short Menus option reduces the number of menu commands you see when you pull down the menus at the top of the screen.

But business and professional writers aren't interested just in ease of use. They're busy people, and their organizations depend on their productivity. Unfortunately, that's where the trouble starts. Even with a Macintosh program, a computer's manuals don't always make obvious how you can apply the program to get those big gains in productivity—gains that people frequently assume are all but automatic. They aren't. Experience in applying word processing technology in business and professional environments is necessary to learn how to realize the promise of higher productivity—just learning which button to press when is not enough.

This book was written to show you how to apply word processing in business and professional environments, which is also why this book is not like the manuals that come with Word. The goal of this book is to show you the pathway to high-productivity word processing in business and professional settings. To be sure, this book teaches you how to use Word—you will find step-by-step tutorials, which assume that you're a beginner with the program. But this book moves far beyond that level, revealing the techniques professional writers have developed to realize big gains in the productivity and the quality of their work. You will find ample guidance in the form of Power-User Tips and keyboard shortcuts, both of which are highlighted by icons in the margins, and summary sections outlining the high-productivity techniques introduced in each chapter.

A computer manual tries to say at least a little about every program feature. In what follows, I say a great deal about the Word features that can count big for you in improving the quality and productivity of your work. For this reason, this book uses an approach that brings high-productivity techniques to the fore, even if they may seem too advanced for beginning users. As you surely will agree after reading this book and trying these features, anyone can learn how to put Word's amazing productivity features to work.

How This Book Is Organized

Part I, "Getting Started with Word 4," presents two in-depth tutorials that introduce the professional writer's approach to Word. Far from elementary, these tutorials are intended to do more than merely introduce the program on an elementary level. Guided step-by-step, you also will take a tour to some of the more sophisticated levels of Word, such as outlining and page design. You will learn to conceptualize word processing in an entirely new way, a way that emphasizes the seamless integration of text editing features with page design features. Even if you're already familiar with Word, your time will be repaid if you skim Part I's two chapters. If you're new to Word—and especially if you're new to word processing—work through the tutorials step-by-step.

Part II, "Word 4 Fundamentals," covers the basics of Word in detail, going back over many of the subjects introduced in Part I and building a foundation of program knowledge. Included among the fundamentals, along with the usual features such as character and paragraph formatting, is Word's powerful style sheet formatting feature, which some people still consider to be an "advanced" feature. But as you will see, style sheet formatting really is fundamental to the use of Word at high levels of productivity. And with the Version 4 enhancements of this feature, it's now so easy to use that ordinary formatting techniques seem difficult in comparison. To master Microsoft Word, you should read all these chapters in sequence.

In Chapter 3, "Writing and Editing Strategies," you will learn a high-productivity approach to creating text with Word. In this approach, which is used extensively by professional writers, you perform some editing and formatting operations as you write.

Chapter 4, "Fundamentals of Document Design I: Character Formatting," details Word's tools for page design. This chapter features character formats, including fonts, font sizes, and character emphasis. You learn how to take full advantage of your Mac's fluency with fonts and specific characters.

Chapter 5, "Fundamentals of Document Design II: Paragraph Formatting," discusses the second of Word's formatting domains: paragraph formats. You learn how to control indents, alignment, and line spacing. In addition, you learn how to use custom tabs and borders, which Word treats as paragraph formats.

Chapter 6, "Fundamentals of Document Design III: Section and Document Formatting," covers the basics of page formats, such as page numbers, headers, footers, margins, and footnotes.

Chapter 7, "Formatting with Style Sheets," explains what is probably Word's most powerful feature: styles, which you create and name. You can create as many styles as you want, and each can contain several formats. When you apply a style, then, you apply several formats with just one command. Mastering this technique can save you time and increase your productivity significantly.

Chapter 8, "Checking Spelling, Saving, and Printing," covers the techniques you use to proofread your document, archive your work, and print your document.

Part III, "Word 4's Features and Applications," delves into seven areas of the program and its uses that are most susceptible to high-productivity enhancement. You needn't read all these chapters, nor do you need to read them in sequence.

In Chapter 9, "Customizing Word 4's Menus and Keyboard," you will learn how you can use new Version 4 features that enable you to redesign Word's screen and keyboard precisely the way you want. If you plan to use the program at advanced levels, and especially if you're a good typist and you like to use keyboard shortcuts, this chapter will amply repay your close attention.

Chapter 10, "Organizing Your Document with Outlining," is for anyone who writes long complex documents, such as proposals, business reports, technical documentation, or dissertations. You will learn how you can develop an outline structure that parallels the headings in your document, and how Word dynamically updates this outline as you restructure your document. You will even learn how you can restructure your entire document just by making a few quick changes on the outline. If you have ever struggled with the organization of a lengthy, complex document and wished for a better way, here's some excellent news: Word has a better way, and it's explained in this chapter.

Chapter 11, "Creating and Using Glossaries," reveals the mysteries of Word's glossaries, which you can use to store standard passages of text (called boilerplate). As you will quickly discover, there's no reason on earth to type the same passage of text twice when you can store and retrieve oft-used passages in glossaries. You will learn, in fact, how you can use Word's glossaries to create a comprehensive system for responding rapidly and consistently to business inquiry letters. The glossary feature is one of the biggest productivity boosters revealed in this book.

Chapter 12, ''Creating Tables and Lists,'' introduces the remarkable new Table commands, which create a spreadsheetlike matrix of rows and columns (without the old hassle of setting tabs). You still can set all the tabs you want, but you surely will agree after trying the Table commands that this new Version 4 feature is a blessing for anyone who types tables or lists. As you master the Table commands, you will cut significantly—by as much as 50 percent in typical cases—the time you will have to spend fussing with table formatting.

Chapter 13, ''Creating Business Forms,'' continues the discussion of Version 4's new Table commands by highlighting their application for the design and printing of business forms. If you have ever spent big bucks and big time hassling with a professional layout artist and printer about a business form, only to find that you had left out something and had to repeat the whole process, you will find this chapter immensely appealing. In it, you will learn how you can use the Table commands to design and print business forms that will equal, if not surpass, the work done by professional layout artists. And if you discover that you have left out something or if your business changes, a new version of the form will pop out of your printer in minutes!

Chapter 14, ''Page Layout Strategies with Text and Graphics,'' is in many respects the highlight of this book. You will learn how to create multiple-column text for applications like in-house newsletters. You will learn to use Word's text-and-graphics integration features, which allow you to import, size, and scale graphics as a key element in your document design. And you will also learn how to position text and graphics in fixed positions on the page so that text ''floats'' around them. With the knowledge you will gain in this chapter, many document processing applications you have considered beyond your reach, such as illustrated newsletters, price lists, and brochures, will be well within your grasp.

Chapter 15, ''Adding an Index and Table of Contents,'' is for anyone who prepares reports, proposals, or technical documents that will be reproduced directly from Word printouts. You will learn all about Word's outstanding indexing features, which you can use to code terms in your document so that Word will automatically compile them into a professional-looking index. And if you have created an outline for your document, you will learn how Word can generate a table of contents for your document after you give just one command!

Chapter 16, ''Creating Form Letters and Mailing Labels,'' presents a completely new approach to form-letter generation with Word, an approach that features Word 4's new Table commands. An application that has always been rather formidable becomes, in Version 4, approachable even for beginning users. If you have ever wanted to compile a mailing list, send the same letter to many people, or print mailing labels, by all means read Chapter 16 in detail.

Three appendixes round out this book's treatment of Microsoft Word 4.

Appendix A, "Installing Word 4 and Configuring Your System," helps you get started with Microsoft Word. If you haven't installed Word, begin this book by reading this appendix.

Appendix B, "Mathematical Typesetting with Word," shows you how to use powerful Word features that generate complex mathematical formulas from commands you place in the text.

Appendix C, "Word 4's Keyboard Shortcuts," provides a handy reference guide to Word's keyboard commands.

A Word of Encouragement

If you're just getting started with Word 4, you may feel daunted by the program's complexity—this is big league ball, after all. But you will be surprised at how far you can get if you take just one step at a time. You're not a failure at personal computing if you don't understand some features right away. And remember, too, that you don't need to memorize long lists of commands and procedures. In this book, you will find that any procedure requiring more than a step or two is explained in a handy step-by-step format. Make your own index (or just dog-ear the pages) to highlight the procedures you think you will need to look up again, and keep this book by your computer.

Before you know it, Word 4 will come naturally to you, even when you're exploiting the program at its intermediate and advanced levels. And as your knowledge of the program grows, you will learn how to customize it so that it's truly an extension of your preferences and ways of doing things. All in all, it's a journey well worth making!

Part I

Getting Started with Word 4

Includes

Word 4 Quick Start:
Creating a Business Letter

Microsoft Word is well known as one of the most powerful word processing programs available for the Macintosh. The program is also quite easy to use at an elementary level. You can start producing letters, memos, and brief reports right away. With the Macintosh's intuitive user interface, you don't need much instruction to produce simple letters right away.

If you are familiar with the Macintosh and Word, you still should pay special attention to the tutorials in this chapter and in Chapter 2. The tutorials introduce you to high-productivity Word techniques—the same ones developed by business and professional writers to maximize this marvelous program's efficiency. If you have already created simple letters with Word, this chapter can still prove valuable. At the most elementary level, tricks and strategies can help you improve the quality and quantity of the work you produce with Microsoft Word. This chapter starts right in with Power-User Tips, keyboard shortcuts, and other high-productivity techniques.

Note: This chapter assumes that you have installed Word (see Appendix A if you haven't). The text also assumes that you have basic Macintosh skills, such as opening and sizing windows, clicking and dragging, and using pull-down menus. For an introduction to these skills, see the lessons in the manual that came with your Macintosh.

Preparing To Use Word 4

Start Word from the Finder by double-clicking the Word icon. Word displays a blank, untitled document. On-screen you see the features in the following list (see fig. 1.1).

Fig. 1.1.

*Word's initial
display screen.*

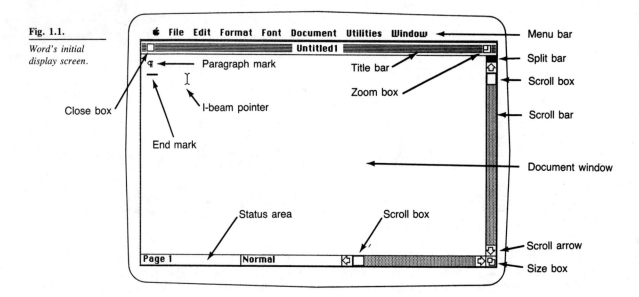

- *Menu bar*. At the top of the screen are Word's pull-down menus. These menus contain the commands used to open, save, print, edit, format, and display documents.

- *Document window*. Below the menu bar is the window in which Word displays a document. You can open more than one window at a time—up to 22, in fact—although you seldom open more than two or three at the same time. You can display a different document in each opened window.

- *Window features*. In the document window are the window moving, sizing, and scrolling features common to all Macintosh applications. These features include the *close box*, the *title bar*, the *zoom box*, the *split bar*, the *scroll arrows*, the *size box*, the *scroll boxes*, the *scroll bars*, and the *insertion point*. For a review of window skills, see table 1.1.

- *I-beam pointer*. The mouse pointer takes the shape of an I-beam when it's in the document text area. When the pointer looks like an I-beam, it's ready to click a new insertion point (or to highlight text). When you move the pointer to the window borders, the pointer changes to an arrow shape. The shape change lets you know that the mouse is ready to scroll, size windows, or pull down a menu.

❑ *Status area*. The last line of the window displays the page-number indicator. Because Word 4 inserts page breaks dynamically as you type and edit, the page number in the status area is accurate. You can turn off the page-number indicator by clicking the Background Repagination box in the Preferences dialog box, accessed from the Edit menu.

❑ *End mark*. The end mark appears as a dark horizontal line and shows the end of your document. You cannot move the insertion point past the end mark. Don't conclude that Word allows you to create only one-line documents! By entering text and pressing Return, you push the end mark down, creating a virtually unlimited amount of document space. The theoretical maximum length of a document is 16 million characters, or well over 10,000 double-spaced pages of text. In practice, Microsoft recommends a maximum document length of 1,000,000 characters, or about 650 pages.

Table 1.1
Review of Macintosh Window Skills

Task	Technique
To reduce size of window	Drag size box up or left
To zoom window to full size	Click zoom box
To unzoom window to reduced size	Click zoom box again
To move window	Drag title bar
To make a window active	Click anywhere in document area
To close a window	Click close box
To scroll line-by-line	Click scroll arrows
To scroll screen-by-screen	Click scroll bar above or below scroll box
To scroll longer distances	Drag scroll box

Full Menus and Short Menus

Because Word is such a big, complex, powerful program, it can be intimidating to new users. To reduce the complexity of the program, Word is preset to display shortened versions of the pull-down menus. For this tutorial, however, you use the longer, full version of the menus. To display the full menus, choose the Full Menus option from the Edit menu, as shown in figure 1.2.

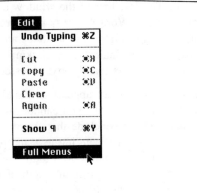

Fig. 1.2.

Choosing the Full Menus option from the Edit menu.

Speed
Keys

⌘-Y

Before you proceed with the program, turn on the display of paragraph marks. Paragraph marks show where you pressed the Return key to start a new paragraph. As you will see, editing and formatting your document is easier when these marks are displayed.

To turn on the display of paragraph marks, choose Show ¶ from the Edit menu or use the ⌘-Y keyboard shortcut.

Note: When you choose Show ¶, you see tab and space marks on the screen too. The space marks appear wherever you press the space bar and are rather disconcerting when you first see them. The space marks closely resemble periods. If you examine the screen closely, however, you find that the space marks are positioned just above the text baseline, unlike periods.

Writing the First Draft

Professional and business people write letters every day, and it's a big responsibility. Every time you send a first-class letter, you put yourself and your organization on the line. You have the opportunity to create a favorable impression of your organization, but you also can leave a *negative* impression, one that may have damaging consequences. For this reason, preparing letters with a fine word processing program like Word is an excellent idea. If you do, you can experiment with the wording of the letter until you get it just right.

This chapter presents a single Quick Start tutorial that walks you through a "real world" writing experience. You start with a poorly written letter and alter it until it meets the professional standards of today's business environment.

To get in the mood for this tutorial, imagine yourself in this situation: You're the director of a small training firm that specializes in training corporate employees in security techniques. You frequently make use of videos to show potential security problems. Last week, you spent a day training some employees at Atlantic Electronic Enterprises, Inc. Everything went fine, except that the video projector bulb blew in the final moments of the presentation. You had a backup, however, and before long you were back in action.

This week, you received a letter from Mr. Nelson T. Jones, your contact at Atlantic Electronic Enterprises, Inc. In the letter, Mr. Jones thanked you for the presentation but complained—rather unfairly and gruffly—about the equipment breakdown. The ball's in your court now; you have to answer the letter. You have a problem, however: you're annoyed at Mr. Jones and your annoyance probably will show in your first draft of the letter.

To begin the tutorial, make sure that a blank, untitled document is on your screen (refer back to fig. 1.1). If you have another document displayed, pull down the File menu and choose the New option.

Centering the Return Address

The first step in entering the letter to Mr. Jones is to type your company's return address. It is your company style to center the return address. Use the following steps to enter and center the return address:

1. To display the ruler in your document, choose Show Ruler from the Format menu. Alternatively, use the ⌘-R keyboard shortcut. The ruler appears as shown in figure 1.3.

⌘-R

You learn about the features of the ruler elsewhere in this book. The ruler is useful for choosing paragraph formats, setting and moving tabs, and using styles. The ruler takes up four lines of text space on the screen, however. For this reason, you may want to hide the ruler after using it.

To hide the ruler, pull down the Format menu. Notice that the Show Ruler option has changed to Hide Ruler. If you choose Hide Ruler (or press ⌘-R again), Word hides the ruler, and the Format menu displays the Show Ruler option once more. The ruler option in the Format menu is, in short, a *toggle*—a command that switches an option on or off.

For now, display the ruler and locate the centered paragraph alignment icon on the ruler (see fig. 1.3)

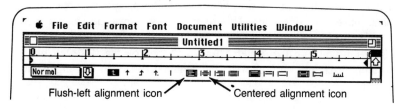

Fig. 1.3.

The ruler.

To write and revise effectively, you should see as much text as possible on the screen. The more text you can see, the easier it is to keep track of what has been said and where you're going with the text. The ruler takes up four lines of text space and can make your screen appear complex and distracting. Keeping the ruler hidden when you're not using it may be best. Practice toggling the ruler on and off by pressing ⌘-R. When you need the ruler, toggle it on; toggle it off when you resume writing.

2. To create a format for centered text, click the centered paragraph alignment icon on the ruler. Alternatively, use the ⌘-Shift-C keyboard shortcut. The insertion point moves to the middle of the screen.

You can use the ⌘-Shift-C keyboard shortcut even when the ruler is not displayed. When you format paragraph alignment or use other ruler formats, therefore, keyboard shortcuts have a big advantage: you don't have to toggle the ruler on and off to give the command.

3. Type *Albemarle Valley Associates* and press Return. If you make a typing mistake, press the Delete key (also called Backspace on some keyboards) to rub out the error. Then type the correct characters.

   The text you typed is centered. When you press Return, Word inserts a paragraph mark. Notice that Word copies the centered format to the next line.

4. Type the rest of the return address as shown in figure 1.4, pressing Return where you see paragraph marks.

5. Press Return three times after you type the telephone number to leave two blank lines under the return address.

6. Click the flush-left alignment icon on the ruler. Alternatively, use the ⌘-Shift-P keyboard shortcut.

⌘-Shift-P

   The insertion point jumps to the left margin, but the lines already centered stay centered.

Note: If you have used other Macintosh word processing programs, notice that Word documents have only *one* ruler. This ruler always shows the *current* formats for the paragraph in which you place the insertion point. Verify this by clicking the insertion point on the centered lines and then on the flush-left line. The highlight jumps back and forth between the centered and flush-left alignment icons on the ruler.

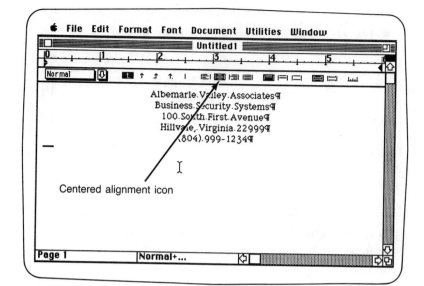

Fig. 1.4.

Entering the return address.

Keep this document on the screen. The tutorial continues in this chapter.

If you want to take a break at any point in this chapter, choose Save As from the File menu and type *Letter* in the Save Current Document As box. Then choose Quit from the File menu. You will see the Finder on-screen after you quit Word. To resume work, find this document's icon and double-click it. Word starts up and opens the Letter document automatically so that you can resume the tutorial.

Boldfacing the Firm's Name

You have already learned how to enter one kind of Word format, *paragraph alignment* (specifically, centered and flush-left alignment). Now you learn how to format *character emphasis* (specifically, boldface). To attach emphasis to characters already typed, you select the characters to highlight them on the screen. Then you choose the desired emphasis from the Format menu (or use one of the keyboard shortcuts).

To boldface the name of the firm in the Quick Start document, do the following steps:

1. Move the pointer toward the left window border so that it changes shape to an arrow pointing up and to the right (see fig. 1.5). When the pointer takes on this shape, you have moved the pointer to the *selection bar*, a special area of the screen that selects lines and paragraphs quickly.

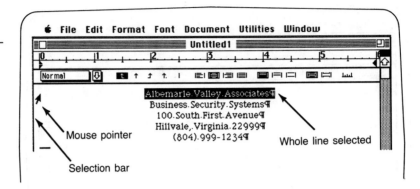

Fig. 1.5.

The pointer changes shape in the selection bar.

⌘-Shift-B

2. Click to select the whole line.

3. Choose Bold from the Format menu. Alternatively, use the ⌘-Shift-B keyboard shortcut. Word boldfaces the firm's name (see fig. 1.6).

The following steps explain how to format the company name in a different way. Word lets you format text in two ways: after it is typed (as you have just done with steps 1, 2, and 3), and as you type it (as shown in the following steps). You should understand how to use both methods.

Fig. 1.6.

Boldfacing the firm's name.

> **Albemarle.Valley.Associates**¶
> Business.Security.Systems¶
> 100.South.First.Avenue¶
> Hillvale,.Virginia.22999¶
> (804).999-1234¶

4. Highlight the entire return address except for the last paragraph mark. Choose Cut from the Edit menu. All the text disappears.

5. Choose Bold from the Format menu (or press ⌘-Shift-B), and type *Albemarle Valley Associates, Inc.* again. The text you type appears in bold.

6. Press Return. Word copies the centered format *and* the bold format to the next line. Because you don't want to boldface the rest of the return address, you must cancel the boldface formatting. Step 7 explains how to do this.

⌘-Shift-Z

7. To cancel the boldface formatting for the rest of the return address, choose Plain Text from the Format menu. Alternatively, use the ⌘-Shift-Z keyboard shortcut.

8. Type the rest of the return address.

One of the wonderful things about the Macintosh is the ease with which you can switch fonts and font sizes. If you use more than one font and font size in a document, you will be glad to know that the Plain Text option on the Format menu (and its ⌘-Shift-Z equivalent) does *not* cancel fonts and sizes. The Plain Text option cancels only styles; position, font, and size aren't affected by the option. If you want to cancel *all* special character formats, including style, position, font, and size, press ⌘-Shift-space bar.

About the Formatting Just Entered

Basic to Word is a distinction between *paragraph formatting* and *character formatting*. You also should distinguish between *formatting as you type* and *formatting later*. The following sections help clarify these differences.

Paragraph Formatting and Character Formatting

Paragraph formats include the *alignment* of text (flush left, centered, flush right, or both margins justified); the *indentation* from the right or left margin and the position of the paragraph's first line; *line spacing*, such as single-spaced or double-spaced; and *blank lines* before or after the paragraph. Additional paragraph formats include tabs and borders.

A paragraph format applies to all the text in a paragraph. A paragraph, as Word defines it, is all the text between paragraph marks. A paragraph can consist of just one word, a heading, or, as you have already seen, a single line in a return address.

Character formats include *style* (such as boldface, italic, and underlining); *position* (subscript, superscript, or flush with the base line); *font* (such as New York, Times Roman, or Palatino), and *size* (such as 12 point or 24 point).

A character format applies only to selected characters. You can apply character formats to any unit of text, ranging from one character to the entire document.

Formatting as You Type and Formatting Later

You can attach character and paragraph formats to your text in two ways:

❏ *Formatting as you type*. To format this way, you choose the format you want and type. As you type, Word "lays down" the format (or formats) chosen. When you press Return, Word copies the current formats to the next paragraph. The formats remain in effect until you change or cancel them.

❏ *Formatting later.* To format this way, you type the text first. Then you highlight the text you want to format and choose a format or formats.

Which method of formatting is best? The decision is up to you.

Some writers don't like to format as they type; they would rather concentrate on the text and reduce the number of variables to keep in mind while they compose. For these writers, the formatting-later approach is best. Other writers want to see how their document looks as they type, and they prefer to format as they type.

Experiment with both techniques. You probably will find that you can use both.

Inserting the Date Automatically

You can type the current date manually, if you want, but a new Word 4 feature can do it for you automatically. To insert the date automatically, use the following steps:

1. Place the insertion point on the flush-left paragraph mark below the return address.

2. Choose the Glossary option from the Edit menu. If you don't see the Glossary option, choose Full Menus from the Edit menu and try again.

3. When the Glossary dialog box appears, as shown in figure 1.7, highlight the Date—Now—Long option.

4. Click the Insert button to close the Glossary dialog box.

You can see what this option does by looking at the line below the Name box. Highlight other date options to see how the format of the date appears, and choose the date format that you want.

Fig. 1.7.

The Glossary dialog box.

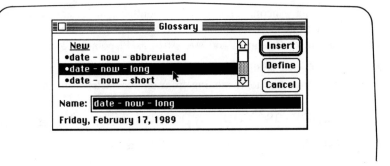

Word inserts the date in your document as shown in figure 1.8. Don't worry about adding extra space under the return address; you will take care of that later.

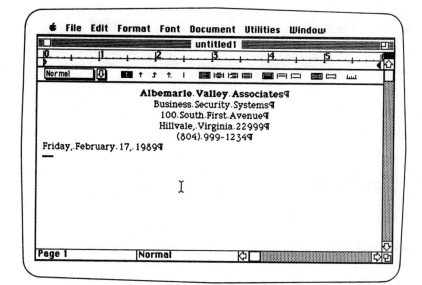

Fig. 1.8.

The date is automatically inserted in the document.

You have just used one of Word's *built-in glossary entries*. A *glossary* is a storage place for certain types of information that can be inserted in your document as you please. The built-in glossary entries include several date and time options. You can create your own glossary entries and display them in this dialog box, as explained in Chapter 11, ''Creating and Using Glossaries.''

The capacity to insert today's date automatically is neat. In fact, you probably have decided to make regular use of this feature already. If you have, putting it on a pull-down menu is easy. Use the following steps to put the date format on the new Work menu:

1. Press ⌘-Option-plus (+). The pointer becomes a big plus symbol.

2. Use the big plus symbol to pull down the Edit menu and choose the Glossary option.

⌘-Option-Plus

3. Choose the desired date format, just as if you were inserting a date into your document (see fig. 1.9). Because you don't actually carry out the command, don't worry about inserting an extra date in your letter.

4. Click the Cancel button. Alternatively, press Esc.

Esc

If you haven't used ⌘-Option-plus before, Word creates a new pull-down menu called the Work menu. The glossary entry you chose is added to this menu (see fig. 1.10). To add the current date to your letters in the future, choose the desired glossary entry from the Work menu.

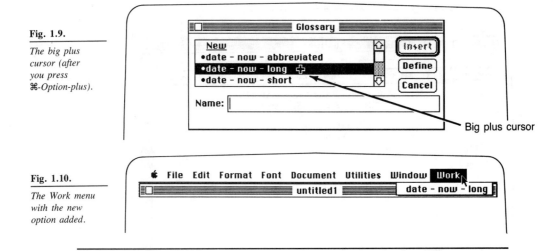

Fig. 1.9.

The big plus cursor (after you press ⌘-Option-plus).

Fig. 1.10.

The Work menu with the new option added.

Typing the Inside Address and the Text of the Letter

When you finish typing the return address and the date, press Return twice to create two blank lines. Then type the correspondent's address and the salutation as shown in figure 1.11. Then type the text of the letter as shown in figure 1.12. By the way, the letter is dreadful—especially the part about engineers knowing better! Type the letter as shown; you need something horrible so that you can fix it later.

As you type, don't press Return until you start a new paragraph. Words that go past the right margin are automatically "wrapped" to the next line. When you're finished typing, your letter should look like the one in figure 1.12.

Revising the Letter

As you reread the body of this letter, you hear—distantly, through the mists of time—the voice of your business communication teacher. She's saying, "Write positive letters! Emphasize the reader's point of view!" When you look critically at what you have written, you see that it strikes out on both counts.

You must revise the letter—another victory for professional standards in business communication! As a first move, you decide to join the first two paragraphs to see whether an improvement results.

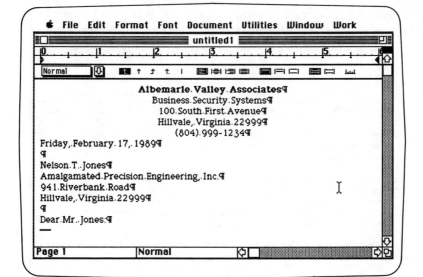

Fig. 1.11.

Typing the correspondent's address and the salutation.

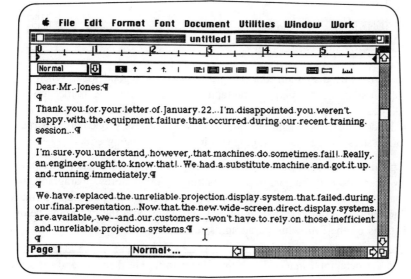

Fig. 1.12.

A dreadful first draft of a business letter.

Joining Paragraphs

To join two paragraphs, follow these steps:

1. At the end of the first paragraph (the one ending with *training session*), click the first paragraph mark and drag down to select the second mark. If you don't see the paragraph marks, choose Show ¶ from the Edit menu.

Speed
Keys

⌘-X

2. Choose Cut from the Edit menu or use the ⌘-X keyboard shortcut. The paragraphs are joined as shown in figure 1.13. You may need to enter a space or two to separate the sentences you just joined.

Fig. 1.13.

The letter with the first two paragraphs joined.

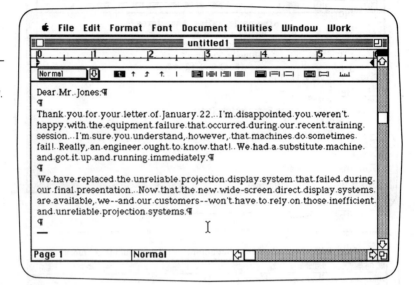

Now you know why displaying the paragraph marks is a good idea. When you can see the marks, you can join paragraphs more easily. If the marks are not displayed, you have to grope in the dark to find them. What's more, you may delete a hidden mark accidentally. Many new Word users become frustrated when, for mysterious reasons, paragraphs join as they're being edited.

Another good reason to avoid accidentally deleting paragraph marks exists. As you learn when you explore paragraph formatting, Word "stores" paragraph formats in paragraph marks. If you delete a mark, you lose all the paragraph formats attached to the paragraph. The paragraph not only joins with the paragraph below it, but it takes on the following paragraph's formats.

Power
User
Tip

If you find the paragraph marks distracting, learn to toggle them on and off with the ⌘-Y keyboard shortcut.

Splitting Paragraphs

Now that you know how to join paragraphs, take a moment to learn how to split them again. You will have many occasions to do so. A real paragraph—the grammatical paragraph, not the artificial paragraphs defined by Word—is unified: it expresses and develops a single idea. If more than one idea is in a paragraph, you may want to split the paragraph. To split paragraphs, use the following steps. Experiment on the first paragraph of your letter—you will undo the change later.

1. Place the insertion point where you want the split to occur. Normally, place the insertion point on the first character of what is to become the second paragraph.

2. Press Return. Word splits the paragraphs. Press Return again to leave a blank space between the paragraphs, if you want.

3. Because you're just experimenting, join the paragraphs again by deleting the paragraph marks you just inserted.

Deleting and Replacing a Paragraph

As you inspect your letter after joining the two paragraphs, it becomes obvious that the whole first paragraph must go. The paragraph is too negative, and besides, it violates the first principle of excellence in business communication: focus on the customer, not your own feelings and preoccupations. You should not bite the bait when you receive a letter that provokes you! To get rid of this paragraph, follow these steps:

1. Move the pointer to the selection bar next to the letter's first paragraph.

2. When the pointer changes shape to an arrow pointing up and to the right, *double-click* the mouse button. This action selects the whole paragraph.

3. To delete the paragraph, choose Cut from the Edit menu (see fig. 1.14). Alternatively, use the ⌘-X keyboard shortcut.

When you choose Cut or press ⌘-X, Word removes the highlighted text from your document and places it on the clipboard, a special, temporary storage area. To see what's on the clipboard, choose the Show Clipboard option from the Windows menu. To close the clipboard, click the Clipboard window's close box.

You can recover a deletion, whether it is large or small, in two ways:

⌘-Z

❑ *Undo.* After you cut text with the Cut option, the Undo option on the Edit menu changes to read Undo Cut. If you choose this option (or use the ⌘-Z keyboard shortcut), Word restores your document to the state it was in before you cut the text. If you want to recover deleted text by using Undo, you must do so immediately after performing the deletion. If you enter more text or choose another command, the Undo command changes and you cannot recover the deletion with this option.

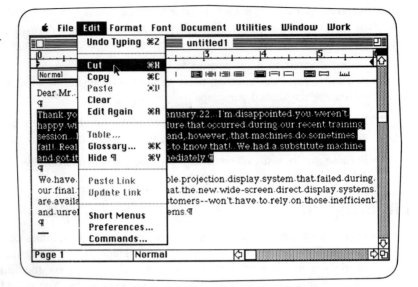

Fig. 1.14.

Deleting a paragraph.

Speed Keys

⌘-V

❑ *Paste.* When you delete text by using the Cut option, Word places it on the clipboard. The text you cut remains on the clipboard until you perform another deletion. (The clipboard holds only one deletion at a time; a new deletion replaces the contents of the clipboard.) If you cannot use Undo to recover the text, you may be able to recover the deletion from the clipboard. To do so, position the insertion point where you want the text to reappear and choose Paste from the Edit menu (or use the keyboard shortcut ⌘-V).

After you delete the first paragraph, choose Undo from the Edit menu to recover the deletion. Alternatively, use the ⌘-Z keyboard shortcut.

Pull down the Edit menu again. Notice that the Undo option has changed to Redo Cut. Choose Redo Cut from the Edit menu (or press ⌘-Z) to delete the paragraph again. Notice that ⌘-Z always undoes your last editing action, whatever it was. When you pull down the Edit menu, look to see what Word considers your last editing action and what will be undone if you press ⌘-Z.

Adding More Text to the Letter

When you look over the remaining text of the letter, you realize that you goofed when you deleted the whole first paragraph. You could have left the sentence, *Thank you for your letter of January 22.* You can bring the deleted paragraph back by choosing Undo or Paste, but it's time to learn how to insert additional text in text you have already typed. To do this, use the following steps:

1. Place the insertion point on the second paragraph mark below the salutation.

2. Type *Thank you for your letter of January 22*. To continue your new effort to be positive, type the rest of this new paragraph: *Mr. Jones, it was a pleasure serving you and your staff! Won't you consider firming up your plans for training your staff in the security techniques we detailed in our presentation? If you will give me a call or drop me a note, I'll have a proposal for you right away.*

3. Press Return when you finish typing this paragraph. Your letter should look like the one in figure 1.15.

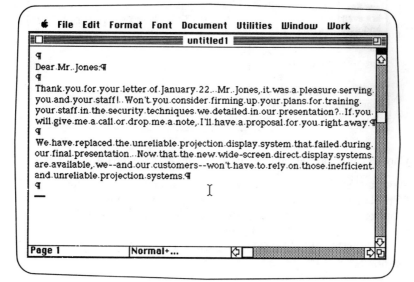

Fig. 1.15.

The letter after adding text to the first paragraph.

Moving Text

The letter is looking better, but in examining what you have written, you realize that what you just typed belongs at the end of the letter, not at the beginning. (You remember your business communication teacher again: "End with a call for action! End on a personal note and invite a response!") You decide to move part of the first paragraph to the end of the letter.

Moving text is easy with Word. Follow these steps to move text:

1. In the first paragraph, double-click the word *Mr.* and continue holding down the mouse button. Drag right and down to select the rest of the text shown highlighted in figure 1.16.

   Important: Don't select the paragraph mark at the end of the paragraph.

Fig. 1.16.

Highlighting the text to be moved.

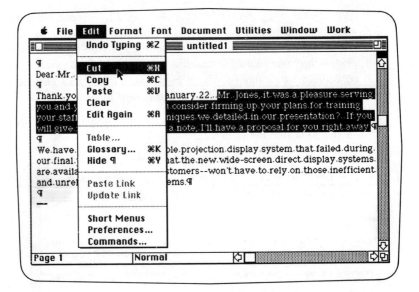

2. Choose Cut from the Edit menu or use the ⌘-X keyboard shortcut.

    Word moves the text you cut to the clipboard. If you select Show Clipboard from the Window menu, you can see the clipboard's contents (see fig. 1.17). Normally, you don't bother with this step, but if you forget what's on the clipboard, it's nice to know that you can view it. To close the Clipboard window, click the close box on the title bar.

Fig. 1.17.

The cut text is stored temporarily on the clipboard.

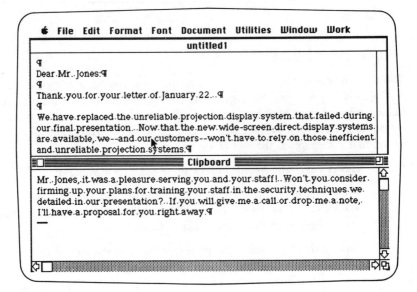

3. Place the insertion point just before the last paragraph mark.

4. Press Return twice to provide a blank line between the last paragraph and the text you will insert.

5. Choose Paste from the Edit menu. Alternatively, use the ⌘-V shortcut. The text you cut appears at the insertion point's location (see fig. 1.18).

Speed Keys

⌘-V

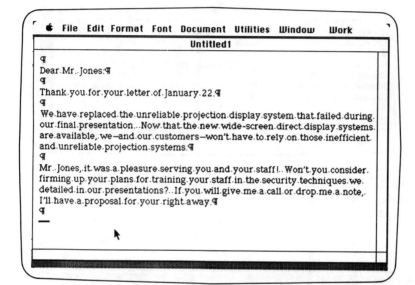

 File Edit Format Font Document Utilities Window Work

Untitled1

¶
Dear.Mr..Jones:¶
¶
Thank.you.for.your.letter.of.January.22.¶
¶
We.have.replaced.the.unreliable.projection.display.system.that.failed.during. our.final.presentation...Now.that.the.new.wide-screen.direct.display.systems. are.available,.we—and.our.customers—won't.have.to.rely.on.those.inefficient. and.unreliable.projection.systems.¶
¶
Mr..Jones,.it.was.a.pleasure.serving.you.and.your.staff!..Won't.you.consider. firming.up.your.plans.for.training.your.staff.in.the.security.techniques.we. detailed.in.our.presentations?..If.you.will.give.me.a.call.or.drop.me.a.note,. I'll.have.a.proposal.for.your.right.away.¶
¶

Fig. 1.18.

The text inserted from the clipboard.

You have moved the text successfully. Welcome to computer-assisted writing!

Learn the keyboard shortcuts for cutting (⌘-X) and pasting (⌘-V). You will use these shortcuts so frequently that they're worth memorizing.

Power User Tip

All that remains now is to address Mr. Jones's concerns in a positive way. Add the new text to the first paragraph as shown in figure 1.19.

Finishing the Letter

Now it's time to add the complimentary closing. To do this, follow these steps:

1. Place the insertion point just before the last paragraph mark and press Return twice.

Fig. 1.19.

Adding a positive opening to the letter.

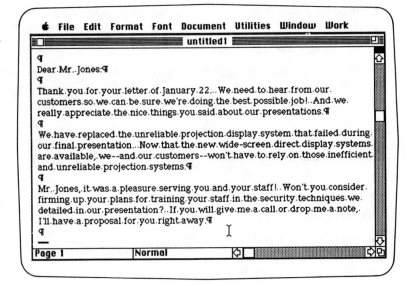

2. Find the left-tab icon on the ruler (see fig. 1.20). If the ruler isn't visible, choose the Show Ruler option on the Format menu or press ⌘-R.

Fig. 1.20.

Locating the left-tab icon.

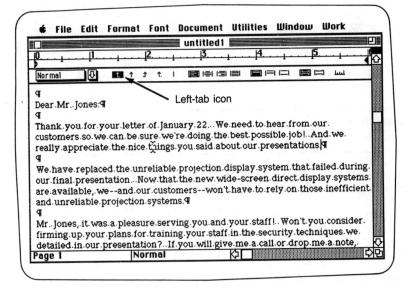

3. With the insertion point next to the last paragraph mark on the screen, drag the left-tab icon to the 3.5 inch position on the ruler (see fig. 1.21).

As you drag the left-tab icon, watch the status line in the lower left corner of the screen. The status line displays the tab's exact location. When the status line shows 3.5in, release the button.

You have just set a tab at 3.5 inches. When you set a tab in this way, Word cancels the default tabs to the left of the new tab. Default tabs appear every half inch.

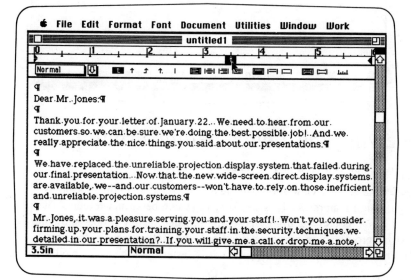

Fig. 1.21.

Setting a left tab at 3.5 inches.

4. Press Tab to move the insertion point to the tab stop you created. Type *Sincerely,*.

Notice that Word inserts tab marks (arrows) where you press Tab. If you find the tab marks distracting, you can hide them by choosing Hide ¶ from the Edit menu.

5. Press Return four times and press Tab again.

6. Type *Diane B. Smith* and press Return.

7. Press Tab again and type *Corporate Training*.

You're done. The closing of your letter should look like that shown in figure 1.22.

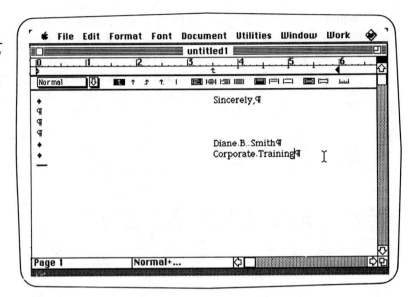

Fig. 1.22.

The complimentary close of the letter.

Previewing the Letter before Printing

With Word 4, you can look at your document in four ways:

❑ *Galley view*. This view shows the text you create and edit, but omits page design features such as headers, page numbers, and footers. The term *galley* is derived from typesetting practice: galley proofs show the text for proofreading purposes. In Word, the Galley view is the best for creating and editing text because it is faster than the other modes.

❑ *Outline view*. As you will learn in Chapter 2, you can view any document with internal subheadings as an outline in which the body text is hidden from view.

❑ *Page view*. In this mode, new to Word 4, you see on-screen a precise visual representation of your document's pages. You see headers, margins, page numbers, multiple columns, and all other page design features (except line numbers). You can edit in Page view, but this mode is considerably slower than Galley view.

❑ *Print Preview*. This mode displays miniature representations of your document's page layout, showing two pages at a time. You cannot read the text on a standard-sized monitor, but you can preview the overall balance of design elements.

So far, you have been working in Galley view because your concern has been with the text of the letter, not with its appearance when printed. Now you are ready to use the Print Preview option to preview the formats you selected. To do this, follow these steps:

1. Choose Print Preview from the File menu. Alternatively, use the ⌘-I keyboard shortcut.

2. When the Print Preview window appears as shown in figure 1.23, notice how the text is laid out relative to the page as a whole.

Speed. Keys

⌘-I

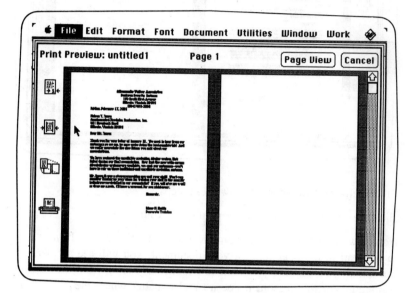

Fig. 1.23.

The Print Preview window.

As you can see, the text is too high—it's jammed up against the return address. To cure the problem, take these steps:

1. Click the Cancel button to exit the Print Preview window.

2. Click the insertion point just to the left of the date, and press Return three or four times.

Choose the Print Preview option from the File menu again; as you can see in figure 1.24, the letter now is balanced on the page. Click the Cancel button to exit Print Preview.

Checking Spelling

Letter-perfect spelling is indispensable for effective business communication. Like it or not, conclusions frequently are drawn about a person's taste, professionalism, and intelligence from such superficial matters as dress and spelling mistakes. Don't let your letter wear blue jeans!

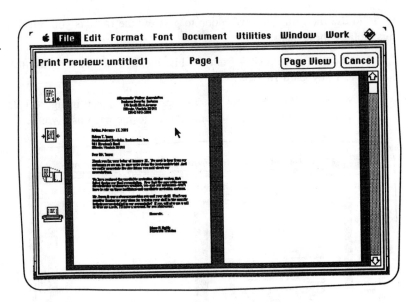

To check the spelling of the letter, follow these steps:

1. Click the insertion point at the beginning of your letter.

   Word always checks spelling from the insertion point down. If you do not start at the beginning of your document, you will see an alert box asking you whether you want to continue checking from the beginning. For this reason, it doesn't really matter where the insertion point is positioned when you choose Spell—you will always have the option of checking the whole document. You can save yourself the trouble of responding to the alert box, however, by positioning the insertion point at the beginning.

Speed Keys

⌘-L

2. Choose Spelling from the Utilities menu. Alternatively, use the ⌘-L keyboard shortcut. The Spelling dialog box appears (see fig. 1.25).

3. Click the Start Check button on the Spelling dialog box.

   When Word finds in your document a word that isn't in Word's dictionary, the unknown word is displayed next to Unknown Word in the Spelling dialog box (see fig. 1.26).

   Check the spelling in your document, using the instructions in the following paragraphs.

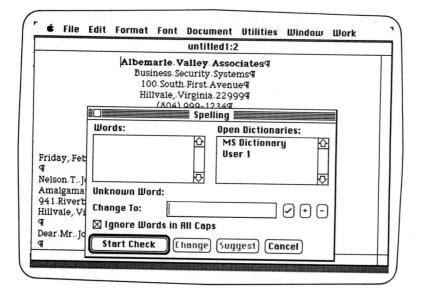

Fig. 1.25.

The Spelling dialog box.

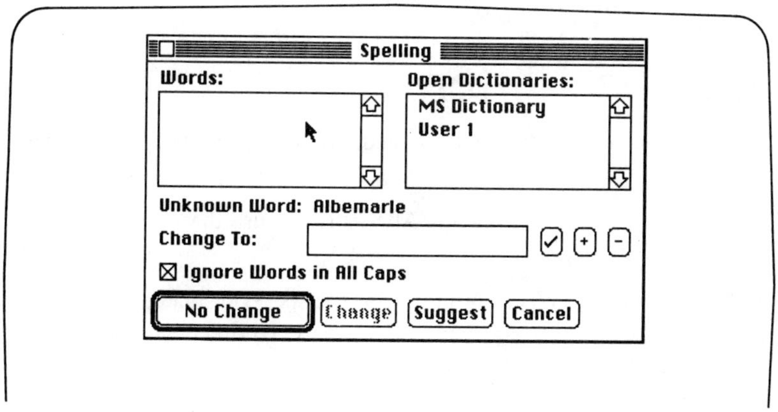

Fig. 1.26.

An unknown word displayed in the Spelling dialog box.

4. When you reach the end of your document, click the Cancel button.

When Word encounters an unknown word, you have several options:

❑ Change the word by typing the correct spelling in the Change To box in the Spelling dialog box and clicking the Change button.

❑ Click the unknown word so that the program inserts it in the Change To box. This action saves you from retyping the word. Edit the word in the Change To box. Alternatively, click the Suggest button. Word suggests possible correct spellings. If you see the correct spelling, highlight the correct word and click the Change button.

❏ Click the No Change button to leave the word as it is. Do this when the word is spelled correctly but is used too infrequently to warrant adding it to the dictionary. (For speedy performance, do not add more than 1,000 words to the dictionary.)

❏ Click the plus (+) button to add the word to the dictionary. Use this option for your name, your business's name, your street, and other correctly spelled words that you use often.

If you were typing a real letter, you would want to add your own name and your business's name to Word's dictionary. For now, just click the No Change button when Word encounters an unknown, correctly spelled word.

You can save your work if you want (choose Save from the File menu and type a file name in the Save This Document As box). Because you're practicing, however, you may not want to clutter your disk with sample files. When you write real letters, you may decide not to save letter files—keeping a printed copy in a file folder may be easier than dealing with dozens or hundreds of document files on disk. If you saved this document so that you could take a break, you can abandon the file later by dragging it to the trash can in the Finder window.

Printing the Letter

Speed Keys

⌘-P

To print two copies of your letter (one to send, the other to file), follow these steps:

1. Choose Print from the File menu. Alternatively, use the ⌘-P keyboard shortcut.

   If you have an ImageWriter printer, you see the Print dialog box shown in figure 1.27. If you have a LaserWriter printer, you see the dialog box shown in figure 1.28.

Fig. 1.27.

The Print dialog box for the ImageWriter printer.

ImageWriter	v2.7	**OK**
Quality: ⦿ Best ○ Faster ○ Draft		
Page Range: ⦿ All ○ From: [ ] To: [ ]		**Cancel**
Copies: [1]		
Paper Feed: ⦿ Automatic ○ Hand Feed		
Section Range: From: 1 To: 1 ☐ Print Selection Only		
☐ Print Hidden Text ☐ Print Next File		

```
┌─────────────────────────────────────────────────────────────┐
│  LaserWriter  "LaserWriter"                    5.2    ┌──────┐ │
│  Copies:▐█▌          Pages:◉ All  ○ From:    To:       │  OK  │ │
│                                                        └──────┘ │
│  Cover Page:   ◉ No ○ First Page  ○ Last Page         ┌────────┐│
│                                                        │ Cancel ││
│  Paper Source: ◉ Paper Cassette  ○ Manual Feed         └────────┘│
│  Section Range: From:  1      To:  1      ┌────┐        ┌──────┐ │
│                                           │    │Print Selection Only│ Help │ │
│  ☐ Print Hidden Text   ☐ Print Next File   ☐ Print Back To Front └──────┘ │
└─────────────────────────────────────────────────────────────┘
```

Fig. 1.28.

The Print dialog box for the LaserWriter printer.

2. If you have an ImageWriter, click Faster or Best.

   The Best option produces the densest output on ImageWriters, but it is slow. The Faster option produces a lower quality printout. (The Draft option prints the text quickly using the ImageWriter's native font, not the fonts you see on your screen, and does not print graphics.)

   Make sure that your printer is turned on and selected and that the paper is positioned correctly. If you haven't installed your printer yet, see Appendix A.

3. Type *2* in the Copies box of the Print dialog box, and click the OK button.

Word prints two copies of your letter. If this were a real letter, you would mail one copy and file the other.

Quitting Word

Speed Keys

⌘-Q

Now that you have printed the letter, it's time to quit Word. To do this, choose Quit from the File menu or use the ⌘-Q keyboard shortcut. If you haven't saved your letter, you see an alert box. This box asks you whether you want to save the document you have created. Click No to abandon the letter. If you want to save the letter, click Yes. (If you have not already saved the document in a previous session, Word displays the Save As dialog box so that you can name the document.) If you have changed your mind about quitting Word, click Cancel or press Esc.

High-Productivity Techniques To Remember

Note: The following techniques are covered in greater detail in Part II of this book.

❏ Learn to toggle the ruler quickly by pressing ⌘-R. Toggle the ruler on to format paragraphs and tabs; toggle it off again so that you can see more lines on the screen.

❏ Keyboard shortcuts save you time—particularly when you choose a format that must otherwise be selected from the ruler or one buried deep in a pull-down menu.

❏ If you frequently use a command buried deep in a menu, such as the date glossary, add it to the Work menu using ⌘-Option-Plus.

❏ The ruler always shows the formats in effect for the currently selected paragraph or paragraphs. If you have selected two or more paragraphs with different formats, the ruler is gray.

❏ Basic to Word is the distinction between character and paragraph formatting.

Character formats, such as font, style, and position, apply to individual characters. You can select any number of characters to receive character formats.

Paragraph formats, such as alignment and indentation, apply to entire paragraphs (in Word, a paragraph is defined as all the text between two paragraph marks).

❏ You can format as you type or format later.

To format as you type, choose one or more formatting commands and start typing. Word "lays down" the formats selected. When you press Return, Word copies the formats to the next line. The formats remain in effect until you change them or cancel them.

To format later, select the existing text you want to format and then choose the formatting command or commands.

❏ Learn to toggle paragraph marks with ⌘-Y.

To join and split paragraphs and avoid unintentional losses of formatting by deleting paragraph marks, display the marks while editing.

Turn the marks off if you find the paragraph and space marks distracting when you write.

❏ Learn the keyboard shortcuts for cutting (⌘-X) and pasting (⌘-V). You will use these commands so frequently that they're worth memorizing.

❏ Select lines and paragraphs rapidly by moving the pointer to the selection bar. Click once to select a line; click twice to select a paragraph.

❏ Preview your document's formatting before printing. Previewing the formatting on-screen is much faster than printing the whole document and then discovering an error!

2

Word 4 Quick Start:
Business Reports

When a new technology comes along, it takes time before people fully understand the uses of the new products. The telephone, for instance, initially was thought to be most useful for listening to distant musical concerts! The same can be said of today's new generation of document processing software. Only a small proportion of users have grasped just how dramatically programs like Word can increase writing productivity and quality.

Word's outlining capabilities are a case in point. According to Microsoft's own user surveys, only a small proportion of Word users create outlines for their documents. Many users probably think Word's outlining capabilities are little more than an electronic version of a paper-and-pencil outline. Some people think that outlines are good to do before writing, but they think outlines are an extravagance to be dispensed with if at all possible.

If you think outlines are an extravagance, you're missing out on one of Word's most amazing and powerful features. Word's outlining feature offers much more than a way to *plan* your document. A Word outline isn't something separate from your document, like a paper outline. *A Word outline is another way of looking at the document you're creating*. You can use the outline to get a quick view of your document's overall structure and organization. What's more, by moving outline headings, you can actually *restructure* a huge document in a few keystrokes! Word moves the text under the heading as well as moving the heading itself! If you have ever struggled with a lengthy document, trying to reorganize it by moving big blocks of text around, you will appreciate how much time and effort this remarkable feature can save.

For anyone who writes business reports, proposals, contracts, dissertations, articles, or other multisection documents, Word's outlining capabilities are worth their weight in gold. The outline feature is useful not just because it can bring you big gains in productivity. Writing experts agree that the most important criterion of writing excellence is the quality of the document's overall organization. A well-structured document achieves your aims: it gets your message across, and it leaves an excellent impression of *you* and your organization's commitment to quality.

This chapter, like Chapter 1, presents an extended tutorial that introduces you to some of Word's most powerful features. Outlining is only one of these features. You also learn how to integrate graphics into Word documents, how to redefine Word's default heading styles, and how to "anchor" graphics so that text "floats" around the positioned images. After reading this chapter, you will understand why Word 4 is the program of choice for high-powered writing applications in business and professional settings.

This chapter assumes that you have installed Word and learned the basic skills for using Word (discussed in Chapter 1). If you have not installed Word, see Appendix A.

Note: You can learn much more about the Word features mentioned in this chapter—if you learned it all in this chapter, you wouldn't need the rest of this book! In this chapter, you find just enough explanation to get you through the tutorial, which shows some of Word's most powerful features. Subsequent chapters deal with these and other subjects in detail. For now, concentrate on learning a new way of thinking about word processing!

Creating the Graphic

For this chapter's tutorial, you need a graphic. This chapter begins by creating the one shown in figure 2.1. Word 4 comes with SuperPaint, a high-quality graphics program. You use SuperPaint to create the graphic you need for this tutorial.

Note: If you're in a hurry, you can save time by creating a simplified version of the graphic or by using some other SuperPaint file you have already created. To use an existing graphics file, open SuperPaint, choose Open from the File menu, and double-click the name of the file. Copy the graphic to the clipboard by following the instructions in step 12.

SuperPaint is included on the Word Utilities 1 disk. If you haven't already installed SuperPaint, place the Utilities 1 disk in the drive, double-click the disk icon to open the disk directory, and double-click the SuperPaint icon. Make sure that the Paint Layer is selected (the paintbrush should be superimposed on the drafting tool at the top of the tool palette). See figure 2.2 for a quick guide to the SuperPaint screen features used in this tutorial.

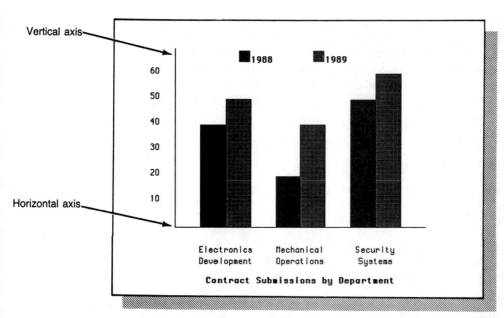

Vertical axis

Horizontal axis

Fig. 2.1.

A business graphic created with SuperPaint.

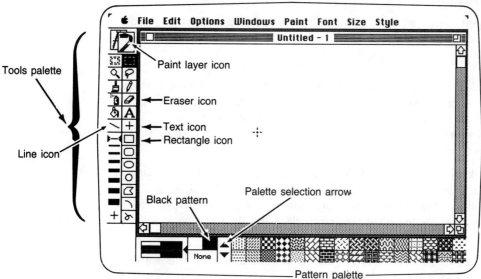

Tools palette

Line icon

Paint layer icon

Eraser icon

Text icon
Rectangle icon

Black pattern

Palette selection arrow

Pattern palette

Fig. 2.2.

The SuperPaint screen features on the Paint Layer.

To create the graphic shown in figure 2.1, using SuperPaint, follow these steps:

1. Choose the Grid and Rulers option from the Options menu.

2. When the Grid and Rulers dialog box appears, type .25 in the Grid Spacing box. Then click the Grid Snap On and Show Grid boxes. These options help you create a rectilinear graph quickly and efficiently. Click OK.

3. Click the line icon on the tools palette. Position the insertion point near the upper left corner of the window and drag straight down. Release the mouse after creating a vertical axis of sufficient length, as shown in figure 2.1. Then click at the bottom of this line and drag right to create the horizontal axis. Notice that the lines you draw "snap" to the grid lines on the screen, even if you don't align the insertion point exactly with the grid.

4. Click the black pattern on the pattern palette (see fig. 2.2).

5. Click the rectangle icon (see fig. 2.2).

6. Place the pointer on the bottom axis and drag right and up. As you drag, you create a black rectangle. Continue until you have created a column like the first black one in figure 2.1.

   If you need to start over, choose Undo from the Edit menu. When you have sized the rectangle correctly, release the mouse button. Create the other columns as shown in figure 2.1.

7. Click the palette selection arrow in the patterns palette and choose a gray pattern.

8. Repeat steps 5 and 6 to create a gray column like the first gray one shown in figure 2.1.

9. Create additional black and gray columns as shown in figure 2.1.

10. Click the text icon in the tool palette. Click the insertion point where you want the text to appear, and type the text, as shown in figure 2.1. If you make a mistake, you can press Delete to rub out characters you just typed, or click the eraser icon to turn the pointer into an eraser.

11. Click the black pattern in the pattern palette. Then click the rectangle icon. Click and drag above the first pair of columns to draw the small rectangle for the legend at the top of the graphic. Repeat these steps to create the small gray rectangle. Click the text icon and add the legend text as shown in figure 2.1.

12. Pull down the Edit menu and choose Select All. Then pull down the Edit menu again and choose Copy.

13. Choose Save from the File menu and type a file name in the text box. Click OK. Then choose Quit from the File menu.

Creating the Outline

The next step in this tutorial involves creating an outline with Word. You will learn how to link outline headings with document headings. This link allows you to restructure major text domains simply by changing the order in which headings appear in your document. Follow these steps:

1. Place the Word program disk in the internal drive and double-click the disk icon to open the disk directory window. If you have a hard disk, double-click the folder in which you placed Word.

2. Double-click the Word icon to start Word and display a new, blank document.

3. Choose Outlining from the Document menu. Alternatively, use the ⌘-U keyboard shortcut. You have toggled Word into the Outline view of the document.

   After you choose this option, you see the outline icon bar below the title bar, as shown in figure 2.3. Complete information on the meaning of these icons is found in Chapter 10, ''Organizing Your Document with Outlining.'' For now, you learn about only the icons relevant to this tutorial.

   The style indicator on the status line reads Heading 1, indicating that the insertion point is positioned at the top level of the outline.

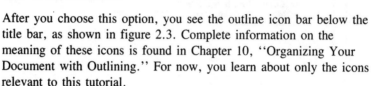

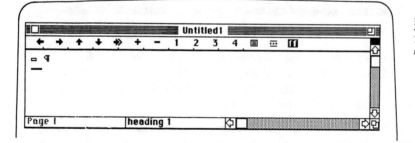

Fig. 2.3.

The outline icon bar.

4. On the first line of the document, type the title of the report: *Report on Contract Proposal Activity, 1988-1989.* Then press Enter.

   Important: If you make a mistake, correct it by using one of the techniques that does not place the deletion on the clipboard. If you delete to the clipboard, you erase the graphic stored there! (If this happens, save your Work, quit Word, open SuperPaint, and copy the graphic to the clipboard again.) To erase text without cutting to the clipboard, use the Delete key or choose Clear from the Edit menu.

5. To indent the next heading one level, click the right arrow on the icon bar below the title bar. Alternatively, press the right-arrow key.

   The status line now says Heading 2.

6. Type *Executive Abstract* and press Enter. The insertion point stays at the second level of the outline when you press Enter.

7. Type the rest of the second-level headings as shown in figure 2.4.

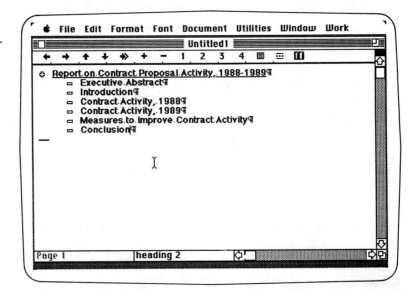

Fig. 2.4.

The second-level headings in Outline view.

8. Choose Outlining again from the Document menu or press ⌘-U to toggle off Outline view and go back to Galley view. The same headings remain on-screen, but they lose the indentations assigned them in Outline view (see fig. 2.5).

Notice that Word has formatted the headings on-screen. The first-level heading is formatted with the Helvetica font, in bold, and underlined; the second-level headings are formatted with Helvetica, in bold, but are not underlined. You may be tempted to reformat these headings now, but don't; you will redefine them with styles after you import and position the graphic.

You should notice that you can look at your document in two ways. The Outline view shows the headings you created as *outline* headings, that is, with a pattern of indentations showing their logical relationship. In Outline view, you see the outline icon bar. The Galley view is the normal document view and shows the same headings, but they are displayed as *document* headings—titles and subtitles. A

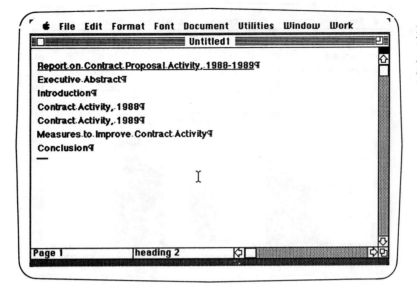

Fig. 2.5.

The first-level and second-level headings in Galley view.

Word outline, in short, gives you two ways of looking at the same document. You learn how to benefit from the two views of the document later in this tutorial.

Importing the Graphic

The clipboard should still contain the graphic copied from SuperPaint. To make sure that it does, choose Show Clipboard from the Window menu. If the graphic does not appear in the Clipboard window, choose Save from the File menu, quit Word, open SuperPaint, open the graphics file you created, and recopy the graphic to the clipboard. Open Word again.

When you are sure that the graphic is on the clipboard, perform these steps to import the graphic into the Word file:

1. Click the insertion point at the end of the heading titled, *Contract Activity, 1989*, and press Return.

2. Choose Paste from the Edit menu. Word inserts the graphic at the location of the insertion point (see fig. 2.6).

Fig. 2.6.

The graphic pasted from the clipboard into a Word document.

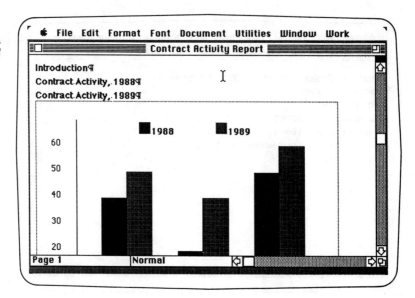

 If you have 2M of RAM or more, you can run SuperPaint and Word simultaneously under MultiFinder. Using MultiFinder greatly speeds the process of pasting graphics into Word documents. MultiFinder also enables you to use Word's QuickSwitch command to move the graphic back to SuperPaint for revision. For more information, see Chapter 14, "Page Layout Strategies with Text and Graphics."

Positioning the Graphic

 The graphic just pasted into your document looks best when positioned dead center on the page, with text above and below it. You can manually position the graphic in this way after you write the rest of the document's text. Word 4's new Position command on the Format menu, however, does the job automatically.

Use the Position command whenever you want to fix the position of a graphic (or a paragraph of text) on the page. With this command, you can tell Word to print the graphic at the exact location you specify relative to the margins, page edges, or column edges. In the following tutorial, you position the graphic to print dead center on the page, relative to the margins. Word automatically fills the rest of the page with text, producing an attractive result.

The position command is fully discussed in Chapter 14, "Page Layout Strategies with Text and Graphics." For now, try an experiment with this important new feature.

To anchor the graphic in the center of the page, follow these steps:

1. Click the insertion point within the graphic and choose Position from the Format menu.

2. When the Position dialog box appears, as shown in figure 2.7, click the arrow next to the Horizontal box. Drag down to select the Centered option. Then click the Margin button in the Relative To list underneath the Horizontal box.

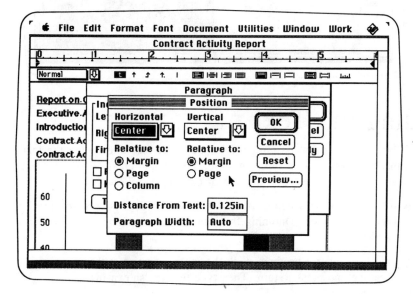

Fig. 2.7.

The Position dialog box.

3. Click the arrow next to the Vertical box and drag down to select the Center option. Click Margin in the Relative To list underneath the Vertical box.

4. Click the Preview button to view the graphic's position in the Print Preview window, as shown in figure 2.8.

5. Click Cancel to exit the Print Preview mode.

Fig. 2.8.

Viewing the graphic's position in the Print Preview window.

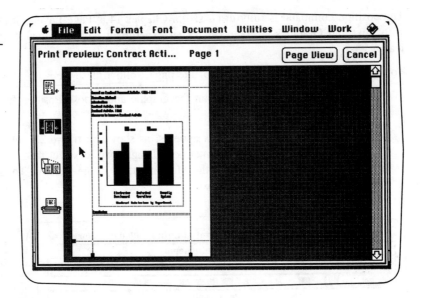

Adding the Text

Now add the text of the business report. If you don't feel like typing the text verbatim, make up your own or type nonsense. You should create *something* that you can work with later. To create the text of the report, follow these steps:

1. Add the text to the headings in Galley view. If Word is currently in Outline view, choose Outlining from the Document menu or press ⌘-U.

2. To add text under a heading, click the insertion point at the end of the heading and press Return. Then type the text shown in figure 2.9.

   Important: Don't press Return to enter blank lines. You add blank lines later in this tutorial.

Reformatting the Document Headings

You probably have noticed already that the headings you create in Outline view are formatted differently from ordinary text, and what's more, the formatting doesn't go away when you switch to Galley view. Mysteriously, the first-level

Report on Contract Proposal Activity, 1988-1989

Executive Abstract
Measures to increase the Company's performance in preparing contract proposals were implemented in January, 1989, leading to an increase of nearly 75 percent in proposal output in calendar year 1989. The measures appear successful, and this report recommends increased implementation of them for 1990.

Introduction
Under the direction of Ms. Suzanne Smith, the Company's Chief Executive Officer, the External Contract Development Committee was formed in November, 1987 and charged with two responsibilities: (1) to investigate the Company's current level of contract submission performance, and (2) to recommend measures to improve the level of contract submissions.
The Committee investigated contract activity in the Company's three divisions (Electronics Development, Mechanical Operations, and Security Systems) from December to March, 1988. The Committee analyzed the data from June to September, 1988, and the analysis was forwarded to the Chief Executive Officer on September 16, 1988. Under the directions of the Chief Executive Officer, the committee's recommendations were implemented beginning January 1, 1989. The current report compares contract performance in 1988 and 1989. Have the new measures been successful?

Contract Activity, 1988
In 1988, Security Systems led the company's proposal-production rate with 50 contract proposals. Second was the Electronics Development section, with 40 proposals. Mechanical Operations turned in a disappointing level of performance, with only 20 proposals submitted.

Contract Activity, 1989
In 1989, Electronics Development and Security Systems improved their already-impressive levels of performance, submitting 50 and 60 proposals, respectively. Mechanical Operations doubled their output, submitting 40 proposals.

Fig. 2.9.

The text of the business report.

Fig. 2.9—Continued

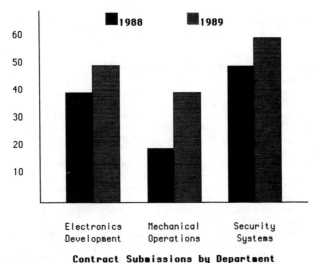

Measures to Improve Contract Activity
In its investigation, the Committee determined that the Company's performance in this area could be improved by (1) creating a position for a Contract Information Officer, whose responsibilities include disseminating information about external contract opportunities and assisting Company personnel with proposal development, and (2) equipping Company departments with Macintosh computer systems capable of integrating text and

Contract Submissions by Department

graphics. Both measures were implemented in January, 1989.
Conclusion
Judged by the nearly 75% increase in the number of proposals generated in 1989, the measures should be judged a success. The Committee recommends the retention and promotion of the Contract Information Officer and the installation of additional Macintosh systems in all Company units.

headings appear in bold underlined Helvetica, and the second-level headings appeared in bold Helvetica without underlining. The headings are formatted this way because Word's default style sheet contains predefined character styles for each heading level. You can change the style definition, if you want. If you do, you will learn how easy it is to format your document with Word's most powerful formatting feature.

A *style sheet* is a list of styles. *Styles* are named collections of formatting choices. The style that defines the first-level heading in the outline is named Heading 1 and includes the following formats:

❑ Flush-left, single-spaced paragraph with 12 points of blank space
before Helvetica font, 12-point size

❑ Bold and underlined character formats

Word automatically applies the default style sheet to every new document. The
default style sheet includes style definitions for all the heading levels in an outline. Figure 2.9 shows the styles for Heading 1 and Heading 2, the first-level and
second-level outline headings, as they appear in Galley view.

When you select Full Menus from the Edit menu, you see the name of the style
attached to the text in which the insertion point is positioned. The name appears
in the style name area and the style selection box (see fig. 2.10).

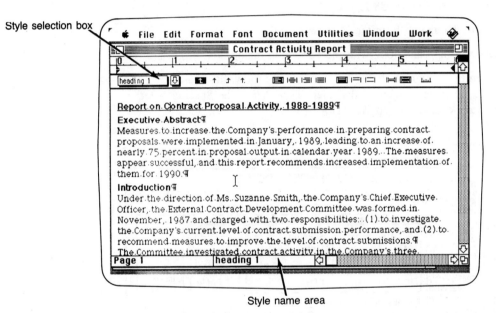

Fig. 2.10.

*The style selection
box and style
name area.*

You can see the definitions of the various styles by choosing Styles from the
Format menu. When you highlight one of the styles in the list box, the definition
appears in the style description area (see fig. 2.11). The check mark next to the
style name indicates the style of the current selection (the text in which the insertion point is positioned).

Although the Heading 1 and Heading 2 formats are predefined, the styles aren't
satisfactory for most report-writing applications. You may want to center the document's title and leave additional blank space under it, for example. Redefining
the heading formats makes good sense. Begin the redefinition of the heading formats by following these steps:

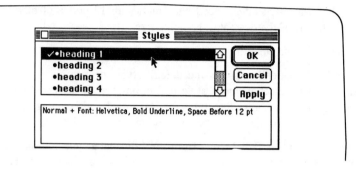

Fig. 2.11.

*The Styles
dialog box.*

1. Place the insertion point on the document's title (*Report on Contract Proposal Activity, 1988-1989*).

2. Choose Paragraph from the Format menu.

   The ruler appears along with the Paragraph dialog box.

3. When the Paragraph dialog box appears, as shown in figure 2.12, click the centered icon on the ruler. Type *2 li* in the Spacing After box and click the Keep With Next ¶ box.

Fig. 2.12.

*The Paragraph
dialog box.*

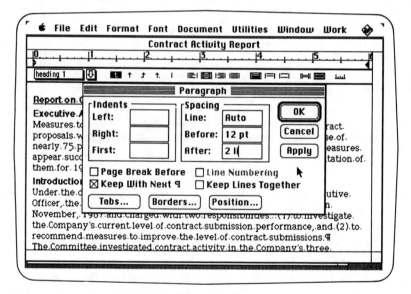

4. Click OK to close the paragraph dialog box.

Formatting the document's title with a larger type face and a different font is appropriate. The underlined format assigned to the first-level heading can be removed as well. To make these formatting changes, follow these steps:

1. Move the pointer to the selection bar. When the pointer takes on the shape of an arrow pointing up and to the right, click to highlight the whole heading.

2. Choose Underline from the Format menu to toggle off underlining.

3. Choose Geneva from the Font menu. Then choose 14 Point from the Font menu.

The document's title now is attractively formatted, as shown in figure 2.13.

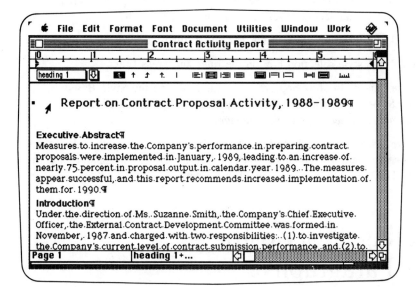

Fig. 2.13.

The document title in 14-point Geneva.

The second-level headings could be reformatted as well. You can define each heading individually, if you want, by using the ruler and the dialog boxes on the Format and Font menus. The best way to do the job, however, is to redefine the style for Heading 2. Once you change the default style definition, all the second-level headings you enter in this document's outline automatically have the formats selected.

To change the default style setting for the second-level headings, follow these steps:

1. Place the insertion point on the *Executive Abstract* heading, which is the first second-level heading in the document.

2. Choose Paragraph from the Format menu. When the Paragraph dialog box appears, type *.5 li* in the Spacing After box and click the Keep With Next ¶ box. The Keep With Next ¶ option prevents Word from breaking a page after the heading. Leaving a widowed heading at the bottom of the page is an unsightly formatting fault.

3. Click OK.

4. Move the pointer to the selection bar, the leftmost column on the screen, directly across from the *Executive Abstract* heading. When the pointer changes shape to an arrow pointing up and to the right, click to highlight the whole heading.

5. Choose Geneva from the Font menu.

   You have reformatted the second-level heading. The following steps explain how to redefine the Heading 2 style and change the default settings for all second-level headings in this document.

6. Click the insertion point in the *Executive Abstract* heading.

7. Click the style selection box on the ruler and press Enter.

8. When the dialog box appears, click the Redefine the Style Based on the Selection button and click. You have now reformatted *all the second-level headings in your document!*

As you have just seen, one of the best things about formatting with styles is that with just one formatting command, you can redefine styles throughout an entire document. That's high-productivity word processing!

Creating a Style for Text Paragraphs

Now that you have formatted the Heading 1 and redefined the Heading 2 styles, create a style for text paragraphs. Use the following steps to create a new default style for the text in your business report:

1. Move the pointer to the selection bar next to the first text paragraph. When the pointer changes to an arrow pointing up and to the right, double-click the mouse button to select the whole paragraph.

2. Choose Geneva from the Font menu.

3. Choose Paragraph from the Format menu. When the ruler appears, click the double-space and justification icons, as shown in figure 2.14.

4. In the Paragrapn dialog box, type *0.5 in* the First box. Type *0.5 li* in the Spacing After box. These options create an automatic first-line indentation of a half inch and leave some blank space after each paragraph. Click OK to close the Paragraph dialog box.

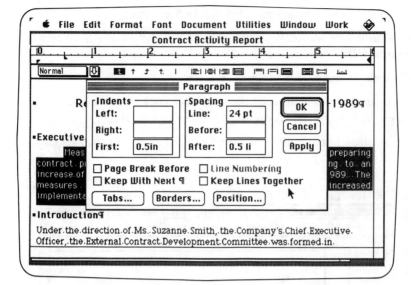

Fig. 2.14.

The Paragraph dialog box and ruler settings for text paragraphs.

You have changed the format of the first paragraph. The following steps explain how to turn these format settings into a new style that you can use for text.

5. Click the style selection box on the ruler.

6. In the style selection box (see fig. 2.15), type *Report* ¶ and press Return. To enter the ¶ symbol, press Option-7.

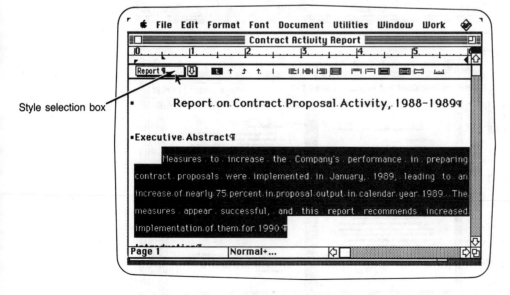

Style selection box

Fig. 2.15.

Naming a style in the style selection box.

7. When the dialog box appears, click the Define button.

To apply the new style named *Report* ¶ to the rest of the paragraphs of text in your document, follow these steps:

1. Click the insertion point in a text paragraph.

2. Click the drag-down arrow on the style selection box on the ruler. When the list appears, choose Report ¶ (see fig. 2.16).

3. Repeat steps 1 and 2 until you have formatted all the text paragraphs (see fig. 2.17).

Fig. 2.16.

Choosing the Report ¶ style from the style selection box.

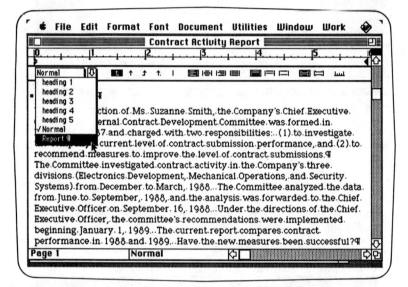

Fig. 2.17.

The Print Preview window showing the new style formats of text paragraphs.

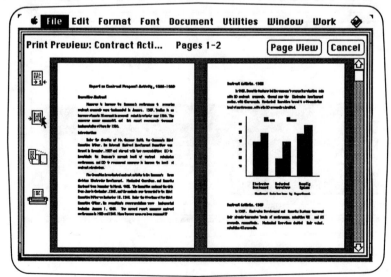

You can see the advantage of formatting with styles. When you redefine a default style (or create a new style), you can apply several character and paragraph formats with just one command. What's more, the command affects all the text to which the style has been applied. After you apply the Report ¶ style to all the text paragraphs, for example, you can reformat all three paragraphs just by redefining the style (as you did when you redefined the Heading 2 style). Style formatting is the royal road to high-productivity formatting with Word 4!

You can redefine the default font for your document by modifying the Normal style. To begin, apply the Normal style to some text by choosing Normal in the style selection box. Then select the text and choose the font and type size you want as the new default. Click the style selection box on the ruler and press Return. When the dialog box appears asking you whether you want to apply the style or redefine, choose the option that redefines the style.

Adding Headers

By default, Word doesn't print page numbers. You can add page numbers by clicking the Auto box in the Section dialog box (on the Format menu). You also can add page numbers to headers or footers. If you add page numbers in headers or footers, you also can add a shortened version of your document's title to print at the top or bottom of every page.

To create a header that prints page numbers, follow these steps:

1. Choose Open Header from the Document menu. The Header dialog box appears (see fig. 2.18).

   When you choose Open Header, Word uses the Normal style to define your document's header formats. The New York font appears in your document again.

2. Type *Report on Contract Proposal Activity, 1988-1989* and press Tab.

   When you press Tab in the Header or Footer dialog box, Word moves the insertion point to the right margin. The text you enter after pressing Tab is formatted flush right.

3. Type *Page*, press the space bar once, and click the page-number icon (see fig. 2.19). The page-number icon places a special character in the header. This character always displays the current page number.

   The header has been created. The following steps explain how to change the default header font from New York to Geneva.

Fig. 2.18.

The Header dialog box.

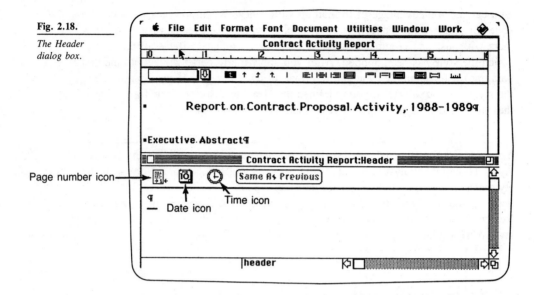

Page number icon ——→

Date icon   Time icon

Fig. 2.19.

Including the page number in a header.

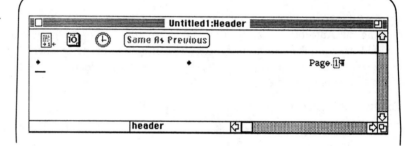

4. Move the pointer to the selection bar next to the header's text. When the pointer turns into an arrow pointing up and to the right, click.

5. Choose Geneva from the Font menu.

6. Click the close box.

Power User Tip

An obvious advantage of redefining the default font is that you don't have to perform steps 4 through 6 to change the font of the header. If you had chosen Geneva as the default font for your document, for instance, Geneva would have been the font you saw when you started typing in the Header dialog box. For instructions on defining a default font for your document, see the preceding Power-User Tip. For instructions on defining a default font for all documents, see Chapter 7, "Formatting with Style Sheets."

You're not quite done with the header yet. By default, Word prints headers and footers on the first page, as well as on all subsequent pages. A header or footer on the first page of the document is usually not necessary. You can disable headers and footers on the first page by using the Section dialog box, as described in the following steps:

1. Choose Section from the Format menu.

2. Click the First Page Special box (see fig. 2.20). Then click OK.

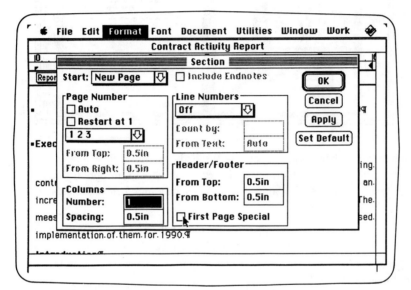

Fig. 2.20.

The Section dialog box.

Now Word does not print the header on the first page. The header appears on the second and subsequent pages of the document (see fig. 2.21).

Restructuring the Document

Once your document is attractively formatted, review its structure. When you do, you will see that a change is in order. The section entitled *Measures to Improve Contract Activity* ought to come *between* the *Contract Activity 1988* and the *Contract Activity 1989* sections. The report claims that these measures were responsible for the increase in activity. Logically, therefore, the section explaining the measures belongs between the sections on 1988 and 1989 activities.

To reorganize your document, follow these steps:

1. Choose Outlining from the Utilities menu or press ⌘-U.

Fig. 2.21.

*The Print Preview
window showing
the headers on the
document.*

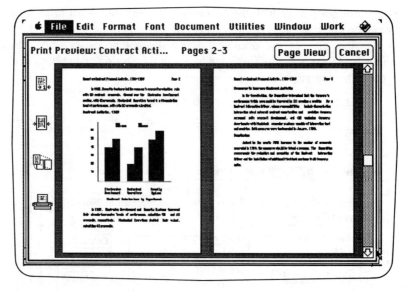

When the outline appears, you see the body text as well as the
outline headings. To hide the body text, you choose an option that
collapses, or hides, the body text and any headings below second-
level headings.

2. Click 2 on the outline icon bar at the top of the window. The body
text disappears and only the first-level and second-level headings
appear (see fig. 2.22). The gray underlining tells you that body text
is hidden beneath the headings.

Fig. 2.22.

*Document outline
with body text
hidden.*

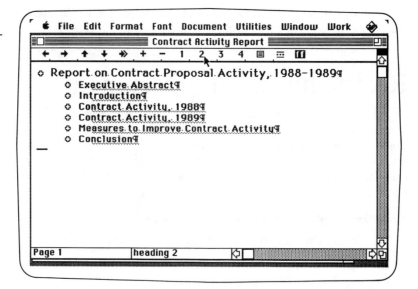

3. Move the pointer to the selection bar next to the heading entitled *Measures to Improve Contract Activity*. When the pointer becomes an arrow, click the mouse button to select the heading.

4. Choose Cut from the Edit menu.

5. Click the pointer in front of the first character of the heading entitled *Contract Activity 1989*.

   Important: Do not select the entire *Contract Activity 1989* heading. If you do, Word replaces the selected heading with the text you insert. If this happens, chose Undo from the Edit menu immediately.

6. Choose Paste from the Edit menu. Word inserts the section entitled *Measures to Improve Contract Activity* between the sections on 1988 and 1989 contract activity (see fig. 2.23).

Selection bar

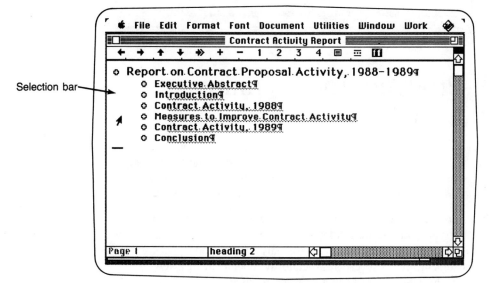

Fig. 2.23.

The restructured document in Outline view.

Switch to Galley view by pressing ⌘-U and examine your document (see fig. 2.24). As you can see, Word didn't move just the heading; Word also moved all the body text under the heading. By rearranging headings in Outline view, you can restructure the entire document in just a few keystrokes.

For a document as short as this one, moving sections in Outline view may not seem much better than moving text in Galley view. Think of the power of this technique when you work with a report dozens of pages long!

Fig. 2.24.

The restructured document in Galley view.

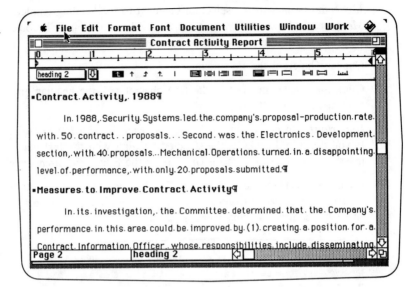

High-Productivity Techniques To Remember

❏ If you have stored on the clipboard something that you plan to paste later, be sure to delete additional text by using one of the techniques that doesn't erase the clipboard's current contents. Such techniques include pressing the Delete key or choosing Clear from the Edit menu.

❏ When you create a document containing headings and subheadings, begin by typing the heading titles in Outline view. When you type the headings in Outline view first, you not only have a good plan for your document, you also can restructure the document in a few keystrokes by rearranging headings on the outline.

❏ Use the Position command to ''anchor'' a graphic image (or a paragraph of text) on the page. Once anchored, the text or graphic always prints precisely where you positioned it, regardless of how much text you insert above it or below it.

❏ A *style* is a collection of formats. The collection can include character, paragraph, and other formats. When a style is defined, it is applied with just one command (you choose the style name from the style selection box or use the Styles command in the Format menu). For high-productivity formatting, make full use of Word's style formatting feature.

❑ Word's heading styles are predefined, but you almost certainly will want to change the definitions. Be sure to click the Keep With Following ¶ box in the Paragraph dialog box so that Word does not break the page below a heading.

❑ Instead of using several formatting commands each time you format a unit of text, create a new style. Then apply the style by choosing it from the style selection box on the ruler.

❑ You can use a font other than New York as the default for your document. To specify a new default, redefine the Normal style to include the font and size you want.

❑ By default, Word doesn't print page numbers. You can turn on page-number printing by adding page numbers to a header or footer.

❑ By default, Word's headers and footers print on the first page of a document. To disable this feature, click the First Page Special box on the Section dialog box.

❑ To restructure your document, choose Outlining from the Document menu and collapse the body text by clicking 2 on the outline icon bar. Then use the usual cutting and pasting techniques to rearrange the headings. As you move headings, Word moves the associated body text as well.

Part II

Word 4
Fundamentals

Includes

Writing and Editing Strategies

Fundamentals of Document Design I:
Character Formatting

Fundamentals of Document Design II:
Paragraph Formatting

Fundamentals of Document Design III:
Section and Document Formatting

Formatting with Style Sheets

Checking Spelling, Saving, and Printing

3

Writing and Editing Strategies

In Chapters 1 and 2, you learned many fundamentals of writing and editing with Microsoft Word. This chapter extends and develops your Word knowledge by examining writing and editing techniques in detail.

As you quickly discover, writing, editing, and formatting aren't rigidly separated pigeonholed tasks with Word. For this reason, this chapter introduces the formatting techniques you will most likely use as you create documents. As you create text, you may find it helpful to begin by choosing the font and margins you want. As you type, you can make full use of the Macintosh's fluency with symbols, adding technical characters, arrows, bullets, and diacritical marks. You are wise, too, to control line and page breaks as you type; if a problem with line or page breaks comes up, you can see the problem right on the screen, and fix it then and there.

You may find that you stop in the middle of writing to edit something—if so, fine! Most writers do. To work at peak productivity with Word, use a repertoire of techniques for moving the insertion point and scrolling. Commands to move the insertion point include Go To, Go Back, and Find. When the time comes to perform editing operations, you need to know how to select (highlight) text; you also need to know which command to use for maximum speed and efficiency. You find complete coverage of all these commands in this chapter.

Because Word is designed to please keyboard users as well as mouse users, most mouse techniques are duplicated by one or more keyboard commands. You needn't learn both methods in order to use Word effectively. If you're planning to use the mouse, however, exploring the keyboard techniques still makes sense. When you use the keyboard techniques, you don't remove your hand from the keyboard, so they're somewhat faster than the mouse techniques. Try the keyboard analogues for mouse actions, and if some of them seem particularly sensible or useful to you, highlight them in the keyboard command list at the end of this book.

Using Commands

To make Word easier for beginners to use, the program gives you a way of hiding its complexity: the Short Menus option in the Edit menu. When you start Word for the first time, you will find Short Menus in effect. For the material covered in this and the rest of the chapters of this book, however, choose the Full Menus option in the File menu.

Note: If you're trying the techniques in this chapter and you cannot find a menu option, you may have forgotten to choose Full Menus. Choose this command from the Edit menu. When you exit Word by choosing Quit from the File menu, Word saves your choice so that it becomes the default.

Choosing Commands with Keyboard Shortcuts

Standards of good practice for computer programmers state that keyboard commands should be mnemonic or easily memorized. At the minimum, they should use the command's first letter. So how come ⌘-U chooses Outlining, and ⌘-H chooses the Change command? By any standard, Word's keyboard equivalents for mouse commands is one of the weaker aspects of the program. Table 3.1 lists the assignments, but it's a safe guess that few users will memorize the whole list.

In fairness to Microsoft, note that the programming team was constrained by standard Macintosh key assignments. One of the appealing characteristics of the Macintosh environment is that the same skills work for most programs. For instance, Macintosh applications all use the same window features—once you have learned how to scroll in one program, for instance, you have learned how to scroll in the others too. The same goes for certain ⌘-key assignments. ⌘-S is supposed to be used for the Save command, for instance, while ⌘-V is Paste. ⌘-O is for the Open command—and therefore Microsoft cannot use it for choosing Outlining, at least not without violating the spirit of the Macintosh environment.

Table 3.1.
Keyboard Equivalents for Menu Commands

Command	Keyboard equivalent
Again	⌘-A
Calculate	⌘-equal
Change	⌘-H
Character	⌘-D
Close	⌘-W
Copy	⌘-C
Cut	⌘-X
Define Styles	⌘-T
Find	⌘-F
Find Again	⌘-Option-A
Footnote	⌘-E
Glossary	⌘-K
Go Back	⌘-Option-Z, or Keypad 0
Go To	⌘-G
New	⌘-N
Open	⌘-O
Outlining	⌘-U
Page View	⌘-B
Paragraph	⌘-M
Paste	⌘-V
Print	⌘-P
Print Preview	⌘-I
Quit	⌘-Q
Repaginate Now	⌘-J
Save	⌘-S
Show ¶/Hide ¶	⌘-Y
Show Ruler/Hide Ruler	⌘-R
Spelling	⌘-L
Undo	⌘-Z

Microsoft didn't violate the Macintosh standards for ⌘-key assignments—but you can. In Chapter 9, you will learn how easy it is to reassign command keys. You can set up keyboard equivalents for menu commands any way you want.

Power
User
Tip

If you have used previous versions of Word, you will be pleased to know that Word's dialog boxes have been reorganized and improved. Dialog boxes appear when you choose a menu command followed by three dots. These boxes allow you to choose ⌘-key options. Compared to previous versions, Word 4 has less clutter, and new features (such as dropdown list boxes) make Word 4's dialog boxes even easier to use, despite Version 4's many new features.

As you explore Microsoft Word and learn the program, you will use these dialog boxes frequently. It pays to spend a few minutes now learning about the options you will see in dialog boxes—and how to use these options effectively.

Selecting Options in Dialog Boxes

Figure 3.1 shows the Character dialog box, which appears after you choose Character in the Format menu. This dialog box illustrates all the features you will see in Version 4's dialog boxes.

❑ *Option group*. In most dialog boxes, related options are grouped and boxed (see fig. 3.1).

❑ *Check boxes*. When you see a square check box, you can click the box to turn the option on (so that an X appears in the box) or off (the X disappears). In an option group containing several check boxes, you can choose more than one option.

❑ *Option buttons*. When you see a round option button, you can click the button to turn the option on (a dot appears in the box) or off (the dot disappears). Unlike check boxes, however, you can click only one option button in a group. When you choose one option, Word turns off the other ones in the group.

❑ *Command buttons*. These buttons set actions in motion. When you click Apply, Word carries out the choices you have made in the dialog box but does not remove the dialog box from the screen. When you click OK, Word carries out the choices you have made and closes the box. When you click Cancel, Word closes the box without carrying out your choices. In some menus, command buttons open up second-level dialog boxes (dialog boxes within dialog boxes). In the Save As menu, for instance, clicking the File Formats button brings up the File Formats dialog box.

❑ *Text box*. To use a text box, you click it to select it and then type in it directly. If you highlight the box and start typing, Word erases the box's current contents.

❑ *Dropdown list boxes.* To reduce clutter in dialog boxes, Word 4 uses a new feature, the dropdown list box. To use a dropdown list box, you click the arrow, and the list appears (see fig. 3.2). After you choose the item you want, your choice appears in the box and the list disappears. Some dropdown list boxes also are text boxes, meaning that you can type in your own option instead of choosing one from the list. An example is the Size dropdown list box in the Character format menu. You can choose a size from the list or type the size you want.

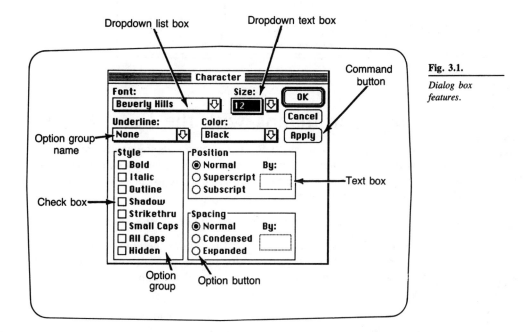

Fig. 3.1.

Dialog box features.

To restore the default settings in an option group, click the option group name. To restore the default character emphasis style (plain) in the Character dialog box, for instance, click the word Style at the top of the emphasis option group (see fig. 3.1).

Fig. 3.2.

Dropdown list box.

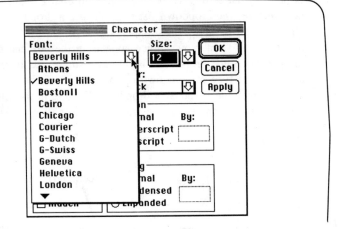

Choosing Commands with the Period Key

Speed Keys

⌘-Tab
Keypad-
period

Because Word's keyboard equivalents for menu commands frequently aren't mnemonic, you may prefer an alternative approach to selecting menu commands from the keyboard. This alternative approach gives you a way to choose commands by typing the command's first letter.

To choose menu commands from the keyboard, follow these steps:

1. Press ⌘-Tab or Keypad-period. Word highlights the command menu. The menu will remain highlighted for five seconds. If you do not press another key within five seconds, the highlighting disappears and Word returns to normal operation.

2. Type the first letter of a menu command. Alternatively, type a number from 0 to 8, or press the right-arrow key. Word pulls down the first menu to the left that begins with the letter you type. The number 0 pulls down the Apple menu, 1 pulls down the File menu, and so on. If you press the right arrow-key, Word opens the next menu right. Keep pressing the arrow key to move farther right. If you go too far, press the left-arrow key to go back.

3. After Word pulls down a menu, use the down- and up-arrow keys to highlight a menu item. Alternatively, press the item name's first letter on the keyboard.

4. To cancel a menu selection, press ⌘-period or Esc.

Keyboard Techniques in Dialog Boxes

If you like to use the keyboard, investigate the keyboard techniques for navigating around dialog boxes and choosing options. Particularly useful is the ⌘-letter option, which selects an item in a group. In the Character dialog box, for instance, pressing ⌘-B selects the Bold option in the Style group.

Table 3.2.
Keyboard Techniques for Dialog Boxes

Key	Effect
Tab	Move to next text box
Shift-Tab	Move to preceding text box
Up arrow	Select next item up in list box
Down arrow	Select next item down in list box
Right arrow	Move to next group right
Left arrow	Move to next group left
⌘-Tab	Move to next option
⌘-Shift-Tab	Move to preceding option
⌘-letter	Chooses option in group
Return	Same as clicking OK
Esc	Same as clicking Cancel
⌘-period	Same as clicking Cancel

More about Creating Text with Word

As distinguished from mere writing, *document processing* involves creating text that finds its expression in carefully designed, beautifully printed pages. You needn't concern yourself with all the minutiae of formatting as you write— indeed, to do so adds another level of cognitive complexity to a process that's already quite difficult! Because your goal is the printed page, making at least a few formatting choices as you type makes sense.

You may find it helpful as you type to choose a default font for your document, understand and use the options for special symbols and characters, choose the margins you want, and control line breaks and page breaks.

Creating a New Default Font for Documents

One of the joys of the Macintosh is its fluency with fonts, but Word's default font—New York—isn't everyone's favorite. Although New York is easy to read on the screen, the ImageWriter printout of this font is far from ideal, even when you choose the best print quality. Chances are that you will soon decide to choose another font for your documents. You may choose one of the other default Macintosh fonts, such as Geneva, or a font added to your Macintosh's System folder using the Font Mover desk accessory.

You can choose the font you want from the Font menu when you start new documents, but doing this for every document is a bother. The solution is to create a new default font for all documents.

⌘-T

To define a default font for all documents, follow these steps:

1. Choose Define Styles from the Format menu or use the ⌘-T keyboard shortcut.

2. Choose Normal in the Define Styles dialog box (see fig. 3.3).

3. Pull down the Font menu and choose the font you want.

4. Click the Set Default button.

5. When the alert box appears, click OK to redefine the Normal style for all documents.

Fig. 3.3.

The Define Styles dialog box.

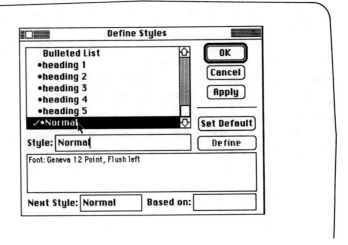

Word records your choices in a file called Word Settings, which the program creates and places in the System folder. If you delete this file, or if you start your Macintosh with a disk containing a different System folder, New York is once again the default font. To restore your font choice, repeat these steps or restart your computer with the start-up disk containing the correct System folder.

You can change the default font again, if you want. Just repeat these steps, and Word creates and saves a new default font definition.

Using Special Characters

For anyone who uses foreign-language or technical characters when writing, the Macintosh is truly a pleasure to use. Depending on the font you use, you can access many special characters by holding down Option or Shift-Option when you press a key. To see the characters available, use the Key Caps desk accessory. This desk accessory, which is part of your Macintosh's system software, displays a keyboard map on-screen. By displaying this map, you can see which characters are available with a given font.

To use Key Caps, pull down the Apple menu and choose Key Caps. Next, choose a font from the Key Caps menu. Then press Option to see the characters available (see fig. 3.4).

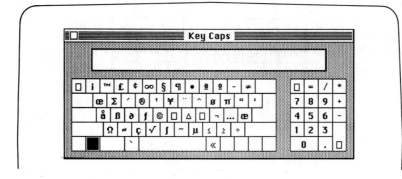

Fig. 3.4.

Key Caps display of special characters available by pressing Option (New York font).

If you press a key on the keyboard while you're using Key Caps, the character you've typed appears in the text box. If you want, you can select the character, choose Copy or Cut from the Edit menu, and paste it in your Word document by choosing Paste from the Edit menu in Word. But it is easier to use Key Caps as a guide to the keyboard layout; you can enter the special character in your Word document directly by holding down the Option key and pressing a key on the keyboard. To enter a bullet (a dot), for example, hold down the Option key and press 8 (on the keyboard, not the keypad).

If you use diacritical marks such as accents or umlauts, you can use the zero-width characters listed in table 3.2 to enter these characters. A *zero-width character* is a character that, when entered, does not advance the insertion point to the next space. To use these characters, press one of the keys listed in table 3.2. (The insertion point doesn't advance.) Then press a letter key; Word enters the mark and the letter together.

Table 3.3
Zero-Width Characters

Press	To Enter
Option-`	Grave accent (`)
Option-e	Acute accent (´)
Option-i	Circumflex (^)
Option-n	Tilde (˜)
Option-u	Umlaut (¨)

If you write in a technical or mathematical field, you will find many more useful symbols in the Symbol font (see fig. 3.5). To install the Symbol font, use the Font/DA Mover desk accessory that came with your Macintosh (see your manual for instructions for using this desk accessory). You will find the Symbol font in the Fonts file on your Macintosh system disk.

Fig. 3.5.

Key Caps display of the Symbol font.

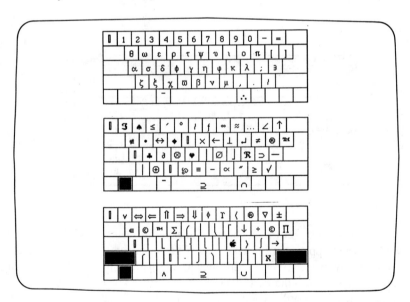

Note: If you create documents that include mathematical formulas, see Appendix B, "Mathematical Typesetting with Word 4."

Creating New Default Margins

By default, Word uses 1.0-inch margins at the top and bottom of the page and 1.25-inch margins at the left and right edges of the page. Unless you write nothing but letters and memos, you may prefer to use 1.0-inch margins all around, producing a line length of 6.5 inches (a standard length). Creating new default margins is easy.

To change Word's default margin settings to 1.0 inch on all sides, do the following steps:

1. Choose Document from the Format menu.

2. When the Document dialog box appears (see fig. 3.6), drag across the Left box and type *1 in*.

3. Drag across the Right box and type *1 in*.

4. Click the Set Default button.

5. Click OK.

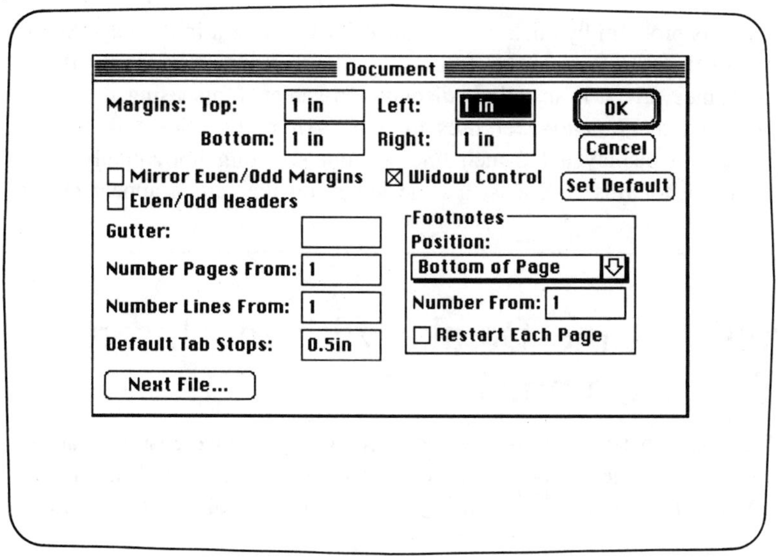

Fig. 3.6.

The Document dialog box.

Why bother with margins? Thanks to Word's graphic text display, you always see precisely where Word breaks lines when printed (even in Galley view). If you begin your document by choosing the margins you will use when you print, you can see line-break problems on the screen as you type. You then can correct the problems as you go, using the techniques discussed in the next section. If you change the margins later, you may not see line-break problems until you print your document. If problems exist, you may have to reprint the document, wasting time, paper, and—if you're using a laser printer—money (toner cartridges are expensive).

If you use an ImageWriter or ImageWriter II printer, you find that the text scrolls off the screen if you choose line lengths wider than 6.0 inches. This scrolling happens because, by default, the Macintosh displays characters using dots 1/80 inch wide. The ImageWriter prints the character dots 1/72-inch wide. When you choose the ImageWriter printer driver in the Chooser (as explained in Appendix A), Word compensates by displaying all the characters that will be printed on a line. The result is that the screen width is exceeded, although the specified line length is still in effect when the document is printed.

You can still write and edit as usual, even though all the text doesn't fit on the screen. Working this way is disconcerting; when the insertion point reaches the right border, the screen scrolls to the right so that you can see the remaining text. When the insertion point moves down to the next line, the screen scrolls back to the left. Keeping track of what you're doing is hard when the screen jumps back and forth.

You can solve this problem by clicking the Tall Adjusted option in the Page Setup dialog box from the File menu. The Tall Adjusted option, available only if the ImageWriter printer driver is installed, displays on-screen fonts using the same 1/72-inch dots that the ImageWriter uses to print. After you click this option, your Macintosh can display a 6.5-inch line without scrolling horizontally. The only price you pay for this choice is that the letters on the screen appear closer together.

Controlling Line Breaks with the Insert Line Break Command

Microsoft Word's "what you see is what you get" user interface ensures that the line breaks you see on the screen are the ones you see in the printed document. By default, Word doesn't start a new line unless one of the following conditions is true:

❏ You type a word that would go beyond the right margin (the program "wraps" the word to the beginning of the next line automatically).

❏ You press Return (Word starts a new paragraph).

❏ You press Shift-Return, the Insert Line Break command. When you use the Insert Line Break command, Word starts a new line without starting a new paragraph. If the Show ¶ option is selected in the Edit menu, Word displays a left arrow where you press Shift- Return.

Shift-Return

The Insert Line Break command is handy in these situations:

❏ You want to create text you can treat as a single paragraph for formatting purposes (see fig. 3.7). All the lines you create with the Insert Line Break command can be selected by clicking the insertion point anywhere within them. You can then choose tabs or paragraph formats as you please, and all the lines are affected with just one command.

❏ You want to keep lines of text together on a page. To keep lines together on a page, create the lines with Shift-Return and choose the Keep Lines Together command in the Paragraph dialog box from the Format menu.

❏ You want to create a multiline unit of text for sorting purposes. The Sort option in the Utilities menu sorts the selected text by paragraph. If you create a unit of text with the Insert Line Break command, the entire unit is kept together when you sort. An example of such a unit is a name and address.

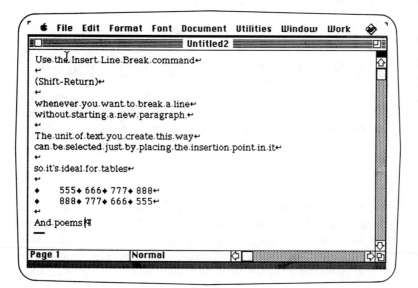

Fig. 3.7.

Controlling line breaks with the Insert Line Breaks command (Shift-Return).

Experiment with the Shift-Return key. You will find it very handy in the situations listed.

Controlling Line Breaks with Hyphens

If you use justified alignment or narrow columns, you may find that Word inserts too much space between words when it tries to align the right margin. If this happens, you may want to use optional hyphens to break long words at the end of lines. You can insert optional hyphens manually or let Word do the job automatically. You see the optional hyphens on the screen only if you have chosen the Show ¶ option in the Edit menu. Word prints the optional hyphens only if they're needed to improve the line break.

To insert an optional hyphen manually, follow these steps:

1. Place the insertion point where you want the hyphen to appear.

⌘-hyphen

2. Press ⌘-hyphen (-).

If you have chosen the Show ¶ option on the Edit menu, you can see where the optional hyphens are entered. Word doesn't print the hyphens unless they're needed to even the right margin. Optional hyphens appear as a hyphen with a tiny dot beneath it.

For information on hyphenating automatically, see Chapter 8, "Checking Spelling, Saving, and Printing."

Using Nonbreaking Hyphens and Spaces

When you type a word using an ordinary hyphen, the one you see on the keyboard, Word treats it as an ordinary character. Suppose that you type a hyphenated name, like Radcliffe-Brown. If this word appears at the end of a line, Word may insert a line break, like this:

    Radcliffe-
    Brown

To prevent Word from breaking a line in a word you have hyphenated, use a nonbreaking hyphen (⌘-'). If you have chosen the Show ¶ option on the Edit menu, Word displays the nonbreaking hyphen distinctively (you see a tilde above the hyphen and a tiny dot below it). The appearance of the hyphen reminds you that you entered a nonbreaking hyphen rather than an ordinary one (see fig. 3.8).

⌘-'

You can prevent line breaks between words that aren't hyphenated by entering a nonbreaking space (Option-space bar or ⌘-space bar). Use this command to prevent line breaks in the proper nouns *El Capitán* or *Sri Lanka*, for instance. If you

⌘-Space,
Option-space

have chosen the Show ¶ option in the Edit menu, Word displays nonbreaking spaces as a tilde over the usual tiny dot that appears when you press the space bar. Figure 3.8 shows how these symbols appear in an ordinary Word document (after you choose the Show ¶ command).

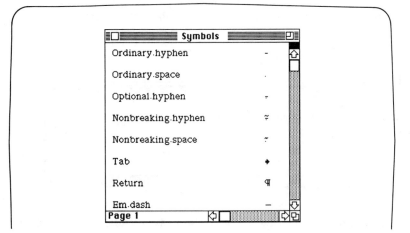

Fig. 3.8.

The screen display of keystroke symbols (after choosing Show ¶ on the Edit menu).

Using the Em Dash

In professional typesetting, the dashes that set off a phrase within a sentence—like this one—aren't created by using two hyphens, as you do on a typewriter or on most computers. Typesetters use a special character, called an *em dash*. You can create an em dash by pressing Shift-Option-hyphen (see fig. 3.8).

Shift-Option -

Breaking Pages Manually

By default, Word inserts page breaks automatically as you type. This feature, called *background pagination*, is controlled by the Background Pagination option in the Preferences dialog box on the Edit menu. To turn off background pagination, click the Background Pagination box in the Preferences dialog box. The page breaks Word inserts are dynamic: the program automatically adjusts them as you insert or delete text.

In some cases, you may want to break a page before it's filled with text (for example, to set off a title page from the body of a document). To enter a manual page break, choose the Insert Page Break option from the Document menu or use the Shift-Enter keyboard shortcut.

Shift-Enter

You can tell the difference between automatic and manual page breaks on the screen: the line marking of a manual page break has twice as many dots (see fig.

3.9). To remove a page break entered manually, move the mouse pointer to the selection bar (the leftmost column on-screen). When the I-beam pointer becomes an arrow pointing up and to the right, click the mouse to select the page break. Then press Delete or Backspace.

You cannot delete an automatic page break this way. To control the placement of automatic page breaks, see the next section, "Preventing Unwanted Page Breaks."

Fig. 3.9.

Automatic and manual page breaks.

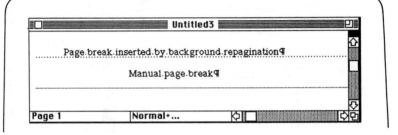

Note: Unlike most other computers, the Macintosh assigns different functions to the Return and Enter keys. If you press Shift-Return, for instance, Word inserts a line break; if you press Shift-Enter, Word inserts a page break.

Caution: Create manual page breaks only when absolutely necessary—for instance, to separate one chapter from another. Don't use manual page breaks to keep text together on a page or to prevent a widowed heading (a heading that appears alone at the bottom of a page, with no text underneath it). If you add or delete text later, you may find that the manual page break produces an unattractive result, such as a page only half filled with text. You then have to remove the manual page break. For most purposes, prevent Word from breaking a page where you don't want a page break to occur as explained in the following section.

Preventing Unwanted Page Breaks

You easily can prevent two common formatting errors (widowed headings and tables broken over two pages) by using commands that prevent page breaks. These commands come into play only if Word finds it necessary to break a page in the middle of the text on which you have used these commands. Because these commands work only when needed, they're much better than manual page breaks, which can become unnecessary if you add or delete text later.

To prevent a page break after a paragraph, use the following steps:

1. Place the insertion point in the paragraph. Remember that, to Word, a paragraph is any text ending with a paragraph mark. A paragraph, in this sense, could be a one-line heading.

2. Choose Paragraph from the Format menu or use the ⌘-M keyboard shortcut.

3. When the Paragraph dialog box appears, click the Keep With Next ¶ box and click OK (see fig. 3.10).

Fig. 3.10.

The Paragraph dialog box on the Format menu.

Paragraph

┌─ Indents ─────┐   ┌─ Spacing ─────┐
Left: `1 in`   Line: `Auto`   `OK`
Right: `     `   Before: `12 pt`   `Cancel`
First: `-0.5in`   After: `     `   `Apply`

☐ Page Break Before   ☐ Line Numbering
☐ Keep With Next ¶   ☐ Keep Lines Together

`Tabs...`   `Borders...`   `Position...`

To keep the lines of a paragraph together on a page, follow these steps:

1. Place the insertion point in the paragraph. If you broke lines with the Insert Line Break command (Shift-Return), all the lines you type are considered a single paragraph by Word. You can type an entire table this way and, as far as Word is concerned, all the lines are a single paragraph.

2. Choose Paragraph from the Format menu or press ⌘-M.

3. When the Paragraph dialog box appears, click the Keep Lines Together box and click OK.

After you choose the Keep With Next ¶ or the Keep Lines Together option, and if you chose Show ¶ on the Edit menu, Word places a small black box, called the *paragraph properties mark*, to the left of the paragraph. This symbol reminds you that you have chosen for the paragraph a format (such as the two just mentioned) that isn't visible on the screen.

You can cancel either of these page-break-prevention choices by clicking the appropriate box in the Paragraph dialog box again so that the *X* disappears.

Finding the Right Word with WordFinder

Word 4 comes with an excellent on-line thesaurus, WordFinder. Once you install WordFinder, you can activate this accessory at any time by choosing WordFinder from the Apple menu. Once you chose WordFinder from the Apple menu, a new menu, WF, appears on the menu bar (see fig. 3.11). Use the thesaurus whenever you want to explore your word-choice options.

Fig. 3.11.

The WordFinder menu.

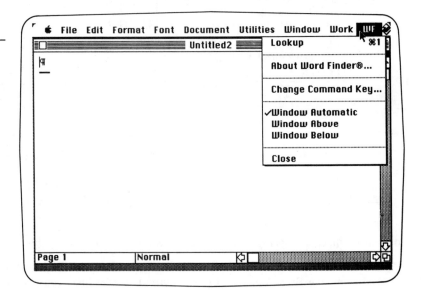

To install WordFinder, follow this procedure:

1. Insert Word Utilities Disk 2 in the external drive.

2. Double-click the WordFinder folder.

3. Double-click the WordFinder DA icon.

   The Finder automatically starts the Font/DA Mover application.

4. Click the Open button at the lower right corner of the Font/DA Mover window.

5. Click Drive until you see the directory of your start-up disk.

6. Highlight System Folder in the list box and click Open.

7. Select WordFinder DA in the left list box and click the Copy button.

8. When you see the WordFinder DA listed in your start-up disk's system folder, click Quit.

   After installing the WordFinder DA, you should see the WordFinder option on the Apple menu.

9. Drag the thesaurus file to the system folder on your start-up disk.

   For more information on the Font/DA Mover application, see the system software manual that came with your Macintosh.

To use WordFinder, follow these steps:

1. Double-click the word you want to look up.

2. Choose Lookup from the WF menu or press ⌘-1.

3. When the thesaurus window appears, examine the list of synonyms (see fig. 3.12). To choose a synonym, click the word, and then click the Replace button.

Speed
Keys

⌘-1

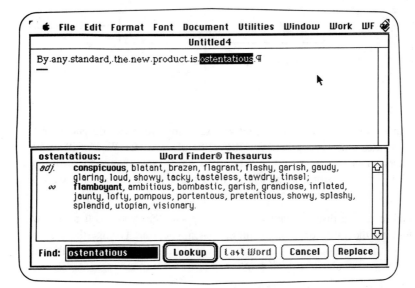

Fig. 3.12.

*The WordFinder
thesaurus window.*

You also can examine synonyms of the words in the list. To do so, click one of the words in the list and then click the Lookup button at the bottom of the thesaurus window. To return to a word that you have looked up already in this editing session, click the Last Word button at the bottom of the thesaurus window.

Moving the Insertion Point and Scrolling

Table 3.4 shows the standard Macintosh techniques used to move the insertion point and scroll the screen. Table 3.5 shows the many keyboard techniques used to move the cursor and scroll the screen. Refer to figure 3.13 for a quick guide to the scrolling features of the standard Macintosh window.

Fig. 3.13.

Scrolling features of the standard Macintosh window.

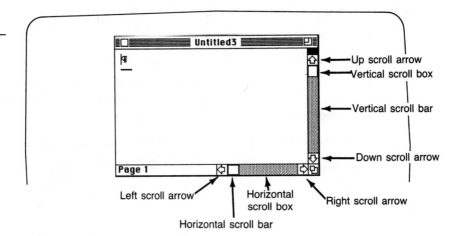

Remember that moving the insertion point and scrolling are two different things. When you move the insertion point, you move the place where Word will insert your characters when you start typing. When you scroll, you change the position of the window on the document, as if you were moving a picture frame over a long strip of paper. When you scroll, the insertion point stays put.

This fact can lead to a disconcerting surprise. Suppose that you scroll to a new location, leaving the insertion point behind. When you start typing, the screen scrolls back to the insertion point's location! To avoid this problem, remember to click a new insertion point after you scroll.

Table 3.4
Mouse Techniques for Moving the Insertion Point

To Move	Action
Up line-by-line	Click the up scroll arrow
Down line-by-line	Click the down scroll arrow
Up one window	Click the scroll bar above the scroll box
Down one window	Click the scroll bar below the scroll box

Table 3.5
Keyboard Techniques for Moving the Insertion
Point and Scrolling

To Move	Press
Up one line	Up arrow or 8 on the keypad. Press ⌘-Option-[(left bracket) to scroll up one line without moving the insertion point.
Down one line	Down arrow or 2 on the keypad. Press ⌘-Option-/ (slash) to scroll down one line without moving the insertion point.
Left one character	Left arrow or 4 on the keypad
Right one character	Right arrow or 6 on the keypad
Left one word	⌘-4 on the keypad
Right one word	⌘-6 on the keypad
Left to start of line	7 on the keypad
Right to end of line	1 on the keypad
To preceding sentence	⌘-7 on the keypad
To next sentence	⌘-1 on the keypad
To preceding paragraph	⌘-Option-Y or ⌘-8 on the keypad
To next paragraph	⌘-Option-B or ⌘-2 on the keypad
To top of window	⌘-5 on the keypad
One window up	9 on the keypad, ⌘-Option-P, or Page Up on the extended keyboard
One window down	3 on the keypad, ⌘-Option-period, or Page Down on the extended keyboard
Beginning of document	⌘-9 on the keypad
End of document	⌘-3 on the keypad

Even if you prefer using the mouse, investigate the keyboard techniques. You may find several keyboard techniques that are particularly useful for you. Make these techniques part of your repertoire of everyday working methods. If you have ever used the MS-DOS version of Word, you will be pleased to know that the Macintosh keypad emulates the MS-DOS keypad's cursor-movement controls.

Because there are so many keyboard commands for moving the insertion point, you may find it helpful to refer to figures 3.14 through 3.16, which show in graphic form the information in table 3.5.

Fig. 3.14.

Moving the insertion point with the keypad.

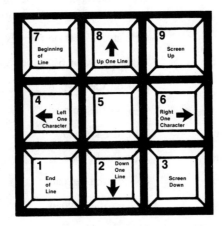

Fig. 3.15.

Moving the insertion point with the keypad (⌘ key held down).

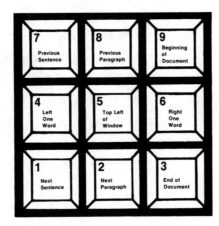

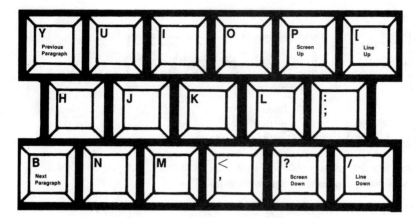

Fig. 3.16.

Moving the insertion point with the keyboard (⌘ and Option keys held down).

Caution: If you try to move the insertion point by using the numeric keypad but Word enters numbers on the screen, you have pressed the Clear key by accident. When you press the Clear key, you change the keypad to its number-entry function, and Word displays the message Num. Lock on the status line. To reactivate the keys that move the insertion point, press Clear again.

In a long document, scrolling line-by-line or screen-by-screen is tedious and slow. Use the techniques described in the following sections to move quickly through the document. Each technique moves the insertion point in large steps through the text or to the precise location you specify.

Using the Go To Command

By default, the Background Pagination option is turned on (this option is controlled by the Preferences dialog box in the Edit menu). With background pagination on, the page numbers that Word displays in the status line are accurate (the program may need a few seconds to update the page numbers as you scroll through your document). You can use the Go To command in the Utilities menu to move around rapidly in a long document.

To move the insertion point to the top of a specific page, follow these steps:

1. Choose Go To from the Utilities menu or use the ⌘-G keyboard shortcut.

2. When the Go To dialog box appears, type the number of the page to which you want to jump (see fig. 3.17).

3. Click OK.

⌘-G

Fig. 3.17.

*The Go To
dialog box.*

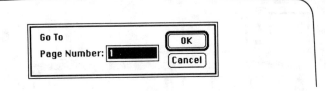

Using the Find Command

If you must scroll to a new location in a long document, but you're not sure of
the page you want, choose the Find command.

To find text in your document, use the following steps:

⌘-F

1. Choose Find from the Utilities menu or use the ⌘-F keyboard
   shortcut.

2. When the Find dialog box appears, type the text you want to find in
   the Find What box (see fig. 3.18).

   You can type up to 255 characters in the Find What box. In general,
   the more you type, the longer the search takes, but the more
   accurate the search will be. If you type *report*, for example, Word
   finds the next instance of the characters you typed, even if they're
   embedded in a word (such as *reporting* or *reported*). If you type
   Quarterly Report 1 of 1989, however, Word matches precisely what
   you specify—and only what you specify.

   A nifty new feature of Word 4 is that you can paste text from the
   clipboard to the Find What text box. You can use this feature to
   avoid retyping a long word or phrase for which you want to search.
   Suppose that you see the phrase "Report: Quarter II, Sections a, b,
   c" on-screen. Retyping this phrase would be tedious, so you select it
   and choose Copy from the Edit menu. Having copied the phrase to
   the Clipboard, you choose Find and then choose Paste from the Edit
   menu. The phrase appears in the Find What text box.

   To restrict the search to whole words, click the Whole Word box. If
   you typed *report* in the Find What box, Word finds *report* but not
   reporting, *reports*, or *reported*.

   To match the precise pattern of uppercase and lowercase letters in
   the Find What box, click the Match Upper/Lowercase box.

3. Click the Start Search button to begin the search.

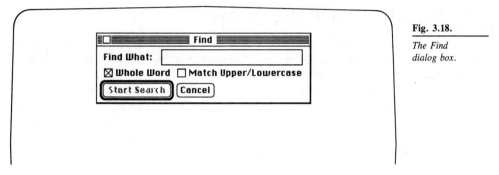

Fig. 3.18.

The Find dialog box.

If Word finds a match, the Find dialog box stays on the screen. Click Cancel to close the box or click Find Again to repeat the search. (The Find Again button replaces the Start Search button after Word finds a match.)

If Word doesn't find a match, an alert box appears, asking whether you want to continue the search from the beginning of the document. Click OK or Cancel. If you click OK and Word still doesn't find a match, another alert box appears, informing you that the end of the document has been reached without finding the text you specified. If Word didn't find a match, check the text you typed in the Find What box. You may have made a spelling mistake or a typographical error. If so, correct the error and click the Start Search button. If not, click the Close box to close the Find window and abandon the search. If no match was found, Word returns to the insertion point's location at the beginning of the search.

After you close the Find dialog box, you can repeat the search by choosing the Find Again command on the Utilities menu (or pressing the ⌘-Option-A keyboard shortcut). Word uses the same settings selected the last time you used the Find command in this editing session.

⌘-Option-A

Finding Text with Wild Cards

In a card game, a *wild card* is card that stands for any other card. In a computer search, a wild-card character is one that stands for any character. You can use a wild-card character when you search with the Find command (or the Change command, discussed later in this chapter). The wild-card character is a question mark (?).

If you type *19?? Report* in the Find What box of the Find dialog box, for example, Word matches *1987 Report*, *1988 Report*, and *1989 Report*.

Note: You can find special characters, such as tab marks, paragraph marks, and optional hyphens. For more information about searching for special characters, see "Changing Text," later in this chapter.

Scrolling in Page View

New to Version 4 of Word is the Page View mode. Page View permits you to type and edit as you view a precise, graphic representation of the page as it is to appear when printed (complete with headers, footers, page numbers, multiple-column text, and "anchored" graphics). Using Page View is like actually editing the pages that come out of your printer (see fig. 3.19). The Page View has many uses, including editing multiple columns on-screen. The concern here, however, is with a congenial feature of Page View: its capability to scroll from the top of one page to the top of the preceding or next page.

Fig. 3.19.

The Page View display of a document.

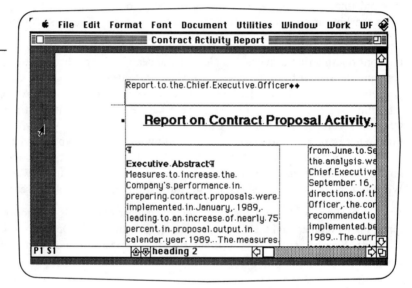

The penalty of using Page View, however, is a sharp reduction in scrolling speed. For this reason, switch to Page View only when you want to take advantage of its special features.

⌘-B

To view your document in Page View mode, choose Page View from the Document menu or use the ⌘-B keyboard shortcut.

When you use Page View, notice the page-forward and page-back icons that appear on the status line. Use these icons to move directly to the top of the preceding or following page. The icons work as if you had used the Go To command and typed the page number.

Using the Go Back Command

Many writers find themselves editing as they write. As they type a sentence, they remember another part of the same document that needs more work. So they stop writing, scroll to a different location, and make changes. Now they have to go back to the original location of the insertion point. To do this with most programs, you have to scroll or search. The little-known Go Back command in the Word Utilities menu, however, moves the insertion point back to its last location—that is, its location before you clicked a new insertion point. Investigate this command—it can save you significant amounts of time if, like most writers, you cycle between writing and editing tasks. If the last location of the insertion point is off the screen, Word scrolls the screen automatically.

Using Go Back takes some getting used to. For one thing, the command's name isn't quite accurate: it may move the insertion point forward (if that was the insertion point's previous location). The command's effects may seem mysterious until you understand what is happening.

Go Back always remembers the last three insertion point locations, so you can use the command three times. The fourth time you use Go Back, you see the location of the insertion point when you gave the first Go Back command. If you keep giving the command, the insertion point cycles among the last three locations and the present location.

A quick and handy way to access the Go Back command is to press 0 on the keypad. If you see the number *0* after pressing this key, press Clear to toggle the keyboard out of Num Lock mode.

Keypad 0

Selecting Text for Editing or Formatting

Basic to Word is the principle that editing and formatting commands act on selected text. This point may be clear to you already. What's not entirely clear from Word's documentation, however, is that you can use two different methods to select text. You can select *fixed* units of text, such as words, lines, or paragraphs, and you can select *variable* amounts of text. Once you have highlighted some text, you can extend the selection if it isn't quite right.

Selecting Fixed Units of Text

Table 3.6 lists the techniques you use to select fixed units of text.

Table 3.5
Selecting Fixed Units of Text with the Mouse

To Select	Do This Action
A word	Double-click the word to select the word and its trailing space
A line	Move the pointer to the selection bar and click
A sentence	⌘-click the sentence to select the sentence and its trailing space
A paragraph	Move the pointer to the selection bar and double-click
A graphic	Click the graphic or drag across it
Entire document	Move the pointer to the selection bar, hold down the ⌘ key, and click

The selection bar is the leftmost column on the screen. You know you have reached the selection bar when the I-beam pointer changes to an arrow pointing up and to the right.

Selecting Variable Units of Text

You can choose from mouse and keyboard techniques to select variable amounts of text.

To select variable units of text with the mouse, follow these steps:

1. Click at the beginning of the block of text you want to select.

2. Hold the mouse button and move the mouse away from the first character you selected. If you move the mouse to the top or bottom window borders, Word scrolls the screen, line-by-line, until you move the pointer away from the border or release the button.

3. When you finish expanding the highlight, release the mouse button.

To select a block of text with mouse using the Shift-click method, follow these steps:

1. Click where you want the selection to start.

2. Move the pointer to the end of the text you want to select. (Scroll the screen if necessary.)

3. Hold down the Shift key and click the last character you want to select.

To select a block of text using the keyboard, follow these steps:

1. Hold the Shift key and use the arrow keys or their keypad equivalents to expand the highlight.

2. When you finish expanding the highlight, release the Shift and arrow keys.

To select a block of text ending with a character you specify, follow these steps:

1. Place the insertion point where you want the selection to begin.

2. Press Option-⌘-H or press the minus key on the keypad. The message Extend to appears on the status line. To cancel the command, press Esc.

⌘-Option-H

3. Type the character to which you want to expand the selection.

Note: This technique is limited in use because you can type only one character, and Word selects up to the next instance of the character, which may not be very far if the character is a common one (such as *a* or *e*). You can extend the selection farther, however, by holding down the Shift key and pressing an arrow key to expand the highlight.

Extending a Selection

Once you have selected text, you can extend or contract the selection if you find that it's not quite right.

To extend the selection with the mouse, follow these steps:

1. Hold down the Shift key.

2. Drag the mouse or press an arrow key to expand or contract the selection.

When you use one of the techniques that selects variable units of text, you may find it tedious to define the end of the selection so that a whole word and its trailing space and punctuation are included. If so, try this trick:

1. Click where you want the selection to start.

2. Use a technique that selects a fixed unit of text, such as a sentence, line, or paragraph.

3. Hold down the Shift key and drag.

Word expands the selection by the fixed unit selected. If you selected a line initially, Word expands the selection line-by-line.

An even easier variation of this technique exists to expand the highlight word by word. This technique can save you no end of frustration, because you don't have to strain your eyes selecting the end of a sentence or paragraph. To expand the selection word-by-word, follow these steps:

1. Double-click the word that starts the selection, but don't release the mouse button after the second click.

2. Drag to the end of the selection. Word expands the highlight word-by-word.

3. When you have reached the end of the text you want to select, release the mouse button.

Deleting Text

The simplest way (and probably the most frequently used) to delete text is to press Delete (called Backspace on some keyboards) in order to rub out the text you just typed.

If you hold down the Delete key, Word deletes left and up. The deletion stops, however, if you try to delete a paragraph mark of a paragraph with different formatting. This feature prevents you from accidentally deleting paragraph formats. (As you quickly learn, Word ''stores'' paragraph formats in paragraph marks. If you delete the mark, you lose the format.)

Another easy way to delete text is to select it and start typing. Word automatically deletes all the highlighted text—even if it's several pages or more in length. If you change your mind, choose Undo immediately.

Neither of these two techniques—pressing Delete or typing over a selection—routes the text to the clipboard. Because this is true, use these techniques only for text you're sure that you don't want. Although you can recover deleted text by choosing Undo, you must choose the Undo command immediately after the deletion. If you're not entirely sure that the deletion is a good idea, choose Cut from the Edit menu or use the ⌘-X keyboard shortcut. If you cut the text to the clipboard, you can recover the text—as long as you haven't cut additional text to the clipboard.

You can use the keyboard commands listed in table 3.7 to delete characters and words.

Table 3.6
Keyboard Commands for Deleting Text

To Delete	Press
Previous character	Delete or Backspace
Next character	⌘-Option-F
Previous word	⌘-Option-Delete or ⌘-Option-Backspace
Next word	⌘-Option-G

Take special note of ⌘-Option-F, the command that deletes the next character to the right. This command is very useful because Word has no other way to delete the next character right with just one command. To delete the next character right with the mouse and keyboard, you need to move the I-beam pointer to the right of the character and press Delete.

This command is especially important if you are accustomed to MS-DOS computers. In DOS, the cursor is always *on* a character, and you always have a command that deletes the character on which the cursor is positioned. In the Macintosh world, the insertion point is always *between* characters, so you have no character to delete at that location. The insertion point is not positioned on a character unless you select the character by dragging over it. Using that method is tedious, however. You will find that it pays to master the use of Delete to erase the character to the left and ⌘-Option-F to delete the character to the right.

Copying and Moving Text

Almost all Macintosh applications, including Word, allow you to copy and move text using the clipboard (as you did in Chapter 1). This technique, however, isn't the easiest or safest. The clipboard holds only one unit of text at a time; if you copy or cut additional text to the clipboard, the new text wipes out the old text without giving you any warning or notification.

Experienced writers know that losing work is not difficult when you move text with the clipboard. Following is a typical situation: You cut a big block of text to the clipboard, planning to move it elsewhere in a major reorganization of your document. As you scroll to the new location, however, you notice something wrong in another area of text, and stop to fix it. Without thinking, you cut more text to the clipboard—perhaps a word or two—and wipe out the huge chunk you're moving. When you get to the new location and use the Paste command, the wrong text appears.

You can avoid this pitfall in two ways:

❏ Move headings in outlining mode if you're moving large blocks of text to reorganize a document, as introduced in Chapter 2, "Word 4 Quick Start: Business Reports."

❏ Use the keyboard copying and moving techniques that bypass the clipboard. These techniques are explained in the following sections.

Copying Text with ⌘-Option-C

To copy text using the keyboard and bypass the clipboard, use the following steps:

1. Select the text you want to copy.

⌘-Option-C

2. Press ⌘-Option-C. The message Copy to appears on the status line. The insertion point becomes a dotted vertical line.

3. Click the insertion point where you want the copied text to appear. You can adjust the location of the insertion point as often as you want. The command isn't complete until you press Return. To cancel the command, press Esc.

4. Press Return to copy the text.

Moving Text with ⌘-Option-X

To move text with the keyboard and bypass the clipboard, use the following steps:

1. Select the text you want to move.

⌘-Option-X

2. Press ⌘-Option-X. The message Move to appears on the status line. The insertion point becomes a dotted vertical line.

3. Click the insertion point where you want the text you're moving to appear.

4. Press Return.

Copying or Moving Text Using Window Panes

As you copy and move text in a document, you may find it helpful to split the window into two panes to display two different parts of the same document. After splitting the window, you can scroll each pane independently, making it easy to copy or move text from one pane to the other. Because you can see exactly what you're doing, keeping your editing plans in mind is easier—and that means fewer mistakes.

To copy or move text from one window pane to the other, use the following steps:

1. Split the screen by dragging the split bar to where you want to divide the window. Alternatively, double-click the split bar to split the screen into two equal parts.

   The split bar is the black bar on top of the right scroll bar. When you split the window, you gain two views of the same document.

2. Scroll each pane until one pane displays the text to be copied or moved and the other displays the final location of the text to be copied or moved.

3. Select the text to be copied or cut in one window pane.

4. Choose Copy or Cut from the Edit menu.

5. Click the insertion point in the other window pane at the point where you want the text to appear.

6. Choose Paste from the Edit menu.

Note: When you split a window into two panes, the screen displays two parts of the same document. To display two or more documents, you open additional documents (up to a maximum of 22 documents) with the Open command on the File menu. When you have opened two or more documents, you can choose among them with the Window menu, which lists the names of each document you have opened. For more information on using two or more documents, see "Using Windows," elsewhere in this chapter.

To remove a window split, drag the split bar to the bottom or top edge of the window, and press ⌘-Option-S (or double-click the split bar).

⌘-Option-S

To copy or move text between two different documents, you must use the clipboard. The keyboard techniques do not work when copying or moving text between documents. To copy or move text between documents, use the following steps:

1. Copy or cut the desired text from the first document to the clipboard.

2. Use the New or Open command to open the document to which you want to copy or move the text. Click the insertion point in the second document where you want the clipboard text to appear.

3. Choose Paste from the Edit menu, or press ⌘-P.

Changing Text

The Change command on the Utilities menu is useful when you decide to replace one word or phrase with another. You can use Change if you decide to substitute the word *use* for the word *utility* throughout your document. You can also use Change to eliminate a word or phrase; you can, for instance, remove all instances of the vague modifier *very*.

When you use the Change command, be sure that you click the Whole Word box. If you click this option, Word does not change or remove portions of words that happen to conform to the text typed in the Find What box.

To change text or remove text throughout your document, use the following steps:

1. Choose Change from the Utilities menu. The Change dialog box appears as shown in figure 3.20.

Fig. 3.20.

*The Change
dialog box.*

```
┌─────────────────────────────────────┐
│▤□▦▦▦▦▦▦▦ Change ▦▦▦▦▦▦▦│
│  Find What: [                  ]     │
│  Change To: [                  ]     │
│  ☐ Whole Word  ☐ Match Upper/Lowercase│
│ (Start Search)(Change)( Change All )(Cancel)│
└─────────────────────────────────────┘
```

2. Type in the Find What box the text you want to change or remove.

   You can type up to 255 characters in the Find What box. The more text you type, the longer the search takes, but the more accurate the search is. If you type *report*, for example, Word finds the next instance of these characters, even if they're embedded in a word (such as *reporting* or *reported*). If you type *Quarterly Report 1 of 1989*, however, Word matches precisely what you specify—and only what you specify.

You can highlight text in the document, cut it to the clipboard, and then paste it in the Find What box with the Paste option in the Edit menu.

3. *Optional but strongly recommended:* To restrict the search to whole words, click the Whole Word box in the Change dialog box. If you typed *report* in the Find What box, Word finds *report* but does not find *reporting, reports,* or *reported.*

4. *Optional:* To match the precise pattern of uppercase and lowercase letters in the Find What box, click the Match Upper/Lowercase box.

5. Type the replacement text in the Change To box. If you want to remove the text specified in the Find What box, leave the Change To box blank.

6. Click the Start Search button.

7. When Word finds the first match, click Change to make the change and continue, click No Change to skip this match and continue, or click Change All to change all matches without confirmation.

Use the Change All button with caution. Inspect a few matches to see how the command is working with your text. Click the Change button to continue to the next match until you're satisfied that the operation is doing what you expected. Then click Change All.

You can locate special characters with the Find and Change commands. The characters you can locate are typed into the Find What box on the Find or Change dialog boxes as shown in table 3.7. To type the caret symbol, hold the Shift key and press the 6 key above the letter keys.

Table 3.7
Searching for Special Characters

To Find or Change	Type
Line break mark	^n
Nonbreaking space	^s
Optional hyphen	^-
Page break or section break	^d
Paragraph mark	^p
Tab mark	^t
White space (any amount)	^w

Using Windows

In the section called "Copying and Moving Text Using Window Panes," earlier in this chapter, you learned how to split a window into two panes, which show two different parts of the same document. To display two or more documents (up to a maximum of 22), you can open two or more windows. The following sections present an overview of the techniques you use to open, size, move, and close windows.

Opening Windows

⌘-N, ⌘-O

Even though a document is open and displayed on-screen, you can open additional documents, up to the maximum of 22, without closing the open document or losing your work. To open an existing document, choose Open from the File menu or use the ⌘-O keyboard shortcut. To open a new document, choose New from the File menu or use ⌘-N.

When you open a new document, the new document's window is placed on top of the first one, filling the screen. For this reason, you cannot see the first document, and you might worry that you have lost your unsaved work. Don't worry! It's still there. You can display the first document by making it active again. And as you will learn, you can display two (or more) documents at once by sizing the windows so that you can see "beneath" the active window.

Making a Window Active

Only one window can be active at once. The active window has a highlighted title bar and contains the insertion point.

⌘-Option-W

To make another window active, choose the window's name from the Window menu or use the ⌘-Option-W keyboard shortcut.

If you haven't saved a document that's displayed in a window, Word gives it the name "Untitled" and assigns a number to it. "Untitled 1" is the first new document you open in an editing session, "Untitled 2" is the second, and so on. Word assigns these names because every window must have its own unique name.

The ⌘-Option-W keyboard shortcut activates windows in a round-robin sequence. If you have opened three new documents (Untitled 1, Untitled 2, and Untitled 3), you will see them activated in that sequence when you press ⌘-Option-W repeatedly. When you press this key while Untitled 3 is displayed, you see Untitled 1 again.

Sizing a Window

You use two important features of the standard Macintosh window border to size windows with Word:

❑ *Zoom box*. Click this box to reduce the window's vertical size automatically by 50 percent, thus revealing the window that is "under" the active window. Click it again to "zoom" the window to full size.

❑ *Size box*. Click and drag this box to size a window manually. You can reduce the size of the window horizontally as well as vertically. Once you adjust the size of a window manually, Word uses this size when you click the zoom box.

Use the following procedure to display two different documents on-screen at the same time.

1. Open both documents using the Open or New command in the File menu.

2. Click the zoom box to reduce the vertical size of the active document window by 50 percent (see fig. 3.21). Alternatively, use the ⌘-Option-] (right bracket) keyboard shortcut.

⌘-Option-]
(right bracket)

Fig. 3.21.

Reducing the vertical size of the active window.

 File Edit Format Font Document Utilities Window Work

Untitled1

Untitled2

Page 1   Normal

Word places the sized window at the bottom of the screen. You see the inactive document beneath the active one.

3. Click the insertion point in the other document's window to make it active. This document fills the screen.

4. Click the zoom box to reduce the size of this document by 50 percent.

   Notice that Word now places the sized window at the top of the screen, a very handy feature (see fig. 3.22).

Fig. 3.22.

Two documents displayed on-screen in two half-size windows.

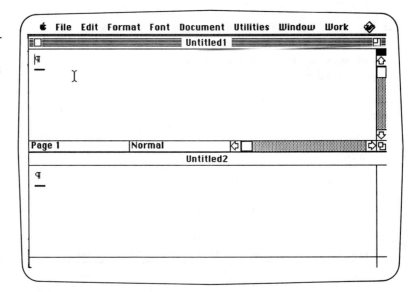

At any time, you can zoom a window to full size by clicking the zoom box. Zooming one window to full size does not affect the size of other windows. While you're working with two windows displayed, in other words, you can zoom one to full size for convenient editing. When you're finished, click the zoom box (or press ⌘-Option-]) to reduce the window to half size again, thus revealing the other window.

Moving Windows

Rarely is it necessary (or even desirable) to do so, but if you want, you can move a window's position on the desktop by dragging the title bar. After moving the window, you can restore its original location by clicking the zoom box.

Closing Windows

To close a window, save your work by choosing Save or Save As from the File menu (or use the ⌘-S keyboard shortcut). Then click the close box, choose Close from the File menu, or use the ⌘-W keyboard shortcut.

⌘-W

High-Productivity Techniques To Remember

❑ If you plan to print with a font other than New York, make your font choice the default. Choose Define Styles from the Format menu, select the Normal style, and choose your font from the Font menu. Then click the Set Default button in the Define Styles dialog box.

❑ Explore the Key Caps desktop accessory, the Symbol font, and the zero-width characters to appreciate fully your Macintosh's fluency with nonstandard characters. Restrict your symbol choices in formal writing to the strictly functional, such as arrows and bullets.

❑ If you don't like Word's 6.0-inch line length and plan to change the margins before you print, start your document by changing the margins. When you change the margins at the start, you can see line breaks the way they will appear when the document is printed. You can fix line-break problems as they arise. To set the margins, choose Document from the Format menu. Set the desired margin values. Click Set Default to make your choices the new default for all documents.

❑ To start a new line without starting a new paragraph (in Word's sense of the term), press Shift-Return or choose Insert Line Break. The lines you create in this way are all one paragraph as far as Word is concerned. You can select all the lines by clicking the insertion point within them. Using this type of line break simplifies the selection of a table of data. Break lines by using the Insert Line Break command when you want to create units of text for sorting purposes.

❑ To improve the right margin when you use justified text or multiple columns, insert optional hyphens in long words at the ends of lines by pressing ⌘-hyphen. Use nonbreaking hyphens (⌘-') or nonbreaking spaces (⌘-space bar) to prevent Word from breaking the line between two words.

❑ Break pages manually by choosing Insert Page Break or pressing Shift-Enter only when absolutely necessary. To keep a table together or prevent a heading from printing at the bottom of the page, format the text with the Keep Lines Together or Keep With Next ¶ option in the Paragraph dialog box, available from the Format menu.

❑ When editing, use Find to scroll precisely to the location of the text you specify. Use the Go Back command to return to the last location of the insertion point.

❑ When selecting variable units of text, double-click the beginning point of the block of text and hold the mouse button to expand the highlight word-by-word.

❑ To delete text quickly, select it and type over it.

❑ When copying or moving text, avoid the clipboard and possible work losses. Use the keyboard copying (⌘-Option-C) and moving (⌘-Option-X) techniques.

Fundamentals of Document Design I: Character Formatting

In *The Psychology of Everyday Things* (New York: Basic Books, 1988), Donald A. Norman enumerates two basic principles of good design. Design elements should be visible, and their relationship to other elements should be natural so that you can interpret them without thinking about them. These two points tell you much of what you need to know to design effective documents. First-level headings, for instance, should be centered, boldfaced, or printed in a larger font to indicate their importance naturally. Second-level and third-level headings, in contrast, should be, by turns, smaller and less conspicuous. You also should do all you can to break up text on the page, for instance, by using lists with bullets or numbers. Good design, in short, isn't a mere matter of aesthetics. Good design is a matter of choosing design elements that communicate effectively and naturally with your readers. Of course, you must use the design elements consistently and conservatively once you have chosen them.

Word's what-you-see-is-what-you-get screen display is ideal for on-screen document design. You can use character formats, such as fonts, font sizes, and character emphasis, to include natural design elements in your document. You can use paragraph formats, such as indentations, alignments, and blank lines, to break up text on the page so that logical relations are clear. Because you see your formatting choices on the screen before you print, judging the effectiveness of the design is easy.

Note: This chapter assumes that you have read Chapter 3, "Writing and Editing Strategies." You also should know the techniques for selecting text, discussed in Chapter 3.

The Four Formatting Domains

Documents are formatted by applying four different kinds of formatting commands: *character*, *paragraph*, *section*, and *document* formats. Following is a brief overview of the four formatting domains:

❑ *Character formats.* The smallest unit of formatting in Word is character formats. This type of format includes font (type design), font size (in printer's points), style (emphases such as boldface, outlining, italic, or underlining), position (superscript or subscript), and spacing (compressed or expanded). You can select precisely the characters you want to format, whether the selection includes just one character or all the characters in the document.

❑ *Paragraph formats.* In Word, a paragraph isn't a unit of *meaning*, as it is for people; a paragraph is any block of text between two paragraph marks (or between the beginning of a document and the first paragraph mark). With this definition, a paragraph can be a single word—or a single character. Paragraph formats, such as indents, line spacing, tabs, and borders, apply to the entire paragraph—or paragraphs, if more than one is selected.

❑ *Section formats.* Section formats are page-style formats that can vary within a document. These formats include page numbers, columns, line numbers, headers, and footers. Most documents aren't divided into sections. For single-section documents, section formats apply to the whole document. If you divide your document into sections by pressing ⌘-Enter, you can change the section formats. Section breaks are useful for creating documents with separate chapters.

❑ *Document formats.* Document formats are page-style formats that apply to the whole document. These formats include margins, footnote position, and default tab width.

This chapter discusses character formats. Chapter 5 discusses paragraph formats, and Chapter 6 examines section and document formatting.

Formatting as You Type and Formatting Later

Following is another distinction that helps to clarify the way you work with Word. Whether the subject is character formatting or paragraph formatting, you can format in two different ways:

❑ *Formatting as you type*. When you format this way, you choose formats before you start typing. As you type, Word enters the formats and text simultaneously. Think of this technique as if you were "programming" the insertion point to "lay down" the formats selected. To stop "laying down" formats, choose commands that cancel character formatting (the Plain Text option on the Font menu or ⌘-Shift-Z) or paragraph formatting (⌘-Shift-P).

❑ *Formatting later*. When you format this way, you choose formats *after* you type. You select the text and then choose a formatting command.

One advantage of formatting as you type is that you don't have to select the text before formatting it. The disadvantage, however, is that you must think about formatting ("What's the command I want?") at the same time you think about the other concerns you have as a writer ("What tense am I using? Is that modifier dangling or not? What the heck am I trying to say?"). If you have trouble writing, you may find it easier to format later, thereby reducing the number of considerations you must keep in mind at once.

Remember, however, that writing may be easier when you can see your text's printed appearance on the screen. In technical writing, for instance, many document elements—such as instructions—are easier to write (and edit) when you set them off from the rest of the text.

Unless you're a beginning writer, document processing theory suggests a very good reason to format as you type rather than formatting later. Character and paragraph formats aren't just variations of the way ink is pounded, sprayed, or fused onto the page—formats have *meaning*. Font choices, list formats, fixed-width characters, and other formats *signal* something to the reader about the *nature* and *significance* of the document. Is the document formal or informal? Is it personal or impersonal? Is it conservative or trendy? Is it solemn or serendipitous? As you become more conscious of the *meaning* of formats, you see that you have two ways to express what you're saying with Word. The first is the meaning of the text you type; the second is the signals you send by the formatting choices you make.

About Character Formatting

With Word, you can vary the following format attributes of any character you can display on the screen:

❑ *Font* (default New York). Font is the type design of the characters you enter. Word uses all the fonts currently available in your System folder. To add more fonts, see Appendix A.

❏ *Size* (default 12 points). Size is the height, in printer's points, of a font. One inch contains 72 points. You can choose fonts in sizes from 2 through 127 points.

❏ *Color* (default black). If you have a color monitor, you can display characters in six colors (blue, cyan, green, magenta, red, and yellow). If you are using another color output device or if you equip your ImageWriter with a color ribbon, you can print colors.

❏ *Style* (default Plain Text). Choose emphases such as boldface, italic, underline, outline characters, and shadow characters. You can choose from four kinds of underlines: single underline, word-only underline, double underline, and dotted underline.

❏ *Position* (default Normal). You can superscript or subscript characters so that they're positioned above or below the line (at a height you specify).

❏ *Spacing* (default Normal). You can adjust the space between the characters. The Expanded option widens the space; the Condensed option narrows it. The Expanded and Condensed options are in the Spacing options group of the Character dialog box.

The following sections look more closely at these aspects of character formatting.

Choosing Character Formats

You can choose character formats in three different ways:

❏ *Format and Font menus*. The Format menu contains character-emphasis options. You can choose fonts and font sizes from the Font menu.

❏ *Character dialog box* (from the Format menu). You can choose fonts, font sizes, emphases, spacing, position, underlining options, and colors from this dialog box.

❏ *Keyboard shortcuts*. You can apply all character formats with keyboard shortcuts.

Which way is best? The decision depends on you and on the format you're choosing. If you're a good typist, you probably will prefer keyboard shortcuts. If you're selecting fonts, choosing them from the Font menu is convenient. If you're choosing colors or spacing options, you use the Character dialog box (because you cannot select these options in any other way).

Regardless of the character-formatting technique you choose, it can be tedious and time consuming to change character formats frequently in a document—too much fussing with the mouse, keys, and menus. To get maximum productivity from Word, you are well advised to develop styles (see Chapter 7, ''Formatting with Style Sheets''). When you create a style, you name a format that combines two or more formatting choices, including character formats.

About Fonts and Font Sizes

Word lets you choose from all the fonts currently stored in the System folder on your Macintosh's start-up disk. To add additional fonts, use the Font/DA Mover application (see your Macintosh's system software manual for more information).

Choosing fonts is fun. For business and professional writing applications, however, you must understand the message you send when you make font choices. The message you send is based on the spacing of the font (whether fixed-width or proportionally spaced) as well as the design of the typeface. The following sections explain these aspects of font design.

Fixed-Width and Proportionally Spaced Fonts

The characters in a *fixed-width font* (such as Monaco or Courier) always occupy the same width, whether the character is narrow (like *l*) or wide (like *w*). Fixed-width fonts look like typewritten characters—not too surprising, considering that typewriters produce fixed-width type. Courier is an excellent choice for business correspondence and memos; the ''typewriterlike'' appearance of this font suggests a document that has been typed especially for the recipient.

In proportionally spaced fonts (such as Chicago, Geneva, or New York), the wide characters take up more space than the narrow ones. The result is a more professional, typeset appearance—but it's also more impersonal. Psychologically, people react to such type in the same way they react to a printed book; they assume that the text has been scrutinized, edited, and proofread. As a result, proportionally spaced type (especially when printed with a laser printer) carries all the authority—and the responsibility for accurate reporting and good judgment—of a printed document. Choose proportionally spaced fonts when you want your document to carry weight. Make sure that you have done your homework so that your work deserves the respect you're seeking. Remember that someone reading your document will assume that the document has been prepared for many people to read. For this reason, proportionally spaced type may be the wrong choice for a personal message.

Font Design

Hundreds of typeface designs exist, each subtly conveying a complex message about the nature of the text and about *you*. Following are the meanings many people associate with the fonts.

❑ *Chicago*. Brash, crude, masculine, and massive, this font works well for the Macintosh system (the font is so distinctive that it functions well to set off command names from other text on the screen). The font is too loud for most business and professional applications, with the exception of business forms. In business forms, the Chicago font can perform the same function it does on-screen (attracting attention).

❑ *Courier*. Simulates the typescript created by office typewriters. This font suggests a *personal* message prepared especially for the recipient and is an excellent choice for letters and memos.

❑ *Geneva*. The Macintosh's version of Helvetica, this airy and pretty font suggests lightness, modernity, and informality. For formal applications, choose Helvetica instead.

❑ *Helvetica*. The "modern" font *par excellence*, Helvetica suggests all that is up-to-date, clean, and sophisticated, like modern corporate architecture. Helvetica is useful when you want to convey the impression of running an intelligent, up-to-date operation. Helvetica isn't as easy to read as Times, however; Times is a better choice for long passages of text. Helvetica produces excellent results with laser printers.

❑ *Los Angeles*. Light, fun, airy, and extremely informal. In business and professional contexts, Los Angeles is useful only for the most informal purposes, such as announcing an office party.

❑ *Monaco*. With its fixed-width spacing and rounded forms, Monaco looks as though it were created by a machine. Monaco suggests mechanical precision.

❑ *New York*. Word's default font, New York is very readable on the screen, but its printed appearance is poor and suggests a lack of attention to detail.

❑ *Times*. Generally regarded to be the most readable font, Times produces excellent results on laser printers. It suggests conservatism and authority and shows a concern for your document's readability. Times creates the impression that the document is being prepared for many people to read (like a book or newspaper) and is rather impersonal.

❏ *Venice*. A pretty italic font that simulates hand calligraphy. Suggests sophistication, grace, and style in a sufficiently "upper crust" way that may imply condescension if used in the wrong context.

Following is a handy guide for font choices for business and professional writing applications.

Application	*Fonts To Use*
Brochures	Use Helvetica to create the impression of a clean, modern enterprise.
Letters	Use Courier for the text. For businesses in a traditional profession, such as medicine, law, or scholarship, choose Times for the letterhead. For more modern enterprises, choose Helvetica for the letterhead.
Memos	Use Courier for serious memos to suggest a personal message. Use Los Angeles for more informal memos.
Reports	If the report is long (more than 3 or 4 pages), use Times for readability. Use Helvetica if suggesting that an up-to-date, sophisticated operation is advantageous.
Forms	Use Chicago to attract attention to headings.

Avoid mixing fonts on the page. Using too many fonts produces a cluttered, visually disjointed appearance. In general, use no more than two fonts on any given page of your document.

Fonts Sizes and "Scaled" Fonts

When you pull down the Font menu, notice that some font sizes appear in outlined characters but others don't (see the Font menu in fig. 4.1). The outlined sizes are the ones for which complete information exists on disk for displaying the font accurately on the screen. You can choose other (nonoutlined) sizes, but Word scales them, producing a jagged, uneven appearance on the screen (notice the difference between the 18-point and 24-point type in fig. 4.1).

If you use an ImageWriter printer, avoid scaled fonts. Scaled fonts don't look any better when you print them than they look on the screen.

If you use a LaserWriter printer, however, scaled fonts print just as well as non-scaled fonts because the LaserWriter "smooths" the fonts to produce excellent results.

Fig. 4.1.

*The Font menu
and examples of
different sizes.*

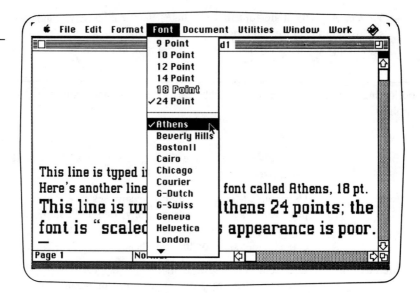

Choosing Fonts and Font Sizes

If you haven't yet redefined Word's default font (see "More about Creating Text
with Word" in Chapter 3, "Writing and Editing Strategies"), you see the default
font, New York, on the screen as you type. You can change the font as you type
or after you are done typing.

To change the font as you type, follow these steps:

⌘-Shift-E

1. Click the insertion point where you want to start typing.

2. Choose the font you want from the Font menu (again see fig. 4.1).
   Alternatively, choose the ⌘-Shift-E keyboard shortcut, and when the
   message Font appears on the status line, type the name of the font
   you want to use.

⌘-Shift-2

3. Type the text.

4. When you are finished typing with the font you have chosen, press
   ⌘-Shift-Z to return to the default font.

To change the font size as you type, follow these steps:

⌘-Shift->
⌘-Shift-<

1. Click the insertion point where you want to start typing.

2. Choose the point size you want from the Font menu. Alternatively,
   press ⌘-Shift-> (greater than) or ⌘-Shift-< (less than) to increase or
   decrease the size of the font by one point size.

3. When you are finished typing with the font you have chosen, press ⌘-Shift-Z to return to the default font.

To change the font after you type, follow these steps:

1. Select the text for which you want to change the font.

2. Choose a font from the Font menu. Alternatively, press ⌘-Shift-E and type the name of the desired font.

To change the font size after you type, follow these steps:

1. Select the text for which you want to change the font.

2. Choose a size from the Font menu. Alternatively, press ⌘-Shift-> to increase the point size, or ⌘-Shift-< to decrease the font size.

⌘-D

You also can choose fonts and font sizes by using the Character dialog box, shown in figure 4.2. To open the Character dialog box, choose Character from the Format menu or press ⌘-D. To open the list of fonts or sizes, click and drag the arrow next to the Font or Size box.

Character

| Font: | Size: | OK |
| Helvetica | 12 | Cancel |

Underline: None   Color: Black   Apply

Style
☐ Bold
☐ Italic
☐ Outline
☐ Shadow
☐ Strikethru
☐ Small Caps
☐ All Caps
☐ Hidden

Position
◉ Normal   By:
○ Superscript
○ Subscript

Spacing
◉ Normal   By:
○ Condensed
○ Expanded

Fig. 4.2.

The Character dialog box.

To restore the default font and font size (and cancel all other character formats), follow these steps:

1. Select the text.

2. Press ⌘-Shift-space bar.

Using Character Emphasis

Word uses the term *style* to refer to character *emphases* such as boldface or under-lining (see fig. 4.3). Because the term *style* invites confusion with the styles entered from style sheets, this book uses the term *emphasis*. You can assign emphasis to any font or font size.

Fig. 4.3.

Character emphasis options.

Character Styles

Plain text

Bold

Italic

Underline

Word Underline

Double Underline

Dotted Underline

~~Strikethrough~~

Outline

Shadow

SMALL CAPS

ALL CAPS

Hidden

To assign emphasis to characters as you type, follow these steps:

1. Click the insertion point where you want to start typing.

2. Choose the emphasis you want from the Format menu. Alternatively, choose Character from the Format menu and choose an Underline or Style option from the Character dialog box. You also can use the keyboard shortcuts listed in table 4.1.

You can choose Bold, Italic, Underline, Outline, or Shadow from the Format menu. To choose other underlining options, Strikethru, Small Caps, All Caps, and Hidden emphases, you must use the Character dialog box or a keyboard shortcut.

To assign emphasis after you type, follow these steps:

1. Select the text you want to format.

2. Choose the emphasis you want from the Format menu. Alternatively, choose Character from the Format menu and select an Underline or Style option. You also can use the keyboard shortcuts shown in table 4.1.

Table 4.1
Keyboard Shortcuts for Character Emphasis

Emphasis	Keyboard shortcut
All Caps	⌘-Shift-K
Bold	⌘-Shift-B
Dotted underline	⌘-Shift-\
Double underline	⌘-Shift-[
Hidden	⌘-Shift-X
Italic	⌘-Shift-I
Outline	⌘-Shift-D
Shadow	⌘-Shift-W
Small Caps	⌘-Shift-H
Strikethrough	⌘-Shift-/
Underline	⌘-Shift-U
Word underline	⌘-Shift-]

If you frequently use an emphasis not on the Format menu, you can add the emphasis to the Format menu using ⌘-Option-Plus.

To add an emphasis option to the Format menu, use the following steps:

⌘-Option-+

1. Press ⌘-Option-Plus.

2. Choose Character from the Format menu. When the Character dialog box appears, click the emphasis option you want.

For more information on adding options to menus, see Chapter 9, "Customizing Word 4's Menus and Keyboard."

To cancel character emphases, follow these steps:

1. Select the text.

2. Choose Plain Text from the Format menu. Alternatively, use the ⌘-Shift-Z keyboard shortcut.

You can determine the formats of a block of text by selecting the text and then choosing Character from the Format menu. When the Character dialog box appears, notice the font, size, color, underline style, and emphasis options listed or checked. The Character dialog box lists all the character formats for the currently selected text.

If you select text that isn't homogeneous in its character formatting, the Character dialog box does not contain the formats of the currently selected text, and the

Style boxes are shadowed (see fig. 4.4). An example of text that isn't homogeneous is a line with one word boldfaced, one word italicized, and the rest formatted as plain text.

Fig. 4.4.

The Character dialog box as it appears for a block of text not homogeneously formatted.

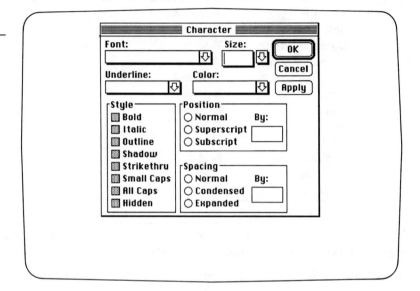

When the Character dialog box appears in its shadowed-and-blank form, you can add a format to those in effect without canceling the formats already selected. (That's why all the buttons and boxes are blank—no formats are entered unless you specifically choose one.)

To see the effects of your choices without leaving the Character dialog box, click the Apply button. To cancel your choices, click Cancel.

Understanding the Underlining Options

You can choose from four underline formats:

❏ *Underline* (⌘-Shift-U). All characters are underlined, including spaces.

❏ *Word Underline* (⌘-Shift-]). Complete words and punctuation marks are underlined, but not white space (tabs and spaces).

❏ *Double Underline* (⌘-Shift-[). A double underline appears beneath all words and spaces.

❏ *Dotted Underline* (⌘-Shift-\). A dotted underline appears beneath all words and spaces.

If you prefer the Word Underline option for day-to-day use, you can replace the Underline option with the Word Underline option on the Format menu by following these steps:

1. Press ⌘-Option-Minus. The pointer changes to a big minus sign.

2. Choose Underline from the Format menu. Word removes the Underline option from the Format menu.

3. Press ⌘-Option-Plus. The pointer changes to a big plus sign.

4. Choose Character from the Format menu.

5. When the Character dialog box appears, click the Word Underline box. Word adds the Word Underline option to the Format menu.

Using Hidden Text

The Hidden character style, grouped with the character-emphasis options, has many uses in Word. With the Hidden style, you can create text that doesn't appear on the screen (or print) unless you want it to. The uses of hidden text include the following:

❏ Entering notes to a colleague in collaborative writing situations.

❏ Hiding special commands that Word enters, such as the commands that mark table-of-contents and index entries (see Chapter 15, ''Adding an Index and Table of Contents'').

❏ Hiding PostScript commands (for owners of LaserWriter or other PostScript-compatible printers who want to include PostScript programming commands in Word documents).

You format text as hidden text by clicking the Hidden box in the Character dialog box (or pressing ⌘-Shift-X). Word displays hidden text on the screen with a dotted underline.

By default, Word displays hidden text. To hide hidden text so that it is not displayed on the screen, or to redisplay text when it is hidden, follow these steps:

1. Choose Preferences from the Edit menu. If Preferences does not appear on the Edit menu, choose Full Menus from the Edit menu and try again.

2. When the Preferences dialog box appears, click the Show Hidden Text box so that there is no X in the box.

3. Click OK.

To remove the Hidden character formatting from text, follow these steps:

1. Select the text formatted as hidden text. If the text isn't visible on the screen, display it by clicking the Show Hidden Text box in the Preferences dialog box from the Edit menu.

2. Choose Plain Text from the Format menu or press ⌘-Shift-Z.

Note: Whether or not you display hidden text, you control the *printing* of hidden text by clicking the Print Hidden Text box in the Print dialog box. Even if hidden text isn't visible on-screen, you can print it by clicking this box. By default, Word doesn't print hidden text. If you want hidden text to print, you must click this box before printing.

If you plan to use hidden text extensively, especially in a collaborative writing situation, add the Show Hidden Text option to the Format menu. Add the Show Hidden Text option to the Format menu by following these steps:

1. Choose Commands from the Edit menu. If Commands does not appear on the Edit menu, choose Full Menus from the Edit menu and try again.

2. When the Command dialog box appears, use the scroll arrows to display the Show Hidden Text option.

3. Select the Show Hidden Text option.

4. Click the arrow next to the Menu box and drag down to select Format.

5. Click the Add button.

6. Click the Do button.

For more information on adding commands to menus with the Commands command, see Chapter 9, ''Customizing Word 4's Menus and Keyboard.''

Controlling Position

For technical and mathematical applications, you can raise (superscript) or lower (subscript) characters from the base line.

To superscript or subscript characters, follow these steps:

1. Position the insertion point where you want the subscript or superscript characters to appear. If you have already typed the characters, select them.

2. Choose Character from the Format menu. When the Character dialog box appears, click the Superscript or Subscript button. To change the default vertical-space adjustment of 3 points, type a new measurement in the By box. Click OK.

3. To return to normal character positioning (no superscript or subscript), press ⌘-Option-2.

Speed Keys

⌘-Shift- −
⌘-Shift- +

Alternatively, use the ⌘-Shift-Plus (superscript) or ⌘-Shift-Minus (subscript) keyboard shortcuts. If you use the keyboard shortcuts, you must accept the default spacing, three points above or below the line.

Using Character Spacing

The Spacing options in the Character dialog box give you a way to condense or expand letters by decreasing or increasing the space after them. When you condense the space after a letter, Word reduces the space by the amount specified in the By box (the default is 1.5 points). You can reduce the space between characters by as much as 1.75 points. When you expand characters, Word increases the amount of space after the letters (the default is 1.5 points). You can increase the space between letters by as much as 14 points (see fig. 4.5).

Normal.spacing

Condensed.by.1.5.pt.

Expanded.by.1.5.pt.

Expanded.by.3.pts.

Expanded.by.6.pts.

Expanded.by.12.pts.

Fig. 4.5.

Controlling character spacing.

To control spacing between characters, follow these steps:

1. Select the characters.

2. Choose Character from the Format menu.

3. Click Condensed or Expanded.

4. Type a measurement in the By box.

5. Click OK.

Word's capability to control the spacing between characters makes it possible to *kern* a font. Kerning is the adjustment of spacing between specific pairs of characters for the best possible aesthetic appearance. Kerning manually is a dreadfully tedious job. You can experiment with manual kerning by kerning a title. A better application is to add space between characters to create attractive chapter titles.

Note: With Version 4 of Microsoft Word, you can make spacing choices as small as 1/20 point. The Macintosh, however, is limited to 1-point increments when it displays your text. If you make choices smaller than 1 point (which frequently is the case in spacing), you must print your text to see precisely how the spacing choices have affected the text. You cannot see such small point-size changes on the screen.

Searching for Character Formats

Suppose that you have created a document with extensive use of italic for character emphasis, only to find that your company's style guidelines forbid italic and require underlining instead. In such situations, you will find it very convenient to let Word track down the unwanted formats for you.

To search for a character format, follow these steps:

1. Select a character that has the format for which you want to search (but doesn't have any other special character formats).

⌘-Option-R
⌘-Option-A

2. Press ⌘-Option-R.

   Word finds the next occurrence of the format and selects it.

3. To continue the search, choose the Find Again command from the Utilities menu or use the ⌘-Option-A shortcut.

   Don't press ⌘-Option-R to continue the search, because Word will use the currently selected text as the basis for the search and this selection may include formats other than the one in the original selection. The Find Again command matches the formats you originally selected.

Copying Character Formats

If you have entered a complex character format and want to use it elsewhere in your document, you don't have to choose the commands all over again. You can use a little-known, but very useful, keyboard shortcut to copy the formats to a new location.

To copy formats, follow these steps:

⌘-Option-V

1. Select a word that has the formats you want.

2. Press ⌘-Option-V.

3. Select the text to which you want the format copied. You will see a dotted underline beneath the selection.

4. Press Return

To cancel, press ⌘-period before pressing Return.

High-Productivity Techniques To Remember

❑ The document-design features you choose should be visible so that the eye can easily tell them apart from other features. The meaning of design features should be obvious. A boldfaced heading is more important than one formatted in plain text. A centered heading is more important than one printed flush left.

❑ With Word, document design involves four formatting domains: character formatting, paragraph formatting, section formatting, and page-style (document) formatting.

❑ You can format as you type or format later. When you format as you type, you "program" the insertion point to "lay down" the character formats you choose. Word keeps entering the formats until you cancel them by choosing Plain Text from the Format menu or by pressing ⌘-Shift-Z. To format after you type, you must select the text before choosing formatting options. If you're a good writer, try to format as you write; doing so saves you the trouble of selecting the text to format it.

❑ You can choose character formats with menus (the Format menu for emphasis options and the Font menu for font and size choices). You also can use the Character dialog box to assign all character formats or use the keyboard shortcuts for most formats. For maximum speed, choose fonts and sizes with the Font menu and choose emphasis options with keyboard shortcuts. You can create styles to enter character formats automatically.

❏ For business and professional writing, choose the Helvetica font for brochures, the Courier font for the text of letters, Times or Helvetica for letterheads, Times for long reports, and Chicago for headings on business forms.

❏ If you use an ImageWriter printer, avoid scaled fonts. Choose only font sizes displayed on the Font menu in outlined characters.

❏ To change the font size quickly, press ⌘-Shift-> to increase the size. Press ⌘-Shift-< to decrease the size.

❏ To increase your productivity in choosing character emphases, add emphases to the Format menu by using the ⌘-Option-Plus technique.

❏ If you write collaboratively, add the Show Hidden Text option to the Format menu, using the Commands dialog box from the Edit menu.

❏ Remember that the ⌘-Option-R shortcut for searching for character formats, and use ⌘-Option-V to copy formats you have already entered.

CHAPTER 5

Fundamentals of Document Design II: Paragraph Formatting

Chapter 4 introduces Word's four formatting domains (characters, paragraphs, section, and document), and discusses character formatting in detail. This chapter examines paragraph formatting, including the formats you expect: alignment, spacing, and indentation. Also covered are some formats you may not expect: tabs and borders (lines and boxes). Tabs and borders are *paragraph* formats in Word; they're applied to the paragraphs you select. Specifically in this chapter you learn

❏ How to break up text on the page with indentations, alignment options, blank lines, and line spacing options

❏ How to surround paragraphs of text (and graphics) with lines, borders, and boxes in a variety of line styles

❏ How to set, move, and clear custom tabs

Topics closely related to this chapter's material are discussed in Chapter 12, "Creating Tables and Lists" and Chapter 14, "Page Layout Strategies with Text and Graphics." Chapter 12 highlights Word 4's new Insert Table command from the Document menu. The Insert Table command creates a spreadsheetlike matrix of cells in which you can enter, edit, and format tables with exceptional ease. Chapter 14 discusses the Position command, another Word 4 feature, which "anchors" a paragraph of text or a graphic to an absolute position on the page so that text "flows" around it.

For this chapter, you need Word's full menus. Choose Full Menus from the Edit menu so that you can explore all the features discussed in the pages to follow.

Note: If you have used other versions of Word, you may have used side-by-side paragraph formatting. In Version 4, that format has been replaced by the Insert Table command. See Chapter 12 for details.

About Paragraphs

Following is a quick review of some fundamental points about paragraphs, that this book has already introduced.

❑ For Word, a paragraph is a block of characters of any length followed by a paragraph mark. A paragraph can be a single paragraph mark with no text preceding it. By this definition, a paragraph can be a one-line heading or a 55-line table, where each line ends with an Insert Line Break command (Shift-Return).

❑ Every time you press Return (or Enter), Word starts a new paragraph. Each paragraph is a unit for paragraph-formatting purposes. For this reason, don't press Return at the end of every line, as you do when working with a typewriter. Let Word start new lines automatically by wrapping text. Press Return only when you want to start a new paragraph of text.

❑ To select an entire paragraph, move the pointer to the selection bar (an invisible line running along the left side of the screen) until the pointer changes to an arrow. When the pointer has an arrow shape, double-click.

❑ If you see a small black box in the selection bar, you have applied ''invisible properties'' to the paragraph, such as Keep With Following ¶.

❑ To split a paragraph, click the insertion point in front of the first character of a sentence and press Return.

❑ To display paragraph marks, choose Show ¶ from the Edit menu.

❑ To join paragraphs, select the first paragraph's mark and press Delete or Backspace.

About Paragraph Formatting

You can assign the following formats to any paragraph in a Word document:

❑ *Alignment* (default flush left). Choose from flush-left, flush-right, right-justified, or centered formats for a paragraph.

❏ *Indents* (default none). You can indent the right margin, the left margin, and the paragraph's first line. Using negative values, you can create hanging indents and other effects.

❏ *Line spacing* (default auto). You can format paragraph spacing with auto (single spacing with automatic adjustment of line height to accommodate the largest font), one-and-one-half space (18 point), and double-space (24 point). You can set other line spacings using measurements specified in lines or points.

❏ *Blank lines* (default none). You can format a paragraph so that Word automatically enters blank space before or after the paragraph.

❏ *Page-break control* (default none). Choose from options that force a page break before a paragraph or prevent one following the paragraph. You also can force Word to keep all the lines of a paragraph together on one page.

❏ *Absolute position on the page* (default none). You can anchor a paragraph of text (or a graphic, which is also a "paragraph" as far as Word is concerned) so that it's position is fixed on the page. You also can choose the size of the frame in which the text or graphic is positioned. If the frame is narrower than the text column, text flows around the frame automatically.

❏ *Borders* (default none). Choose from lines and boxes in a variety of widths.

❏ *Tabs* (default every half inch). Choose from flush-left, flush-right, centered, and decimal tabs. You can also set a vertical tab, which inserts a vertical line at the position you specify.

If you have used other word processing programs, you may think it odd that blank lines, borders, and tabs are paragraph formats in Word. In practice then, every time you start a new paragraph, you have the opportunity to set up a complex new format. The format can include the usual ingredients of paragraph formatting (indents, alignment, and line spacing), as well as the "extras": lines, boxes, a unique pattern of tabs, automatically entered blank lines, and page-break controls.

This chapter discusses paragraph alignment, indents, line spacing, blank lines, borders, and tabs in detail. For information on page-break control, see the sections titled "Breaking Pages Manually" and "Controlling Unwanted Page Breaks" in Chapter 3. For information on absolute positioning, see Chapter 14, "Page Layout Strategies with Text and Graphics."

Choosing Paragraph Formats

You can choose paragraph formats in three ways: with the ruler (by far the easiest way), with the Paragraph dialog box from the Format menu, and with keyboard shortcuts.

As with character formats, you can enter paragraph formats as you type or later. To enter paragraph formats as you type, begin by choosing a paragraph formatting command. You ''program'' the insertion point to ''lay down'' the chosen formats. When you press Return, Word copies the formats to the next paragraph. You cancel the formats by pressing ⌘-Shift-P, clicking the normal paragraph icon (available when Short Menus is selected from the Edit menu), or choosing Normal from the style selection box on the ruler (when Full Menus is selected from the Edit menu).

To format later, you select the paragraph or paragraphs you want to format and choose a formatting command. For a review of paragraph-selection techniques, see the section titled ''Selecting Text for Editing or Formatting'' in Chapter 3, ''Writing and Editing Strategies.''

The following sections explain how to apply paragraph formats by using the ruler, the Paragraph dialog box, and keyboard shortcuts.

The Ruler

⌘-R

Word's ruler always displays the formats of the currently selected paragraph—the one in which the insertion point is positioned. If you haven't chosen any formats, the ruler displays the default formats. If you change the formats, the changes apply to the selected paragraph or paragraphs. To display the ruler, choose Show Ruler in the Edit menu or press ⌘-R.

Following is a list of the ruler icons displayed when Full Menus has been selected from the Edit menu (see fig. 5.1).

❑ *Alignment icons*. Click to select flush-left, centered, flush-right, or justified alignment.

❑ *Line-spacing icons*. Click to select single spacing, one-and-one-half spacing (18 points), or double-spacing (24 points).

❑ *Blank-line icons*. Click to select no blank line before the paragraph (closed paragraph) or one blank line before the paragraph (open paragraph).

❑ *Indent markers*. On the left side of the ruler are two solid triangles. The top left triangle is the first-line indent marker; drag this icon to control automatic first-line indents. The bottom left triangle is the left-

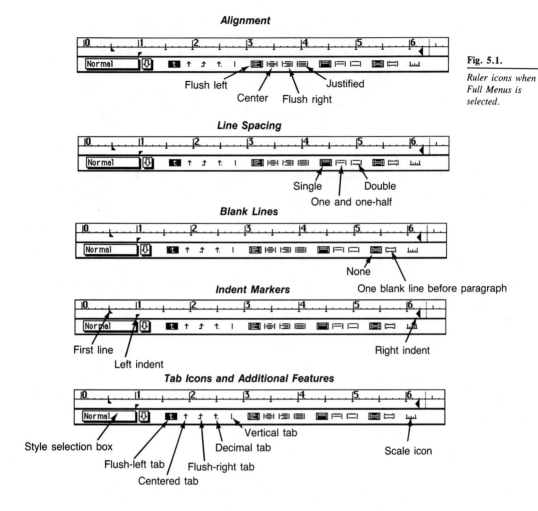

Fig. 5.1.

Ruler icons when Full Menus is selected.

indent marker for all succeeding lines of the paragraph. The larger triangle at the right side of the ruler is the right-indent marker.

❑ *Tab icons.* To set a tab, click one of these icons and drag it to the location you want. You can choose from flush left, centered, flush right, and decimal tab stops. The vertical tab isn't a tab, actually; it enters a vertical line at the position you specify. The line is the same height as the line spacing you specify in the Paragraph dialog box.

❑ *Style selection box.* This dragdown list box, a new Word 4 feature, gives you a handy way to choose styles. For more information on styles, see Chapter 7, "Formatting with Style Sheets."

❑ *Scale icon*. Click this icon to select the mode in which the ruler is to be displayed. The Normal scale measures the line length, starting at zero from the left margin. The Page scale places the zero at the left side of the page and displays the current margin settings with brackets. (You can change your document's margins by dragging the brackets.) The Table scale appears only if you have created a table and positioned the insertion point within it (see fig. 5.2).

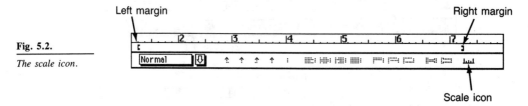

Fig. 5.2.

The scale icon.

When Short Menus has been selected from the Edit menu, fewer options appear on the ruler (see fig. 5.3). The only tab option is flush left. No blank-line icons appear, and the style selection box is gone. The normal paragraph icon on the right edge of the ruler is added. When this icon is clicked, normal paragraph formatting (single space, flush left) is restored.

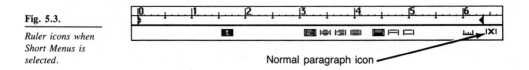

Fig. 5.3.

Ruler icons when Short Menus is selected.

Note: Normally, the ruler shows the current paragraph formatting settings. If you select two or more paragraphs that aren't homogeneous in their paragraph formatting, however, the ruler appears dimmed and no icons are highlighted. Suppose, for instance, that you select a centered paragraph and a flush-left paragraph. The ruler appears dimmed. When the ruler appears this way, you still can choose formats from the ruler. The formats you choose will affect all the paragraphs you have selected.

Speed Keys

⌘-M

The Paragraph Dialog Box

Choosing paragraph formats with the ruler is easy, but not all formats can be chosen that way. To specify indents and line spacing with precision, and to control page breaks, you need the Paragraph dialog box (see fig. 5.4). To use the Paragraph dialog box, choose Paragraph from the Format menu or press ⌘-M.

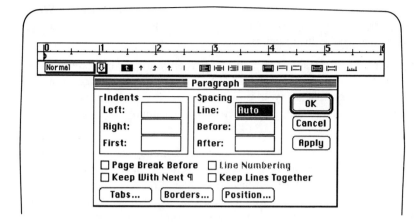

Fig. 5.4.

The Paragraph dialog box.

If you work with the ruler in view, use this super-fast way to access the Paragraph dialog box: double-click the right-indent marker (the big triangle on the right side of the ruler). You also can double-click the paragraph-properties mark to bring up the Paragraph dialog box. The paragraph-properties mark appears as a small black box in the selection bar if you have chosen ''invisible'' formats for a paragraph.

To choose indents and spacing in the Paragraph dialog box, type measurements in one of the measurement formats Word recognizes. Following is a summary of these formats.

❏ *Inches (in or ")*. Word's default measurement format for horizontal formats, such as indents.

❏ *Point (pt)*. Word's default measurement format for line and paragraph spacing. Points are also the default measurement for character spacing and position. Each inch contains 72 points.

❏ *Centimeters (cm)*. One centimeter equals .39 inches, 28.35 points.

❏ *Pica (pi)*. One pica equals 1/6 inch, .42 centimeter, or 12 points.

❏ *Lines (li)*. This measuring format is used for vertical measurements only. One line equals 1/6 inch, 0.42 centimeter, or 12 points.

If you're using Word in a country that has adopted the metric system, you may prefer to use centimeters for measurements. Points and picas are used in typesetting. Point measurements come in handy with Word because they're easier to type than a decimal fraction of an inch.

If you type a measurement without specifying one of the recognized abbreviations (*in* or *"* , *pt*, *cm*, *pi*, or *li*), Word assumes that you're using the default measurement format for that option. When you type a measurement for indents, Word assumes that you're using inches. When you type a measurement for spacing, Word assumes that you're using points.

Keep these points about measurements in mind when you type measurements in the Spacing boxes. If you type *2* in the Line Spacing box, for instance, thinking you will get double-line spacing, you're in for a surprise. What you have entered is a line spacing of 2 points (1/36 of an inch). To enter double-line spacing, type *24 pt, 2 li,* or *2 pi.*

Note: If you select two or more paragraphs that aren't homogeneous in their paragraph formatting, the Paragraph dialog box shows settings for the formats that the paragraphs share. No other format settings are shown. You can choose additional formats for the selected paragraphs without affecting the formats already chosen. You also can override the current settings. Any changes you make in the Paragraph dialog box will be applied to *both* paragraphs.

The Keyboard Shortcuts

The third way to create paragraph formats, and arguably the best way for adept typists, is with keyboard shortcuts. Table 5.1 lists the keyboard shortcuts for paragraph formatting.

Table 5.1
Keyboard Shortcuts for Paragraph Formatting

Format	Keyboard Shortcut
Flush-left alignment	⌘-Shift-L
Flush-right alignment	⌘-Shift-R
Centered alignment	⌘-Shift-C
Automatic first-line indent	⌘-Shift-F
Indent paragraph one tab stop	⌘-Shift-N
Outdent paragraph one tab stop	⌘-Shift-M
Hanging indentation	⌘-Shift-T
Double-line spacing	⌘-Shift-Y
Blank line before paragraph	⌘-Shift-O
Restore normal paragraph formats	⌘-Shift-P

Controlling Paragraph Alignment

Like fonts, alignment options aren't merely so many patterns of ink dots on the page. The alignment choices you make should have *meaning*. Some contexts in which alignments are appropriate are shown in figure 5.5. If you are tempted to use justified alignment to make your document seem more impersonal, dignified, and ''book-like,'' keep in mind that justification makes text more difficult to read. Moreover, Word may introduce unsightly spaces between words in an attempt to even the right margin, producing an unesthetic effect.

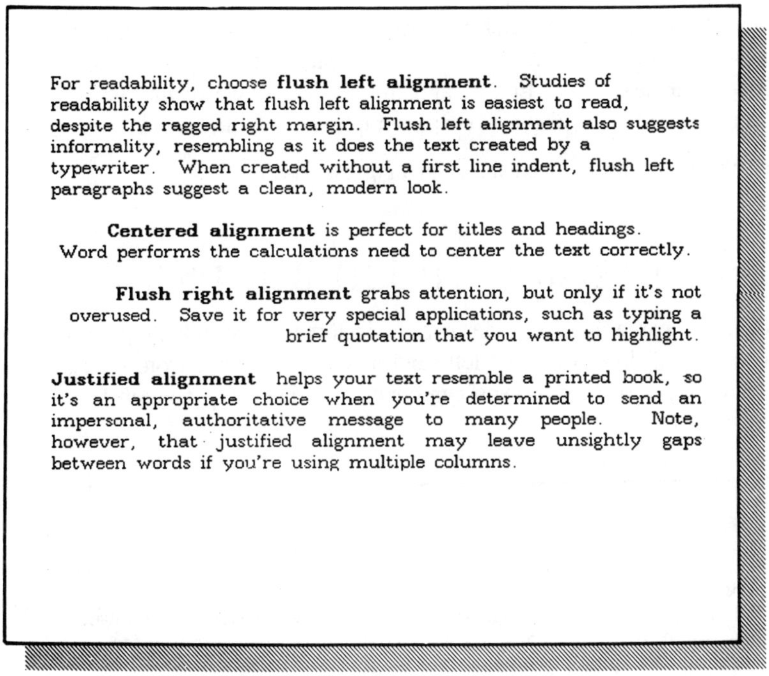

For readability, choose **flush left alignment**. Studies of readability show that flush left alignment is easiest to read, despite the ragged right margin. Flush left alignment also suggests informality, resembling as it does the text created by a typewriter. When created without a first line indent, flush left paragraphs suggest a clean, modern look.

Centered alignment is perfect for titles and headings. Word performs the calculations need to center the text correctly.

Flush right alignment grabs attention, but only if it's not overused. Save it for very special applications, such as typing a brief quotation that you want to highlight.

Justified alignment helps your text resemble a printed book, so it's an appropriate choice when you're determined to send an impersonal, authoritative message to many people. Note, however, that justified alignment may leave unsightly gaps between words if you're using multiple columns.

Fig. 5.5.

Paragraph-alignment options.

To change paragraph alignment as you type, follow these steps:

1. Press Return to start a new paragraph (unless you want to format the current paragraph).

2. Click an alignment option on the ruler or use one of the keyboard shortcuts listed in table 5.1. If the ruler is not visible, choose Show Ruler from the Edit menu or press ⌘-R.

3. Type the text of the new paragraph.

To change paragraph alignment after you type, follow these steps:

1. To select one paragraph, click the insertion point anywhere in the paragraph. (You needn't highlight the whole paragraph; just placing the insertion point in it is sufficient to select it.) To select more than one paragraph, double-click in the selection bar next to the first paragraph and drag down or up until the screen scrolls and the desired paragraphs are highlighted.

2. Click an alignment option in the ruler or use one of the keyboard shortcuts listed in table 5.1.

To cancel the alignment options assigned to text and return to flush-left formatting, follow these steps:

Speed Keys

1. To select one paragraph, click the insertion point anywhere in the paragraph. To select more than one paragraph, double-click in the selection bar next to the first paragraph and drag down or up until the screen scrolls and the desired paragraphs are highlighted.

⌘-Shift-L

2. Click the flush-left icon on the ruler or press ⌘-Shift-L.

Using Paragraph Indentations

You can indent any paragraph from the margins in three ways: indenting the first line only, indenting all lines from the left, and indenting all lines from the right. Using these three types of indents, you can create a variety of paragraph formats (see fig. 5.6).

Fig. 5.6.

Various indented paragraphs.

> Don't press Tab to begin a paragraph with a **first line indent**—let Word do the job for you automatically. With an automatic first line indent, Word tabs to the right every time you press Return. When used for normal text paragraphs, first line indents help the eye to find the paragraphs' beginning.
>
> **Hanging indentations** have many uses, such as lists, bibliographic citations, and other contexts in which it makes sense to set paragraphs off by their first words.
>
> **Nested paragraphs** are useful to show logical relations. Here's a paragraph that's indented one tab stop from the left margin.
>
> Here's a paragraph that's indented two tab stops from the left margin.
>
> And here's one that's indented *three* tab stops from the left margin.

Note: When you indent lines from the left or right, you do not change the margins for the page. The margins stay put; you're just setting up a temporary indentation format. If you want to change the margins for your document, choose Document from the Format menu and type new measurements in the Left and Right Margins boxes.

Automatic First-Line Indentations

Don't press Tab to enter a first-line indentation. Word can do the job for you automatically. To create an automatic first-line indentation, follow these steps:

1. Select the paragraph or paragraphs you want to affect.

2. On the ruler, drag the first-line indent marker to create the indentation. The first-line indent marker is the top left triangle on the left side of the ruler. Alternatively, type a measurement in the First text box of the Paragraph dialog box, or use the ⌘-Shift-F keyboard shortcut.

   ⌘-Shift-F

   ⌘-Shift-F indents the paragraph by one default tab stop, 0.5 inch, unless you've changed the default tab width setting in the Document dialog box.

Creating Hanging Indentations

Hanging indentations are useful whenever you want to emphasize the first few words of a paragraph. Two uses for hanging indentations are shown in figure 5.7: bibliographic citations and word-definitions lists.

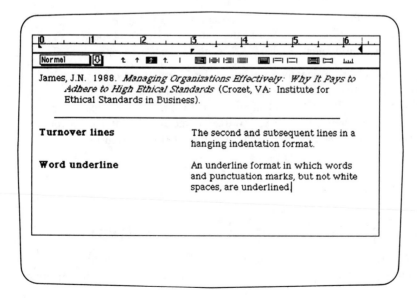

Fig. 5.7.

Applications for hanging indentations.

To create a hanging indentation, you can choose from three techniques. Of these methods, the keyboard technique is by far the easiest.

To create a hanging indentation by using keyboard shortcuts, follow these steps:

1. Select the paragraph or paragraphs you want to affect.

⌘-Shift-T

2. Press ⌘-Shift-T. Word positions the first-line indent marker at 0 inch; the right-indent marker is positioned at 0.5 inch.

3. To increase the indentation an additional 0.5 inch, use the command again.

To create a hanging indentation by using the ruler, use the following steps:

1. Select the paragraph or paragraphs you want to affect.

2. On the ruler, drag the left-indent marker (the bottom left triangle on the left side of the ruler) to the place where you want the paragraph's second and subsequent lines (the *turnover* lines) to be positioned. (The first-line indent marker moves also.) Then drag the first-line indent marker to the left to the place where you want the first line to begin.

To create a hanging indentation by using the Paragraph dialog box method, follow these steps:

1. Select the paragraph or paragraphs you want to affect.

2. Choose Paragraph from the Format menu.

3. When the Paragraph dialog box appears, type a negative measurement (such as *−0.5*) in the Indents First box. Type a positive measurement (such as *1.0*) in the Indents Left box.

   When you type a negative number in the Indents First box, you tell Word, in effect, "Start the first line to the *left* of the left indentation." If the left indentation is 1.0 inch, and you type −0.5 inch in the Indents First box, Word starts the first line 0.5 inch from the left margin and starts the turnover lines 1.0 inch from the left margin.

4. Click OK.

Line Spacing and Blank Lines

The easiest way to choose line-spacing and blank-line options is to click icons on the ruler (again see fig. 5.1). You can choose single, 1.5, and double-line spacing by clicking a line spacing icon. If you click the blank line option, Word adds a blank line before the paragraph.

Word's default line spacing option, Auto, looks like single-spacing on the screen, but Auto has a special characteristic; Auto adjusts the line height automatically to accommodate the font size you use, whether the font is large or small.

To double-space your document, click the double-space icon on the ruler. Alternatively, choose Paragraph from the Format menu or press ⌘-M. Then type *24 pt* in the Line text box and click OK.

Note: If you choose a line spacing other than Auto, Word will increase the line height to accommodate a font size that is greater than the line height. Unlike Auto line spacing, however, the program will not decrease the line height to accommodate a smaller font (see figure 5.8). Therefore, a nine-point font may look triple-spaced if you click the double-line spacing option on the ruler (thus entering a line spacing of 24 points).

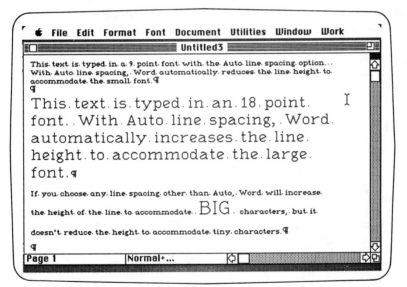

Fig. 5.8.

Examples of Word 4's line spacing.

As a general rule, double the font size to produce double-line spacing. To double-space a nine-point font, click the 1.5 line spacing option or type *18 pt* in the Line box of the Paragraph dialog box. To double-space a 10-point font, type *20 pt* in the Line box.

If you're working on a project that requires precise control over line spacing, enter the line spacing option as a negative number. The minus sign tells Word to turn off automatic line-height adjustment.

To specify values other than those offered by the ruler, you need the Paragraph dialog box.

Additional blank lines are handy when you are formatting headings. Style handbooks and guidelines typically specify precisely how much blank space should precede and follow a heading. A second-level heading, for instance, may require two blank lines before and one blank line after. You can add blank lines to a heading format (or other paragraph formats) by using the Spacing Before and After boxes in the Paragraph dialog box.

To find out how much space is allotted to a line, select it. If you added a blank line before or after the paragraph, Word selects the blank line when you select the paragraph. If you selected 24-point line spacing, Word selects a 24-point line when you select a line of text (even if the text is considerably smaller).

Don't create blank lines in your document by pressing Return. If you do, you cannot control page breaks using the Keep With Next ¶ option because the next paragraph is a blank line. If you create blank lines by adding them to your paragraph formats using the open icon or the Spacing Before and After boxes in the Paragraph dialog box, Word disregards the blank lines when carrying out the Keep With Next ¶ command.

Adding Lines and Boxes

You can add lines and boxes to any paragraph you create with Word (see fig. 5.9). The key lies in the Paragraph Borders dialog box, accessed by choosing Paragraph from the Format menu and, when the Paragraph dialog box appears, clicking the Borders button.

Following is an overview of the line-formatting and box-formatting options in the Paragraph Borders dialog box:

❑ *Box options.* Choose from plain or shadowed boxes.

❑ *Line options.* Choose from single, thick, double, dotted, or hairline. Hairlines print only on PostScript-compatible printers.

❑ *Custom-placement options.* You can place lines above, below, to the left, or to the right of the paragraph. You also can choose any combination of these options. The Outside Bar option prints a vertical line to the right of the paragraph on odd-numbered pages and to the left of the paragraph on even-numbered pages. If you have selected more than one paragraph, you can choose an option that places a border between the selected paragraphs.

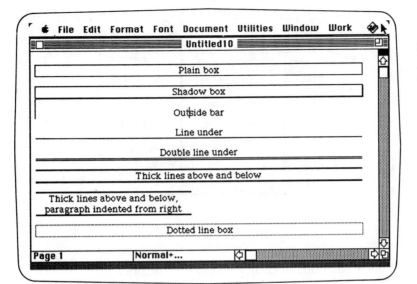

Fig. 5.9.

Paragraphs with lines and boxes.

To box a paragraph, follow these steps:

1. Select the paragraph or paragraphs you want to affect.

2. Choose Paragraph from the Format menu.

3. When the Paragraph dialog box appears, click the Borders button.

4. When the Paragraph Borders dialog box appears, as shown in figure 5.10, choose the border style you want (single, thick, double, dotted, or hairline).

5. To increase the white space between the text and the box (the default is 2 points), type a measurement in the Spacing box.

6. Choose a border option by clicking Plain Box or Shadow Box.

7. Click OK.

8. Click OK again when the Paragraph dialog box appears.

To add additional space in a box, don't press Return. If you press Return, you copy the paragraph format—including the box—to the next paragraph! (If this happens, delete the new paragraph by deleting its paragraph mark.) Add additional lines by pressing Shift-Return, the Insert Line Break command. The Insert Line Break command doesn't start a new paragraph (in Word's sense of the term).

Fig. 5.10.

The Paragraph Borders dialog box.

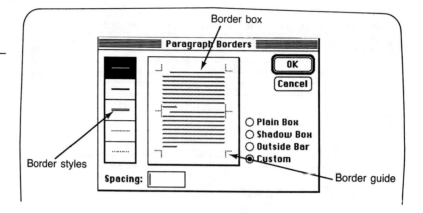

To add lines to paragraphs, follow these steps:

1. Select the paragraph or paragraphs you want to affect.

2. Choose Paragraph from the Format menu.

3. When the Paragraph dialog box appears, click the Borders button.

4. When the Paragraph Borders dialog box appears, choose the border style you want (single, thick, double, dotted, or hairline).

5. To increase the white space between the text and the line (the default is 2 points), type a measurement in the Spacing box.

6. To add a line border above, below, to the left, or to the right of the paragraph, click between the border guides in the border box. To add a border *between* the selected paragraphs, click between the center border guides.

7. To add additional borders, repeat steps 4 through 6.

8. Click OK. When the Paragraph dialog box appears, click OK again.

If you find borders useful, add the Paragraph Borders command to the Format menu for easy access. Use these steps:

1. Choose Commands from the Edit menu. If Commands does not appear on the Edit menu, select Full Menus from the Edit menu and try again.

2. Choose Paragraph Borders from the list box in the Commands dialog box.

3. Click Add.

4. Click Cancel.

For more information on customizing Word's command menus, see Chapter 9, "Customizing Word 4's Menus and Keyboard."

If you decide to remove the lines or boxes attached to a paragraph, you can press ⌘-Shift-P. When you press this key sequence, however, *all* paragraph formats, not just lines and boxes, are canceled and the normal paragraph format is restored. You can then reapply the paragraph formats, if any, that were canceled. Another alternative is to select the paragraph and use the Paragraph Borders dialog box to click off the borders you added. This method can be tedious—particularly if you used more than one line style. The best way to remove the lines or boxes applied to paragraphs is to select the paragraphs and use the ⌘-Option-1 keyboard shortcut.

⌘-Option-1

For information on adding borders to tables, see Chapter 12, "Creating Tables and Lists." For information on adding borders to graphics, see Chapter 14, "Page Layout Strategies with Text and Graphics."

Using Tabs

By default, every paragraph has flush-left tabs every 0.5 inch across the screen. You can change the default tab width for all documents if you want. To do so, choose Document from the Format menu, type the tab width you want in the Default Tab Stops box of the Document dialog box, click Set Default, and click OK. Your choice will affect the default tab width for all your documents, not just the one on-screen. If you want to change the default tab width for the current document but no others, click OK without clicking Set Default.

When you press the Tab key, Word enters a tab mark (a right arrow) in your document. This mark fills up the space taken by the tab. For this reason, you can select all the white space created by a tab by selecting the tab mark. To see the tab marks, choose Show ¶ from the Edit menu. To remove a tab mark, delete it as you would any character; the white space disappears.

In addition to controlling the default tab stops, you can set *custom* tabs. You can set four kinds of custom tabs:

❑ *Flush left*. The text or numbers you type after pressing Tab appear to the right of the tab stop.

❑ *Flush right*. The text or numbers you type after pressing Tab appear to the left of the tab stop.

❑ *Centered*. The text or numbers you type after pressing Tab are centered at the tab stop.

❏ *Decimal*. The numbers you type after pressing Tab are aligned by decimal points; text is aligned flush right.

In addition to these four tabs, you can set a vertical tab stop, which places a vertical line at the place you insert the tab (see the two vertical lines in fig. 5.11).

Fig. 5.11.

The four kinds of tab stops and the vertical tab.

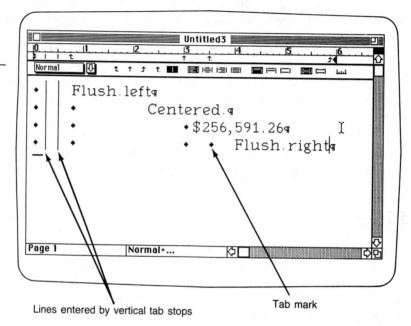

Lines entered by vertical tab stops

Tab mark

Note: When Short Menus is selected from the Edit menu, the ruler displays only flush-left tabs. To choose other tabs from the ruler, first select Full Menus from the Edit menu.

Remember that custom tabs are paragraph formats. When you set tabs, the tab choices you make apply *only* to the paragraph (or paragraphs) selected. When you choose a custom tab stop, Word cancels all the default tab stops to the left of the custom stops. This makes sense, because you will want to tab to the stop you set without tabbing through all the default tabs.

The easiest way to set, move, and cancel custom tabs is to use the ruler. To set custom tabs with the ruler, follow these steps:

1. Select the paragraph or paragraphs that will contain the tabs.

2. Choose Show Ruler from the Format menu if necessary.

3. Click the icon of the kind of tab you want to set. From left to right on the ruler, the icons are flush-left, centered, flush-right, decimal, and vertical bar.

4. Click below the ruler scale at the position or positions where you want to set tabs with the selected alignment.

To move tabs with the ruler, follow these steps:

1. Select the paragraph or paragraphs that contain the tabs you want to move.

2. Choose Show Ruler from the Format menu if necessary.

3. Drag the tab stop to its new position.

To remove a tab stop by using the ruler, follow these steps:

1. Select the paragraph or paragraphs that contain the tabs you want to remove.

2. Choose Show Ruler from the Format menu if necessary.

3. Click the tab stop you want to remove and drag it down and away from the ruler scale.

When you want to clear all the tabs you set or if you want to choose leaders, you need to access the Tabs dialog box. To access the Tabs dialog box, choose Paragraph from the Format menu and click the Tabs button.

To clear all the custom tabs in the selected paragraph or paragraphs and restore the default tabs, follow these steps:

1. Choose Paragraph from the Format menu or press ⌘-M.

2. Click the Tabs button on the Paragraph dialog box.

3. When the Tabs dialog box appears, as shown in figure 5.12, click Clear All.

4. Click OK.

5. Click OK in the Paragraph dialog box.

With the Tabs dialog box, you can set *leaders*, characters that Word enters automatically before a tab stop. You can choose from dot, dash, and underline leaders. Word enters the leaders when you press Tab to move to the stop that includes the leaders. Word automatically adjusts the leader so that there's room for text you type.

To create leaders, follow these steps:

1. Set a tab on the ruler. This tab will receive the leader formatting. For a table of contents, set a flush-right tab at the right margin.

2. Choose Paragraph from the Format menu or press ⌘-M.

3. When the Paragraph dialog box appears, click the Tabs button.

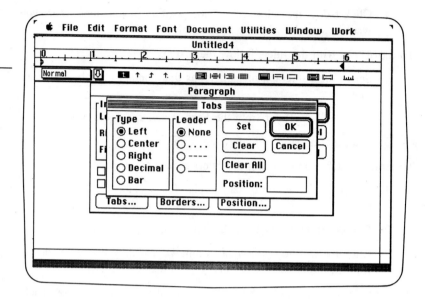

Fig. 5.12.

The Tabs dialog box.

4. When the Tabs dialog box appears, click the tab stop on the ruler that you created in step 1.

5. Click the leader format you want from the Tabs dialog box. Choose from dot, dash, or underline leader formats (see fig. 5.13).

Flush-right tab stop with dot leader

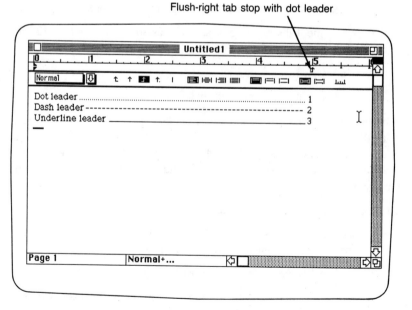

Fig. 5.13.

The types of leaders.

6. Click Set.

7. Click OK to return to the Paragraph dialog box.

8. Click OK from the Paragraph dialog box.

To enter the leader, type some text and press Tab. The insertion point jumps to the tab stop you set, leaving the leader characters in its wake.

Use vertical tab stops to add vertical lines within boxes (see fig. 5.14). Create the box using the Paragraph Borders dialog box, and add white space within the box by pressing Shift-Return. Then select all the lines and set vertical tabs where you want the vertical lines in the box to appear.

Once you create vertical lines in this way, you can tab over them without disturbing them. This feature makes it easy to create and use business forms with Word, as you see in Chapter 13, "Creating Business Forms."

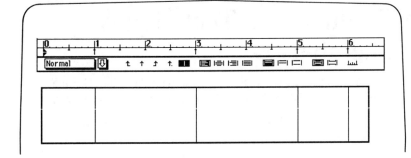

Fig. 5.14.

Vertical tab stops within a box.

Searching for Paragraph Formats

You can search for paragraph formats in much the same way you search for character formats (see Chapter 4). Suppose, for example, that you want to locate and modify all instances of a list format. Word can find the formats for you.

To search for paragraph formats, follow these steps:

1. Double-click the selection bar to select the paragraph containing the formats for which you want to search.

2. Press ⌘-Option-R.

   Word finds the next occurrence of the format and selects it.

3. To continue the search, choose Find Again from the Utilities menu or use the ⌘-Option-A shortcut.

Copying Paragraph Formats

If you have entered a complex paragraph format and want to use it again in your document, you don't have to choose the commands all over again. You can copy the formats by using the ⌘-Option-V shortcut.

To copy a paragraph's formats, follow these steps:

1. Double-click in the selection bar to select the paragraph containing the formats you want to copy.

2. Press ⌘-Option-V.

3. Select the text to which you want the formats copied.

   You will see a dotted underline beneath the selection.

4. Press Return to copy the format or ⌘-. to cancel.

High-Productivity Techniques To Remember

❏ The fastest way to choose paragraph formats is with the ruler. Use the Paragraph dialog box only for formats you cannot enter on the ruler.

❏ To access the Paragraph dialog box quickly, double-click the right indent mark on the ruler.

❏ Remember that Word assumes that you're using measurements in inches for indents and in points for line spacing.

❏ Don't create blank lines by pressing Return. Add blank lines by using the blank line icon on the ruler or by typing measurements in the Paragraph dialog box's Before and After boxes.

❏ To delete borders quickly, select the paragraph containing the boxes and press ⌘-Option-1.

❏ Use the ruler to set, move, and cancel custom tabs. You need the Tabs dialog box only when you choose leaders.

❏ If you plan to create a table, use Word 4's new Insert Table command (on the Utilities menu) rather than set tabs.

❏ Use the ⌘-Option-R shortcut to search for paragraph formats and ⌘-Option-V to copy paragraph formats.

6

Fundamentals of Document Design III: Section and Document Formatting

P*age styles* include a variety of page design elements, such as page numbers, headers, footers, footnotes, margins, and columns. All these styles appear on more than one page. They amount to an overall page design in which your character and paragraph formats are included.

Your page design may range from simple to complex. At the minimum, you can accept Word's default formats for margins, in which case page-style formatting is completely automatic. You just choose Print from the File menu, sit back, and relax. If you're creating a document longer than a business letter, however, you will almost surely want to add page numbers (which you must turn on deliberately) and perhaps a header (repeated text that appears above the body text on every page). At the other extreme, you can create a complex page design by breaking your document into *sections*, such as chapters, each with its own running heads, footnote numbering, and column arrangement.

You use several different commands to control page styles, including the Section and the Document commands in the Format menu and the Open Header, Open Footer, and Footnote commands in the Document menu. This grouping of commands is an improvement over previous versions of Word, in which some page-design elements were tucked away in the Page Setup command in the File menu. Yet first-time voyagers into the realms of document formatting may be puzzled because the formatting options are split up between two menus—and the distinction between the Section and Document menus may seem especially mysterious. But the distinction has a logic behind it:

❏ The Document dialog box controls aspects of page design that affect your *entire* document, such as footnote position (bottom of page or end of section or document), margins, and default tab width.

149

❏ The Section dialog box controls aspects of page design that can *vary* within your document. These formats include the position of page numbers; the number of columns; the use and content of headers and footers; and the use of line numbers. If you create a section break by pressing ⌘-Enter, you can assign a different page style to each section. One section, for instance, can have single-column formatting and the next have double-column formatting.

If you don't divide your document into sections, the options you choose in the Section dialog box affect your entire document—or to put it another way, your document has only one section.

To keep things simple, this chapter discusses single-section documents—that is, documents you *have not* divided into two (or more) sections by pressing ⌘-Enter. For a discussion of multisection documents, see Chapter 14, ''Page Layout Strategies with Text and Graphics.'' Also discussed in Chapter 14 are multiple-column formats, which, for reasons explained in that chapter, are frequently multisection documents as well. Because multisection documents are explained in detail in Chapter 14, some features of the Section and Document dialog boxes aren't discussed in this chapter.

Chapter 14 also discusses the Position command, an important new Word 4 page-design feature. With the Position command, you can ''anchor'' text or graphics to the page so that no matter how much text you add or delete, the anchored material always prints precisely where you anchor it (centered on the page or in the upper right corner, for example). For now, however, this chapter concentrates on the fundamentals.

Using Page View

In Galley view, your text is one long continuous scroll of text, as if you were writing on a roll of paper towels. In actuality, however, Word keeps track of where one page stops and the other starts. (You can see pages on the screen if you have clicked the Background Repagination option in the Preferences dialog box of the Edit menu.) The page breaks are calculated using Word's default page-design settings (1.0-inch margins top and bottom, and 1.25-inch margins left and right). To view an on-screen simulation of the page design, choose Page View from the Document menu.

In Page View mode, you can see the page's margins and other page-design features (except line numbers) while you write and edit. The ruler's zero mark is positioned at the left edge of the paragraph in which the insertion point is positioned; the negative number shows the left side of the page. If you click the Show Text Boundaries in Page View option in the Preferences dialog box (Edit menu), you see dotted lines outlining the various page-design elements, including headers, footers, footnotes, tables, and pictures. (Word is preset to display text boundaries.) Although scrolling is considerably slower in Page view, you can move quickly to the top of the next or the preceding page by clicking the arrows in the status line (see fig. 6.1).

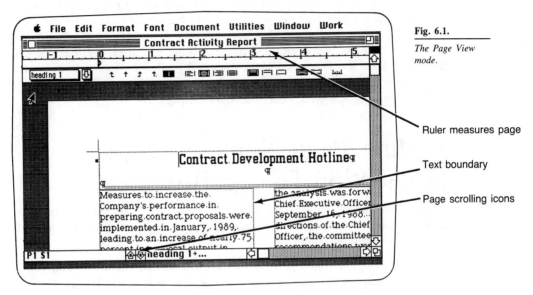

Fig. 6.1.

The Page View mode.

Ruler measures page

Text boundary

Page scrolling icons

As you will quickly discover, scrolling in Page view is a little disconcerting at first. When you get to the bottom of a page, the screen stops scrolling for a moment, and the next page ''pops'' into view—almost as if you were turning an actual page. The new display begins with the first line of text on the page. To see the header, you need to scroll up a few lines to bring it into view. If you scroll right or left, you can see the side margins.

Here's a brief overview of Page view techniques.

Speed Keys

❏ To toggle on the Page View mode, choose Page View from the Document menu (or use the ⌘-B keyboard shortcut).

⌘-B

❏ To toggle off the Page View mode, choose Page View or press ⌘-B again.

❏ To scroll quickly to the top of the preceding or next page, click one of the arrows on the status line.

❏ To toggle the display of text boundaries on or off, click the Show Text Boundaries in Page View box in the Preferences dialog box (Edit menu).

Because Page view slows scrolling considerably, choose it *after* you have chosen page-design elements just to get a final preview before printing. Or toggle Page View on and off quickly by using the ⌘-B keyboard shortcut.

Note: If you have used previous versions of Word, you will notice that the Print Preview mode no longer allows you to magnify the screen so that you can read the text, view fonts, and so on. This function has been replaced by the Page View mode, which allows you to edit and reformat while you display all page-design elements (except line numbers). When you use Print Preview (which is discussed elsewhere in this chapter), you can access Page view quickly by clicking the Page View button or double-clicking anywhere on the page.

Adding Page Numbers with the Section Dialog Box

As you have probably already learned, Word doesn't print page numbers on your document unless you deliberately instruct the program to do so. You can turn on page numbers in three ways:

❑ By clicking the Auto option in the Page Number part of the Section dialog box (Format menu). The page numbers print in the location specified in the From Top and From Right boxes in the same dialog box. Word is preset to print the page numbers 0.5 inch from the top and 0.5 inch from the left.

❑ By adding a page number icon to a header or footer

❑ By dragging the page number icon to one of the pages displayed in the Print Preview mode. Word prints the page numbers at the place where you release the mouse button.

This section discusses the first of these three techniques. The header/footer and Print Preview techniques are discussed later in this chapter.

To add page numbers to your document through the Section dialog box, follow these steps:

1. Choose Section from the Format menu.

2. When the Section dialog box appears, click the Auto box (see fig. 6.2). After you click the Auto box, the From Top and From Right boxes are no longer shaded.

3. To change the page number location, type measurements from the top and the left of the page in the From Top and From Right dialog boxes, respectively.

   To position page numbers centered at the bottom of the page, for instance, type *10.5in* in the From Top box, and *4.5in* in the From Right box.

4. To choose a page number format other than Arabic numbers, click the arrow on the 1 2 3 dropdown list box in order to see your other options: uppercase Roman numerals, lowercase Roman numerals, uppercase letters, or lowercase letters (see fig. 6.3).

5. Click OK to turn on page numbering.

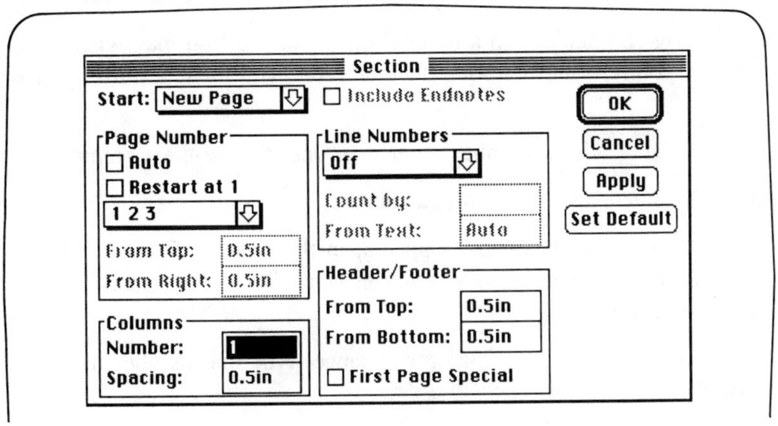

Fig. 6.2.

The Section dialog box.

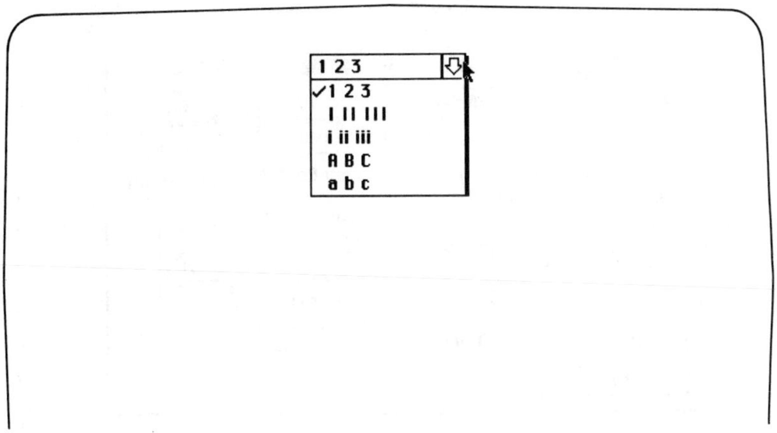

Fig. 6.3.

The page number format dropdown list box in the Section dialog box.

Note: When you choose a page number format, your page numbers print in that format even if you turn on page numbering with headers, footers, or the Print Preview technique.

Caution: If you decide to add page numbers to headers or footers, be sure to turn off automatic page numbering by clicking off the X from the Auto box in the Section dialog box.

When you choose the Auto option to turn on page numbering, page numbers print on all pages of your document, beginning with page 1. But that location is a design flaw—page numbers shouldn't appear on the first page. To suppress the printing of page numbers on the first page, click First Page Special in the Section dialog box.

You can start the page numbers with a number other than 1. You may wish to do so, for example, if you're printing a long document that you divided into separate files.

To start page numbering with a number other than one, follow these steps:

1. Choose Document from the Format menu.

2. When the Document dialog box appears, in the Number Pages From box, type the page number at which you want line numbering to start (see fig. 6.4).

   To start page numbering at 235, for instance, type that number in the Number Pages From box.

3. Click OK.

Fig. 6.4.

The Document dialog box.

Document
Margins: Top: `1 in` Left: `1 in`   **OK**
Bottom: `1 in` Right: `1 in`   **Cancel**
☐ Mirror Even/Odd Margins ☒ Widow Control   **Set Default**
☐ Even/Odd Headers
Gutter: `  `   ⌐Footnotes Position:
Number Pages From: `1`   `Bottom of Page` ⬇
Number Lines From: `1`   Number From: `1`
Default Tab Stops: `0.5in`   ☐ Restart Each Page
Next File...

Adding Line Numbers

If you're preparing legal briefs or other legal documents, you will make extensive use of Word's line-numbering capabilities. Word prints line numbers in the left margin. When counting lines, Word skips white space. If you wish, you can suppress line numbers in part of your document, so that the line numbering skips a heading and continues counting just the lines of text.

To add line numbers to your document, follow these steps:

1. Choose Section from the Format menu.

2. When the Section dialog box appears, click the Line Numbers dropdown list box and choose an option (again see fig. 6.2).

   Choose By Page to start line numbers at 1 at the top of each page. Choose By Section to start line numbers at 1 at the beginning of each section (if your document has been divided into sections). Choose Continuous to number lines sequentially throughout your entire document.

3. To print line numbers by a specified increment, type a number in the Count By box.

   For example, if you type 5, Word prints the line number of every fifth line.

4. To adjust the distance between the line numbers and the text, type a measurement in the From Text box. The defaults are 0.25 inch for single-column text and 0.13 inch for multiple-column text.

5. Click OK.

To suppress line numbering for part of the document,

1. Select the paragraph or paragraphs you do not want numbered.

2. Choose Paragraph from the Format menu.

3. Click the Line Numbering box off.

4. Click OK.

You can start line numbers with a number other than 1, if you wish. To start line numbering with a number other than 1, do the following:

1. Choose Document from the Format menu.

2. When the Document dialog box appears, in the Number Lines From box type the line number at which you want line numbering to start (again see fig. 6.4).

To start line numbering at 20, for instance, type that number in the Number Lines From box.

3. Click OK.

Using Headers and Footers

Headers and footers consist of text that is repeated at the top or bottom of each page, and they add valuable information—and security—to your document. Headers (also called running heads) and footers remind the reader of the document's title or topic—and if your document isn't securely bound, they help the reader identify and reassemble a document that has been scrambled on the top of a cluttered desk. (Yes, it happens!)

Word gives you many header and footer options:

❑ Each section can have its own distinctive header and footer. In a multisection document that is broken down into chapters, for instance, the header or footer can repeat the current chapter's title on each page.

❑ Just by dragging an icon on the screen, you can quickly add page numbers, the current date, or the current time to your header or footer.

❑ Headers and footers are preset with a special tab format (a centered tab stop in the middle of the page and a flush-right tab stop at the right margin). This format simplifies and speeds formatting.

❑ You can create different headers and footers for odd and even pages. If you're planning to duplicate your document on both sides of the page for binding, you can create a visually pleasing pattern in which page numbers always print on the outside margin.

❑ You can create a header or footer with more than one line. Word automatically adjusts the top or bottom margin to accommodate the header or footer.

❑ You can suppress the printing of headers or footers on the first page of a document—or you can create a special header or footer that will print on just the first page.

If you're printing a document that's more than two or three pages long, by all means add headers or footers—the process is easy, and you will improve your document's appearance.

The procedure for adding headers or footers varies depending on which view you're using: Galley view or Page view. I will start with the Galley view techniques.

Adding a Header or Footer in Galley View

You add a header or footer, respectively, by typing and formatting text in the Header or Footer window. To display these windows, you choose Open Header or Open Footer in the Document menu. These windows are truly windows, incidentally, rather than dialog boxes. While the Header or Footer window is open, you can choose commands from the menus, you can paste into these windows text you have stored on the clipboard or in the glossary, and you can turn on the ruler to assist you as you format the header or footer text.

To add a header or footer to your document (Galley view), follow these simple steps:

1. Choose Open Header or Open Footer from the Document menu.

2. When the Header or Footer window appears, type the header or footer text in the window (see fig. 6.5).

3. Format the header or footer as you choose.

   The Header and Footer windows have preset tabs at 3.0 inches (centered) and 6.0 inches (right). You can change these tabs (or add new ones) by choosing the Show Ruler option from the Format menu.

   You can choose other formatting options as you please. Choose character emphases, fonts, alignments, and indentations by using any of the techniques discussed in Chapters 4 and 5.

   To position header or footer text beyond the margins, drag the indent marks on the ruler or type negative numbers in the Left and Right indent boxes of the Paragraph dialog box.

   To create an interesting effect, add borders to your headers or footers. Add a line below the header and a line above a footer to create a symmetrical "frame" for the document's body text.

4. To add page numbers, the current time, or the current date, click the insertion point where you want the number, the time, or the date to appear. Use the preset tabs to align the page number, date, or time. Then click the icon on the header or footer title bar.

   After you add the page numbers, date, or time, Word displays the current value of the page number, date, or time (see fig. 6.6). If you have chosen the Show option in the Edit menu, you see these values in a box.

To delete a value, just select the box or backspace over it. (As far as Word is concerned, the box is a single character.)

5. Click the close box to close the header or footer window.

Fig. 6.5.

The header window.

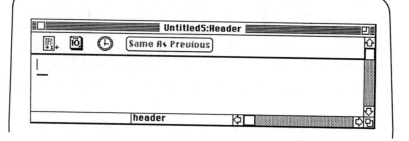

Fig. 6.6.

Header with date and page numbers added.

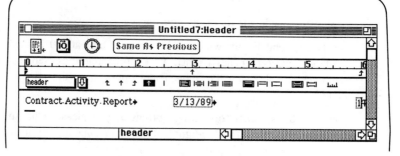

To edit or delete a header or footer you have already added, work through the following steps:

1. Choose Open Header or Open Footer from the Document menu.

2. When the Header or Footer window appears, edit the text or delete it to cancel the header or footer.

3. Close the Header or Footer window.

If you have redefined Word's default margins, you may wish to change the preset header and footer tab stops (3.0 inches centered and 6.0 inches left). Suppose that you redefine the default margins so that they're set at 1.0 inch left and right, producing a 6.5-inch line length. You should set the centered tab at 3.25 inches and the flush-right tab at 6.5 inches so that text aligned with these tabs looks correct on the screen. To learn how to redefine the Header and Footer styles, see Chapter 7, ''Formatting with Style Sheets.''

Adding a Header or Footer in Page View

When you add a header or footer in Page view, you do not see the Header or Footer window. Instead, the insertion point moves immediately to the first header or footer area in your document (see fig. 6.7). You type the header or footer in the top or bottom margin.

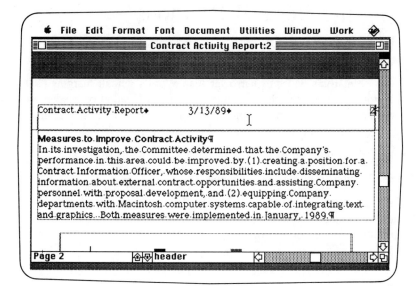

Fig. 6.7.

Adding a header in Page view.

Adding page numbers, dates, and times to headers in Page view isn't quite as straightforward as the process is in Galley view, when you see the icons on the Header or Footer window's title bar. You must choose one or more of the supplied glossary entries.

To add page numbers, dates, or times to headers or footers in Page view, do the following:

1. Move the insertion point to the header or footer area. If you haven't already added a header or footer, choose Open Header or Open Footer and type the header or footer text.

2. Position the insertion point where you want the glossary entry to appear.

3. Choose Glossary from the Edit menu.

4. To add the date or time, choose one of the date or time options.

   For a list of the date and time options available in the Glossary list box, see Chapter 11 "Creating and Using Glossaries."

5. Click Insert to add the glossary entry to your header or footer.

6. Repeat steps 2 through 5 to add additional glossary entries to your header or footer.

For more information on glossaries, see Chapter 11.

Adjusting the Vertical Positions of Headers and Footers

By default, Word prints headers or footers 0.5 inch from the top or bottom margin. If you choose margins wider or narrower than Word's default margins (1.0 inch top or bottom), you may wish to change the vertical location of headers or footers so that they print in the middle of the margin. If you choose a 1.25-inch top margin, for instance, you should position the headers at 0.675 inch.

To change the vertical position of headers or footers, follow these steps:

1. Choose Section from the Format menu.

2. Type a measurement in the From Top box to change the vertical position of headers; type a measurement in the From Bottom box to change the vertical position of footers.

3. Click OK.

Using (or Suppressing) First-Page Headers or Footers

Normally, headers and footers don't print on the first page. Word, however, prints them on page 1 unless you deliberately disable first-page header printing by clicking First Page Special in the Section dialog box. (You also click this option to suppress the printing of page numbers on the first page.)

Sometimes you will want to print a special first-page header or footer. Suppose that you have added a header *and* a footer to your document. You don't want the header to print on page 1 because the header would interfere with the document's title. So you click First Page Special (Section dialog box) to disable headers and footers on page 1. But you *do* want the footer to print on the first page. Fortunately, it's possible!

To print special first page headers or footers,

1. Choose Section from the Format menu.

2. Click First Page Special in the Section dialog box so that an X appears in the box.

3. Click OK.

4. Choose Open First Header or Open First Footer from the Document menu.

   These options appear only if you have clicked the First Page Special option. These options are not available when you are in Page View mode.

5. Type and format the header or footer you want to appear on the first page.

6. Close the header or footer window.

Defining Odd- and Even-Page Headers and Footers

If you're planning to duplicate your document on both sides of the page, take advantage of this Word feature, which allows you to define different headers and footers for odd and even pages. The odd-page headers or footers will appear to the right of the binding, and the even-page headers will appear to the left of the binding.

To create odd-page and even-page headers or footers,

1. Choose Document from the Format menu.

2. Click the Even/Odd Headers box so that an X appears.

3. Click OK.

4. Pull down the Document menu.

   You see four new options: Open Even Header, Open Even Footer, Open Odd Header, and Open Odd Footer.

5. Choose one of these options and create the header or footer.

6. Repeat step 5 until you have created all the headers or footers you want.

To create a pleasing effect, position the page numbers flush-right on odd pages and flush-left on even pages. Add lines below the headers and above the footers to frame the text on the page (see fig. 6.8).

Power
User
Tip

Fig. 6.8.

*Print Preview of
odd- and even-
page headers and
footers.*

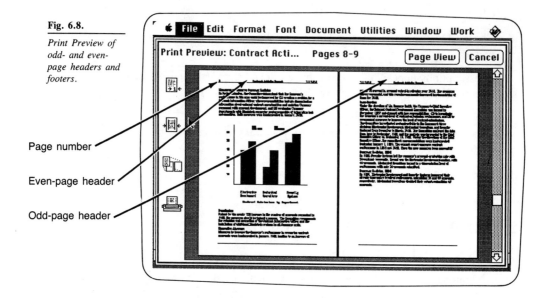

Page number

Even-page header

Odd-page header

Changing Margins

With Word, distinguishing between *indents* (which are *paragraph* formats) and *margins* (which are *document* formats) is important. You can choose indents for each paragraph, including single-line "paragraphs," such as headings. For this reason, you can vary indents as you please, creating in your document complex patterns that serve to highlight important text. In contrast, you choose margins for the whole document. The margin setting doesn't vary, even if you break your document into sections (see Chapter 14, "Page Layout Strategies with Text and Graphics," for more information on sections).

Figure 6.9 illustrates one of the design possibilities that stem from the difference between indents and margins. In this document, the left margin has been set at 2.0 inches. (In this Page view of the document, you can see the left margin as a dotted line down the screen at the zero mark on the ruler. The paragraphs containing the headings, however, have been formatted with a *negative* indent (-1.0 inch), so that they're positioned in the left margin. A double line under each heading, added with the Paragraph Borders command, creates a visually pleasing effect.

You can set or change the margins for your document in three different ways:

❏ By typing measurements in the Document dialog box

❏ By dragging the margin icons on the ruler when it is in the Page Scale mode

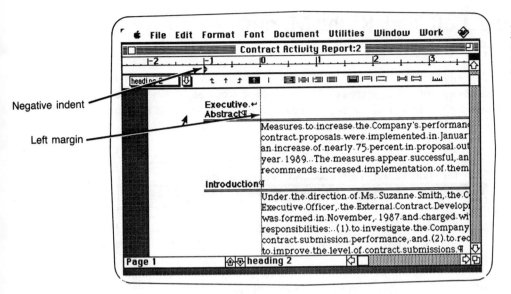

Fig. 6.9.

Use of negative indents in page design.

❏ By dragging the margin boxes in Print Preview

This section deals with the first two techniques; for information on changing margins with Print Preview, see "Controlling Page Style Formats with Print Preview" in this chapter.

Setting Margins with the Document Dialog Box

You can set margins with the Document dialog box, but you must type the measurements. If you work with the ruler displayed, and if you're setting just the left and right margins (not top or bottom), the ruler technique, which is described in the next section, is easier to use.

To set margins with the Document dialog box,

1. Choose Document from the Format menu.

2. Type measurements in the Top, Bottom, Left, and Right boxes.

   If you do not type a measurement abbreviation, Word assumes that you are expressing the measurements in inches.

3. Click OK.

For more information on measurements, see the section "Paragraph Dialog Box" in Chapter 5, "Fundamentals of Document Design II: Paragraph Formatting."

Setting Left and Right Margins with the Ruler

At the extreme right side of the ruler is the page scale icon, which, when you click it, changes the ruler's appearance. The formatting icons are dimmed, the scale measures the whole page (from edge to edge), and the left and right margin marks appear. These marks are left and right brackets (see fig. 6.10).

Fig. 6.10.

The ruler after the page scale icon has been clicked.

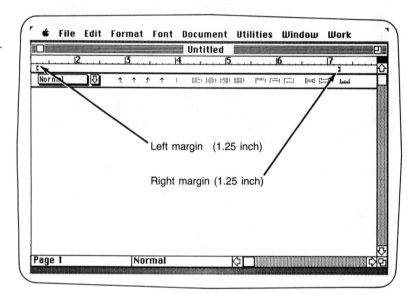

Left margin   (1.25 inch)

Right margin (1.25 inch)

To set the margins with the ruler, follow these steps:

1. If the ruler is not displayed, choose Show Ruler from the Format menu or use the ⌘-R keyboard shortcut.

2. Click the page scale icon.

3. To change the left or right margin, click on the left or right margin mark (the bracket) and drag. As you drag, watch the status line, which displays the mark's current location.

4. Click the page scale icon to restore the ruler's normal mode.

After you reposition the margin marks, Word updates the settings in the Document dialog box. If you change the settings in the Document dialog box, Word repositions the margin marks on the page scale ruler.

If you set the left and right margins at 1.0 inch to produce a 6.5-inch line length and you're using an Apple ImageWriter printer, the lines will be too long to display on the screen. When the insertion point nears the end of the line, the screen scrolls horizontally to display the insertion point. The horizontal scrolling can be disconcerting—so much so, in fact, that you may lose track of what you're doing. You can compensate for this problem by clicking the Tall Adjusted option in the Page Setup dialog box. After choosing this option, you can display 6.5-inch line lengths without horizontal scrolling.

Adding Gutters

If you plan to bind your document, you may wish to add a *gutter*, extra margin space to accommodate the binding. If you're planning to duplicate your document using just one side of the page, add a gutter by increasing the size of the left margin. If you're planning to duplicate your document on *both* sides of the page, however, add the gutter by typing a measurement (such as 0.5 inch) in the Gutter box of the Document dialog box. Word will add the gutter to the left margin of odd pages and the right margin of even pages.

Using Mirror Margins

If you are going to duplicate your document using both sides of the page, click the Mirror Even/Odd Margins box in the Document dialog box. With this option, the Left and Right Margins boxes change so that they read Inside (close to the binding) and Outside (away from the binding). If you type *1.5in* in the Inside box and *1.0in* in the Outside box, Word will print a 1.5-inch left margin and 1.0-inch right margin on odd pages. On even pages, Word will reverse these margin settings, printing a 1.0-inch *left* margin and 1.5-inch *right* margin on even pages.

Note: Setting a 1.5-inch inside margin and 1.0-inch outside margin produces precisely the same result as choosing a 0.5-inch gutter. If you type *0.5* in the Gutter box as well as typing *1.5* in the Inside box, you will get a 2.0-inch margin near the binding. Add a gutter one way or the other, but don't use both.

Controlling Page-Style Formats with Print Preview

The Print Preview command (File menu) provides an on-screen simulation of two full pages at a time (or just one, if you prefer), permitting you to check the relative position of all document formats before you print them. You use Print Preview to examine the overall balance of text on the page and to check the positions of headings and graphics. That much you have probably already learned by experimenting with the Print Preview command.

What's not obvious initially in Print Preview is that you can use this command to set margins and adjust the vertical positions of headers and footers. This technique is especially useful when you need to "finesse" the margins so that the text is nicely balanced on the page. You also can add page numbers to your document.

To adjust the margins and header and footer positions with Print Preview, follow these steps:

1. Choose Print Preview from the File menu.

2. When the Print Preview window appears, click the margins icon (the second from the top).

    After you click the margins icon, you see the margins superimposed on the page (see fig. 6.11). If you added a header or footer, you also see the text areas set aside for these formats.

3. To change the margins, move the pointer to one of the margin handles (the little black boxes on the margin line). When the pointer changes to a crosshair, click and drag. To see the pointer's position, watch the top of the Print Preview window, where the position is shown in inches. When you have adjusted the margin to your satisfaction, release the mouse button.

    If you're not happy with the change you have made, repeat step 3 and move the margin again. Word doesn't execute the margin change until you carry out step 5.

4. To adjust the vertical position of headers or footers within the top or bottom margins, click the header or footer's handle (the little black box) and drag. Watch the number in the top window border to see where you have positioned the header or footer. Release the button when you have finished moving the header or footer vertically.

5. When you're satisfied with the change, double-click the margin icon or click anywhere outside the page.

After you change the margins or header or footer location with the margin icon in Print Preview, Word updates the settings in the Document dialog box.

To add page numbers,

1. Choose Print Preview from the File menu.

Margin icon →

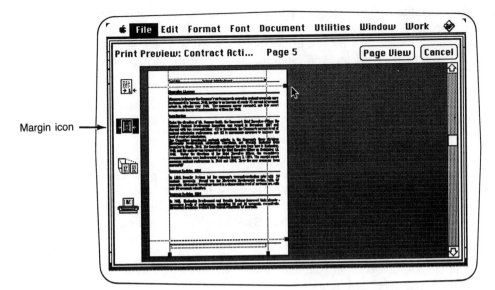

Fig. 6.11.

Adjusting margins in Page View.

2. Click the page number icon and drag it to the location you want.

   Watch the top window border to see the pointer's location in inches.

3. When you have positioned the number where you want it, release the button.

4. Press Cancel to quit Print Preview.

Creating and Editing Footnotes and Endnotes

Many business and professional writers, not just scholars, must back up their claims by citing other experts. A simple way to refer to other works is to include within the text a bibliographic reference enclosed by parentheses and attach a reference list at the end of the document. In many cases, however, writers must use footnotes or endnotes, which are referenced in the text by a number (usually superscripted).

Word's footnote capabilities are superb. The program automatically numbers your footnotes (and renumbers them if you insert or delete footnotes). After you create a footnote, Word opens a "smart" footnote window, which displays the text of the note that's referenced in the document window above. As you scroll through your document, the footnote window scrolls too, so that the relevant notes are always visible. If the footnote text is too long to fit on one page, Word floats the rest of the footnote text to the next page and prints a continuation separator above the notes (a line spanning the page). If you wish, the program will print a continuation notice telling the reader that the rest of the footnote's text will be found on the next page. If you prefer endnotes, you can print the notes at the ends of sections or at the end of the document.

Adding a Footnote or Endnote to Your Document

You add footnotes and endnotes to your document by the same procedure. Choose Footnote from the Document menu. You type the text of the note in a special footnote window, which opens after you click OK in the Footnote dialog box. To return to your document, you choose Go Back from the Utilities menu.

To create a footnote, follow these steps:

Speed Keys

⌘-E
⌘-Shift-Option-S

1. Position the insertion point in your text at the point where you want the footnote reference mark to appear.

2. Choose Footnote from the Document window, or use the ⌘-E keyboard shortcut.

3. When the Footnote dialog box appears, click OK to have Word number the note automatically (see fig. 6.12). Word inserts a 9-point, superscripted number after you click OK.

   If you want to insert a footnote reference mark other than a number (such as an asterisk), type the mark in the Footnote Reference Mark box before you click OK. Word will not number the note. If you have added other notes using automatic numbering, adding the note with an unnumbered reference mark does not affect the number sequence; Word simply skips this note.

   To edit the footnote separator (the line that separates the text from the footnotes), click the Separator button. To edit the continuation separator, which separates the text from continuation footnotes (long footnotes that are "floated" over from the preceding page), click the Cont. Separator button. To create a continuation notice (a warning to the reader that the rest of a long footnote continues on the next page), click the Cont. Notice button.

   After you click OK, Word splits the screen, positioning the footnote window below the document window (see fig. 6.13). Word echoes the footnote reference mark in the footnote window and positions the insertion point so that you can type the note.

4. Type the text of the note.

   By default, Word formats the footnote text with 10-point characters.

5. When you are finished typing the note, choose Go Back from the Utilities menu (or press the 0 [zero] key on the keypad) to return to the footnote reference mark in your document.

6. To close the footnote window, drag the window split bar down to the bottom of the window or use the ⌘-Shift-Option-S keyboard shortcut.

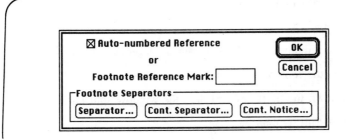

Fig. 6.12.

The Footnote dialog box.

Fig. 6.13.

The Footnote window and the document window.

You can change the default formats for the footnote reference mark (superscript, 9-point characters) and footnote text (single-spaced, flush-left lines with 10-point characters). For details, see Chapter 7, ''Formatting with Style Sheets.''

Power User Tip

Note: The footnote reference mark in your document isn't just a number; the footnote reference mark is a special character that links the reference mark to the footnote text. If you delete the footnote reference mark, you delete all the footnote text too! (If you accidentally delete the reference mark, choose Undo from the Edit menu immediately.)

Editing, Deleting, and Moving Footnotes and Endnotes

Once you have created a footnote or endnote, you can edit the footnote text, delete the note, or move it to a new location in your document.

To edit the footnote text,

1. If the footnote window isn't visible, open the footnote window.

   You can open the footnote window three different ways:

   ❏ Hold down the Shift key and drag the window split bar down.

   ❏ Press ⌘-Shift-Option-S.

   ❏ Double-click the footnote reference mark.

2. Edit the note.

   If you accidentally delete the footnote reference mark, replace it by choosing Footnote from the Document menu and clicking OK.

3. Choose Go Back from the Utilities menu or press 0 (zero) on the keypad to return to your document.

To delete a footnote,

1. Select the footnote reference mark.

2. Press Delete or choose Cut from the Edit menu.

Note: You cannot delete a footnote by deleting the footnote text. You must delete the footnote reference mark in your document. Deleting the mark deletes the text, too.

To move a footnote,

1. Select the footnote reference mark and choose Cut (or press ⌘-X).

2. Position the insertion point at the footnote reference mark's new location.

3. Choose Paste from the Edit menu or press ⌘-V.

Specifying Where Notes Will Print

To specify where notes will print, choose Document from the Format menu and click the Position dropdown list box to see your options:

❑ *Bottom of Page*. Choose this option to place footnotes at the bottom of the page, even if the last page isn't completely filled with text.

❑ *Beneath Text*. Choose this option to place footnotes at the bottom of the page, except on the last page, on which the notes will be positioned just after the last line of text.

❑ *End of Section*. Choose this option if you have created a multisection document and want the notes for each section to be collected and printed as endnotes at the end of each section.

❑ *End of Document*. Choose this option to print all endnotes at the end of your document (even if you have divided it into sections).

After you choose the option you want, click OK. The choice you make affects the entire document.

The End of Section option is handy because you can use it to collect and print all the endnotes for each section at the end of that section (such as a chapter). As you will learn in Chapter 14, "Page Layout Strategies with Text and Graphics," however, sometimes you must create a section break for reasons other than starting a new chapter. (For example, you must create a section break to change from single- to multiple-column formatting.) In such case, you will probably want to stop Word from collecting and printing the endnotes for that section. To do so, place the insertion point in the section and choose Section from the Format menu. Click the Include Endnotes box so that the X disappears. Word will not print the endnotes until the end of the next section.

 # High-Productivity Techniques To Remember

❑ Page styles, such as page numbers, headers, footers, footnotes, margins, and columns, are repeated on the pages of your document. Page styles provide the page context in which your character and paragraph formats appear. By default, Word paginates the text you type so that it prints with 1.25-inch margins left and right as well as 1.0-inch margins top and bottom. To add additional page styles, such as page numbers, you must choose them deliberately.

❏ Some page styles, such as footnote position (bottom of page or end of document) and margins, always affect your entire document. You control these styles with the Document dialog box (Format menu). Other page styles can vary within your document if you divide it into sections by pressing ⌘-Enter. These formats, which include headers, footers, line numbers, columns, and page numbers, are controlled with the Section dialog box (Format menu). If you haven't divided your document into sections, these formats apply to the whole document.

❏ Toggle the Page View mode on and off with ⌘-B to see the effects of your page-style choices after you make them. Page view displays all page styles with the exception of line numbers (which you can see if you choose Print Preview).

❏ To turn on page numbers, click Auto in the Section dialog box and click First Page Special to suppress page numbers on the first page.

❏ If you plan to use headers or footers, don't turn on page numbers with the Section dialog box; use the page number icon when you create your header or footer. If you're using margins other than Word's defaults, be sure to redefine the tab settings in Word's predefined header and footer formats.

❏ To change left and right margins rapidly, choose Show Ruler, click the page scale icon, and drag the left or right margin marks.

❏ If you would like to set margins and add page numbers simultaneously, the fastest way is to choose Print Preview. Click the margins icon and drag the handles to set the margins. To turn on page numbers, click the page number icon and drag the number to the page number location you want.

❏ To toggle the footnote window on and off rapidly, learn the ⌘-Shift-Option-S keyboard shortcut.

Formatting with Style Sheets

When you're formatting a complex document, you will surely find that ordinary formatting techniques (the ones you learned in the last three chapters) have a significant drawback. For example, suppose that you have chosen the Geneva font, justified alignment, and double-line spacing. Then, to type an extended quotation, you choose the Paragraph dialog box and indent the text from both margins. After you finish typing the quotation, you press ⌘-Shift-P to cancel the quotation format, but you must now enter all those formats all over again. You could copy the formats with the ⌘-Option-V shortcut, as explained in Chapter 6, but even this shortcut requires four steps. How nice it would be if you could enter all those formats, whenever you want, with just one command!

If you have been thinking along these lines, here's some excellent news: with Word's styles, you have precisely the commands you need to solve the problem just mentioned (and others too, as you will see).

A *style* is a stored and named list of character and paragraph formats that you can apply to any paragraph in your document. If you're not using styles, you're missing out on the single most important productivity feature of Word 4.

No matter how many formats you have stored in a style, you can apply it with just one command; and if the style includes more than one or two formats, that capability translates into big improvements in your formatting productivity. For instance, suppose that you want to create a bulleted list printed in 10-point Helvetica with a hanging indentation, justified alignment, and a blank line before each item in the list. Using pull-down menus, you have to give several commands to set up this format. And after you finish typing the text, you cancel all the formats and return to normal paragraph formatting. If you want to type another list with the same format, you must give all these commands again. With a style, however, you enter all these formats with just one command, and you can use the command whenever you need the style.

173

Exploring styles is an excellent idea for a second reason. You can use style formatting to redefine many of Word's default format settings. As you already know, Word comes to you with many defined character, paragraph, and document formats. For example, the formats for headers and footers include all the normal paragraph formats plus tab stops at 3 inches (centered) and 6 inches (flush right). These tab stops are convenient if you're using Word's default line length of 6.0 inches. But what if you're using a 6.5-inch line? You need a centered tab at 3.25 inches and a flush-right tab at 6.5 inches. Must you reset the tabs manually every time you use the Open Header command in a new document? No, and here's why.

You can redefine the default header format and make it the new default for all documents you create. What's more, the header style (and many others) are *automatic styles*. Word applies the style automatically whenever you choose the Open Header command. (Other automatic styles include footers, the footnote reference mark, footnote text, page numbers, line numbers, headings, and more.) After you redefine automatic styles, the formats you chose apply automatically to all new documents.

Styles are productivity boosters for a third reason as well. When you redefine a style you have already created, the change you make automatically applies to all the paragraphs to which you have applied that style. Suppose, for instance, that you create a long report in which extended quotations are formatted for 9-point type. But after you print the report, the 9-point type turns out to be too small, so you decide to change to 12-point type. Instead of manually reformatting every quotation, you simply redefine the quotation style. Word automatically reformats every paragraph to which you have applied that style.

In sum, you save time in three ways by using styles:

❑ When you format by applying a style, you enter several formats with one command.

❑ When you redefine automatic styles, new documents automatically have the formats you have chosen.

❑ When you redefine styles you have created, Word applies the changes automatically—and instantly—to every paragraph to which you have assigned the style.

All three features are essential for high-productivity writing with Word 4.

About Style Sheets and Styles

Here's a brief overview of style sheet formatting. The rest of this chapter explores these topics in more detail.

Word has two kinds of style sheets:

❏ *Default style sheet*. Word's default style sheet automatically applies to every new document you create. The default style sheet contains the program's default settings for the normal paragraph style and all other automatic styles (such as header, footer, footnote reference mark, page number format, and more). If you add styles to the default style sheet or if you modify the styles already contained in it, the new styles are available when you create new documents. The default style sheet also includes the formats in effect when you click the Set Defaults button in the Page Setup dialog box (File menu), the Section dialog box (Format menu), and the Document dialog box (Format menu).

❏ *Document style sheet*. When you create new styles or redefine existing ones, Word creates a document style sheet, which is linked to the document you're working on. The next time you open this document, the style sheet also opens. The document style sheet doesn't apply to other documents unless you deliberately apply the style sheet to a another document, as described elsewhere in this chapter.

When you create a style, you decide whether you want to add it to the default style sheet (so that the new style is available for all new documents) or keep the style in the document style sheet (so that the style is available only for the document you're working on). If you create a style you're sure that you will use in many documents, add it to the default style sheet. If the style cannot be used for other documents, add it to the document style sheet.

When you create a style, you give it a name, such as Bulleted List or Quotation. If you wish, you can give a style two names: the first one, a longer one, like Bulleted List, fully describes the style so that you can tell what it's for when you see the name in a list box; and the second name, a short one, like BL, makes typing the name in a text box for retrieval purposes easier and faster. To give a style two names, separate them by a comma (*Bulleted List,BL*). After you name the style with two names, Word "knows" the style by both of its names.

Note: Do not use a comma in a style name unless you want to separate two names.

After you create a style, you apply it to paragraphs in your document by using the ruler's style selection box, the Styles command, or the ⌘-Shift-S keyboard shortcut. Word instantly applies to the paragraph(s) all the formats you have chosen and displays the style name on the status line.

You can redefine styles you have already created. When you redefine a style, the changes you make automatically apply to all the paragraphs in the document you have formatted with that style. Until you have experienced it, it's hard to believe how powerful this feature is and how much time it can save you. You can reformat a lengthy document extensively with just a few keystrokes and clicks, a job that would take far longer with conventional formatting methods.

When you save your document, Word stores the styles you have created or redefined.

If you have used previous versions of Word, you will be pleased to know that choosing styles is easier with Version 4. The ruler now contains a Style Selection box, which makes it easy not only to choose styles, but also to redefine them. If you're planning to use styles, you will find that it pays to display the ruler at all times.

Creating Styles

You can create styles in two ways: by recording formats you have already applied to a paragraph in a document, or by defining a style with the Define Styles command. The styles you create are recorded in a *style sheet*, a list of styles that is attached to the current document.

Recording a Style

As you format a document, you are sure to create a format you want to save and use again. Suppose, for instance, that you have just finished formatting a bulleted list (10-point Helvetica type, justified alignment, a 1-inch left indent with a 0.5-inch hanging indentation, and blank lines before and after each paragraph).

To record a style you have already created, follow these steps:

1. Select the paragraph whose formats you want to record.

2. If the ruler isn't displayed, choose Show Ruler from the Format menu.

3. Place the insertion point in the style selection box on the ruler and type the style name (see fig. 7.1).

   You can give the style two names—a long one (for description) and a short one (for faster typing). To name the style Bulleted List, for instance, type *Bulleted List,BL* in the style selection box.

4. Press Return.

5. When the message box appears, click Define (see fig. 7.2).

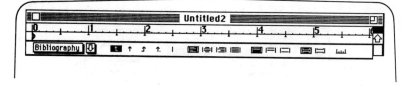

Fig. 7.1.

The style selection box on the ruler.

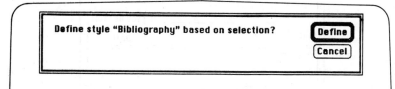

Fig. 7.2.

The style definition message box.

After you record the style, you see its name in the style selection box.

Defining a Style with the Define Styles Command

If your document doesn't contain a paragraph with the formats you want to include in a style, you can create the style with the Define Styles command. Here's how.

⌘-T

1. Choose Define Styles from the Format menu (alternatively, use the ⌘-T keyboard shortcut, or double-click the style name in the status line).

2. When the Define Styles window appears, type the new style's name in the Style text box (see fig. 7.3).

3. Type *Normal* in the Based On box if the box is blank or some other style name is listed there.

4. Choose formats from the Format menu, the Font menu, or the ruler, or use keyboard shortcuts.

   As you choose formats, Word adds them to the style definition, which appears in the box beneath the Style text box.

5. When you finish choosing formats, do one of the following:

   ❑ Click Apply to define the style, apply it to the selected paragraph, and add the style to the document style sheet without closing the Define Styles window. Choose this option if

Fig. 7.3.

*The Define Styles
dialog box.*

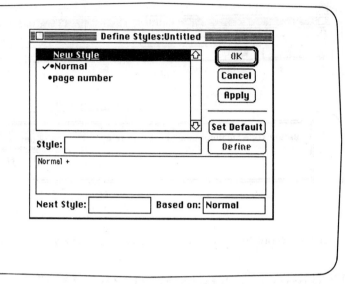

you're not sure that you have chosen the right formats and think that you probably will have to change them. If the style looks OK, click Cancel to close the Define Styles window.

❑ Click Define to define the style and include it in the document style sheet without applying the style to the selected paragraph and without closing the Define Styles window. Choose this option if you want to create another style without leaving the Define Styles window.

❑ Click OK to define the style, apply it to the selected paragraph, include it in the document style sheet, and close the Define Styles window. You normally choose this option when you define a style for the document style sheet.

❑ Click Set Default to add the style to the default stylesheet so that the style is available for all documents.

Basing One Style on Another

As you see from the Define Styles dialog box, you can base one style on another. When the Based On box displays Normal, the style you create is based on the formats stored in the Normal style. (The default Normal style includes the New York 12 font and single-spaced, left-justified lines.) The new style will include the formats of the style on which the new style is based unless you choose new formats that cancel the existing ones. For example, if you base a new style on the default Normal format and then choose justified alignment, the new format will have justified alignment, not flush-left alignment. However, the new style will have any Normal formats that aren't specifically contradicted by your formatting choices. If you don't choose a new font, for instance, the new style will have New York 12 character formatting.

Always define the default font for a document by redefining the Normal style with the font and size you want. Then base all new styles on Normal. If you create your styles this way, you can change the font of every style just by changing Normal. Suppose, for instance, that you define Normal to include Geneva 12. When you create several new styles based on Normal, each is formatted with Geneva 12. Then you decide that the document would look better in Helvetica 12. To reformat your whole document with Helvetica 12, you simply redefine Normal so that it specifies Helvetica 12 instead of Geneva 12. For instructions on modifying existing styles, see "Editing Styles," in this chapter.

Defining the Next Style

After you create a style and apply it (see "Applying Styles," elsewhere in this chapter), you will find that Word returns to Normal formatting when you press Return (instead of copying the format to the next paragraph). To put it another way, Word applies the Normal style automatically when you press Return. If you like, you can control the style Word applies when you press Return.

Controlling the next style is useful when you know that one style will always be followed by another. For example, many corporate style guidelines instruct writers to type their department name just below the document title. In this setting, you can create a Document Title style (14-point Helvetica, boldface type, and centered) that is followed by a Department Name style (10-point Helvetica, centered, with two blank lines before). Every time you apply the Document Title style, type some text, and press Return, Word applies the Department Name style to the next paragraph automatically.

To define a style so that Word enters a second style automatically after you press Return, follow this procedure:

1. Create the two styles.

2. Choose Define Styles from the Format menu (or press ⌘-T).

3. Choose the first style's name in the list box.

4. Type in the Next Style box the style you want to *follow* the first style.

5. Click Define and then Cancel.

Note: Word applies the next style automatically only when you press Return at the end of the paragraph containing the first style. If some text already follows the style, and you don't press Return after typing the paragraph, Word won't change its format.

An attractive document design uses two kinds of paragraphs for body text:

❑ Paragraphs under headings, called *lead paragraphs*, are formatted as block paragraphs without first-line indentation.

❑ The second and subsequent paragraphs under a heading, called *text paragraphs*, do include a first-line indentation.

You can set up styles that enter these formats automatically. Here's how:

1. Using the Define Styles window, create the Text Paragraph style with an automatic first-line indentation. (Type *0.5″* in the First Line box of the Paragraph dialog box when you define the style). Click the Define button in the Define Styles window to define the style. Then type *Text Paragraph* in the Next Style box and click Define again.

   The reason you type *Text Paragraph* in the Next Style box is that text paragraphs are normally followed by text paragraphs.

   You have just defined the Text Paragraph style so that Word will copy the Text Paragraph style to the next paragraph automatically.

2. Use the Define Styles window to create the Lead Paragraph style based on the Text Paragraph style, but with *no* first-line indentation, and type *Text Paragraph* in the Next Style box. Click Define to define the style.

   Your lead paragraphs will always be followed by text paragraphs.

   When you press Return after typing a paragraph formatted with Lead Paragraph, Word will enter the Text Paragraph style automatically.

When you create styles for headings, define them so that the Lead Paragraph style is the next style. For information on defining heading styles, see "Redefining Automatic Styles," elsewhere in this chapter. After doing so, when you press Return after typing a heading, Word enters the Lead Paragraph style automatically. After you finish typing the lead paragraph, Word enters the Text Paragraph format automatically.

Revising and Managing Styles

You can edit, rename, or delete a style after you have created it. When you edit a style, the redefined style applies automatically to all the paragraphs to which you've applied the style.

Editing Styles

You can edit a style you have already created by using the style selection box or the Define Styles window.

To edit a style with the style selection box, follow these steps:

1. Select a paragraph of text to which the style has been applied.

   The style selection box shows the current style name.

2. Choose new formats (or change existing ones) by using the Format menu, the Font menu, the ruler, or keyboard commands.

3. Click the style selection box. Word highlights the box.

4. Click the style selection box's arrow.

5. When the message box appears, click the Redefine option to change the style definition (see fig. 7. 4).

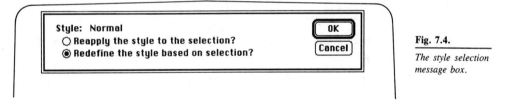

Fig. 7.4.

The style selection message box.

To edit a style by using the Define Styles dialog box, follow these steps:

1. Choose Define Styles from the Format menu.

2. Choose from the list box the style you want to edit.

3. Choose new formats (or change existing ones) by using the Format menu, the Font menu, the ruler, or keyboard commands.

4. Click OK to apply the style to the selected paragraph or click Define and then Cancel to define the style without applying it. Click Set Default to include the style in the default style sheet.

Viewing the Current Style Definition

If you're not sure which formats you have chosen for a style, you can view them by choosing the Styles command.

1. Choose Styles from the Format menu.

2. Choose the style name you want from the list box.

   The current style definitions appear in the Styles box (see fig. 7.5).

3. Click the Apply button to apply the style without closing the Styles dialog box, OK to apply the style and close the box, or Cancel to close the box without applying the style.

Fig. 7.5.

Viewing the current style definition in the Styles dialog box.

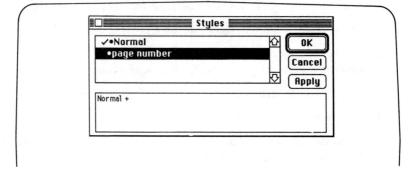

Renaming Styles

Every style should have a unique name. You can rename a style if the new name isn't already in use for another style. Follow these steps:

1. Choose Define Styles from the Format menu.

2. Select from the list box the style you want to rename.

3. Retype the name in the Style box.

4. Click OK.

Deleting a Style

You can delete any style you have added to a document style sheet. Use the following procedure:

1. Choose Define Styles from the Format menu.

2. Choose the style name from the list box.

3. Choose the Cut command from the Edit menu.

4. Confirm the deletion by clicking OK.

If you formatted any text with the deleted style, the text takes the Normal style after you delete the style. If the style also is part of the default style sheet, you will be asked to confirm the deletion from that style sheet as well.

Redefining Automatic Styles

As already explained, Word comes to you with preset automatic styles—33, to be exact (see table 7.1). Among these formats are the Normal paragraph format (New York 12, flush left), Header and Footer formats (which include tab settings), Footnote Reference Mark (superscripted 9-point type), and Footnote Text (10-point type). You can redefine any of these preset styles to suit your formatting tastes and needs. When you redefine these styles, you can choose to redefine them for the document style sheet (in which case they apply only to the document you're creating) or for the default style sheet (in which case they apply to all documents).

These styles are called automatic styles because Word applies them automatically when you perform certain actions:

❑ When you choose Open Header or Open Footer, Word applies the Header or Footer style automatically.

❑ When you choose the Footnote command, Word applies the Footnote Reference Mark style automatically (and when you type the text of the footnote, Word applies the Footnote Text style automatically).

❑ If you add page numbers or line numbers to your document, Word uses the formats defined by the Page Number or Line Number style.

❑ When you create headings in an outline (see Chapter 10, ''Organizing Your Document with Outlining''), Word applies the Heading styles automatically.

❑ The Index and Toc (short for ''table of contents'') styles are applied automatically to the indexes and tables of contents Word creates (see Chapter 15, ''Adding an Index and Table of Contents'').

If you redefine the Normal style and store the new definition in the default style sheet, you redefine all the styles based on Normal, and (as table 7.1 shows) the default style sheet includes all the automatic styles. Therefore, the best way to create a new default font for all automatic styles, including footnotes and page numbers, is to redefine the Normal style and save the definition to the default style sheet. For instructions, see the next section ("Redefining Automatic Styles in the Default Style Sheet").

Table 7.1
Default Format Definitions of Automatic Styles

Automatic Style Name	Default Format Definition
Footer	Normal + Tab stops: 3 inches centered and 6 inches flush right
Footnote Reference Mark	Normal + Font: 9 point, superscript 3 point
Footnote Text	Normal + Font: 10 point
Header	Normal + Tab stops: 3 in Centered 6 in flush right
Heading 1	Helvetica Bold, 12 point, space before 12 point
Heading 2	Helvetica Bold, 12 point, space before 6 point
Heading 3	Normal + Bold, 12 point, indent left 0.25 inch
Heading 4	Normal, 12 point, underline, indent left 0.25 inch
Heading 5	Normal + Bold, 10 point, indent left 0.5 inch
Heading 6	Normal, 10 point, underline, indent left 0.5 inch
Heading 7	Normal, 10 point, italic, indent left 0.5 inch
Heading 8	Normal, 10 point, italic, indent left 0.5 inch

Table 7.1—*Continued*

Automatic Style Name	Default Format Definition
Heading 9	Normal, 10 point, italic, indent left 0.5 inch
Index 1	Normal +
Index 2	Normal + left indent 0.25 inch
Index 3	Normal + left indent 0.5 inch
Index 4	Normal + left indent 0.75 inch
Index 5	Normal + left indent 1.0 inch
Index 6	Normal + left indent 1.25 inch
Index 7	Normal + left indent 1.5 inch
Line number	Normal
Normal	New York 12, flush left
PostScript	Normal + 10 point, hidden, bold
Page number	Normal
Toc 1	Normal + left indent 0.5 inch, 0.5 inch right indent, Tab stops: 5.75 inches flush left with leader dots and 6 inches flush right
Toc 2	Normal + left indent 0.5 inch, 0.5 inch right indent, Tab stops: 5.75 inches flush left with leader dots and 6 inches flush right
Toc 3	Normal + left indent 1.0 inch, 0.5 inch right indent, Tab stops: 5.75 inches flush left with leader dots and 6 inches flush right
Toc 4	Normal + left indent 1.5 inch, 0.5 inch right indent, Tab stops: 5.75 inches flush left with leader dots and 6 inches flush right
Toc 5	Normal + left indent 2.0 inch, 0.5 inch right indent, Tab stops: 5.75 inches flush left with leader dots and 6 inches flush right

Table 7.1—*Continued*

Automatic Style Name	Default Format Definition
Toc 6	Normal + left indent 2.5 inch, 0.5 inch right indent, Tab stops: 5.75 inches flush left with leader dots and 6 inches flush right
Toc 7	Normal + left indent 3.0 inch, 0.5 inch right indent, Tab stops: 5.75 inches flush left with leader dots and 6 inches flush right
Toc 8	Normal + left indent 3.5 inch, 0.5 inch right indent, Tab stops: 5.75 inches flush left with leader dots and 6 inches flush right
Toc 9	Normal + left indent 4.0 inch, 0.5 inch right indent, Tab stops: 5.75 inches flush left with leader dots and 6 inches flush right

Redefining Automatic Styles in the Default Style Sheet

Word's default style sheet contains the default format definitions for the automatic styles.

If you redefine these styles in the default style sheet, the redefined styles apply to all the documents you create (unless you specifically override these styles).

To redefine an automatic style in the default style sheet, follow these steps:

1. Hold down the Shift key, and pull down the Format menu. Then choose Define All Styles from the Format menu.

   When you press the Shift key before pulling down the Format menu, the Define Styles command changes to the Define All Styles command, and the list box includes all the automatic style names.

2. Choose from the list box the automatic style you want to redefine.

3. Choose formats from the Format menu, the Font menu, or the ruler, or use keyboard shortcuts.

4. Click the Set Default button.

5. When the alert box appears, click OK.

6. Click Cancel to close the Define Styles window or click OK to apply the style to the currently selected paragraph.

You may find this brief overview of some style redefinitions helpful:

❑ *Header and Footer.* If you're using a 6.5-inch line, use the ruler to change the tab settings to 3.25 inches (centered) and 6.5 inches (flush right).

❑ *Footnote Text.* Add a blank line before each footnote text paragraph in order to make your footnotes easier to read.

❑ *Headings.* Click the Keep with Next option (Paragraph dialog box) and add blank lines after the headings in order to keep Word from leaving a heading alone at the bottom of the page.

Restoring Word's Default Style Settings

If you have made default style sheet changes that you regret, you can edit them individually. This method is probably the best way to proceed. You may, however, wish to restore Word's default formats to their pristine state—just the way they were when you first started the program.

To restore all Word's default formats, follow these steps:

1. In the Finder, double-click the System Folder icon.

2. Drag the Word Settings (4) file to the trash.

Caution: When you delete the Word Settings (4) file, you delete all the changes you have made to Word, including choices in the Preferences dialog box, the additions and deletions you have made to menus, and changes to defaults you have made by clicking the Set Default button in the Page Setup, Section, and Paragraph dialog boxes.

Redefining Automatic Styles in the Document Style Sheet

Every document style sheet contains the automatic styles and uses the current default formats for these styles. If you wish, you can modify the automatic style definitions in the document style sheet. These changes apply only to the current document (the one that's active when you choose the Define All Styles command).

To redefine an automatic style in the document style sheet, follow these steps:

1. Hold down the Shift key, and pull down the Format menu. Then choose Define All Styles from the Format menu.

   When you press the Shift key before pulling down the Format menu, the Define Styles command changes to the Define All Styles command, and the list box includes all the automatic style names.

2. Choose from the list box the automatic style you want to redefine.

3. Choose formats from the Format menu, the Font menu, or the ruler, or use keyboard shortcuts.

4. Click the Define button.

5. Click Cancel to close the Define Styles window.

Applying Styles

Once you have created or redefined styles, you can choose one of three techniques to apply the styles to selected paragraphs in your document. You can use the style selection box, the Style command, or the keyboard commands.

Applying Styles with the Style Selection Box

By far the easiest way to apply a style is to use the style selection box in the ruler. To apply a style by using the style selection box, follow these steps:

1. Select the paragraph or paragraphs to which you want to apply the style.

   If you're selecting just one paragraph, don't bother highlighting the whole paragraph. Just place the insertion point anywhere within the paragraph.

   If the ruler isn't displayed, choose Show Ruler from the Format menu.

2. Click on and drag the arrow next to the style selection box.

3. When you have highlighted the style you want to apply, release the mouse button.

Applying Styles with the Style Command

If the ruler isn't displayed, you can choose Show Ruler to display the ruler so that you can use the style selection box. Alternatively, you can choose the Styles command from the Format menu and select the style you want from the list box.

You can add frequently used style names to the Work menu by following these steps:

1. Press ⌘-Option-Plus (+).

   The pointer changes to a big plus symbol.

2. Click the drag-down arrow on the style selection box and drag the highlight to the style name you want to add to the Work menu.

3. Release the mouse button.

Word adds the style name you have chosen to the Work menu. If the Work menu isn't on the menu bar, Word creates the menu.

Assigning Styles with the Keyboard

The third way to apply a style is to choose the ⌘-Shift-S keyboard shortcut. Follow these steps:

⌘-Shift-S

1. Select the paragraph or paragraphs to which you want to apply the style.

2. Press ⌘-Shift-S.

   The word Style appears highlighted in the status line (see fig. 7. 6).

3. Type the style name.

   You needn't type the whole name—just enough of it so that Word can distinguish the style you want from other styles with similar names. If you have given two names to the style (such as Bulleted List and BL), type the shorter name.

4. Press Return.

You can assign styles to keyboard commands. For instructions, see Chapter 9, "Customizing Word 4's Menus and Keyboard."

Fig. 7.6.

*Applying a style
with ⌘-Shift-S.*

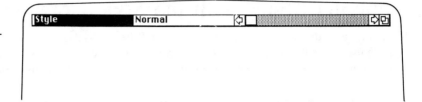

| Style | Normal | | |

Adding and Deleting Formatting in Text Formatted with Styles

After you have applied a style to a paragraph (or paragraphs), you can add additional character or paragraph formats. The formats you add affect only the selected paragraph(s); the added formats don't apply to other paragraphs with the same style.

If you want to delete these additional formats and return to just the formats listed in the style definition, follow these steps:

1. Select the paragraph or paragraphs containing the formatting you want to delete.

2. Click the style selection box.

3. Click the style selection box's arrow.

4. When the dialog box appears, click the Reapply the Style to the Selection option.

Speed Keys

To restore the character format you have assigned to a style, choose the Plain for Style command (Format menu) or use the ⌘-Shift-space bar shortcut.

**⌘-Shift-
space bar**

Copying a Document Style Sheet to a New Document

After you have created a useful document style sheet, you may want to copy it to a new document. Once you do, all the styles you have created are available for the new document.

To copy a document style sheet, use the following procedure:

1. In the new document, choose Define Styles from the Format menu.

2. When the Define Styles window appears, choose Open from the File menu.

3. When the Open dialog box appears, choose the document to which the style sheet you want is attached.

4. Click the Open button.

Word combines the new document's style sheet with the one you have just opened. If a style name in the new document conflicts, Word uses the incoming style's name and formats.

High-Productivity Techniques To Remember

❑ Styles provide a quick way to enter two or more formats with just one command. You also can use styles to redefine many of Word's default formats; and when you redefine a style, Word changes all the text to which you have applied that style—throughout your whole document.

❑ By saving styles to Word's default style sheet, you make them available for every document you create or edit.

❑ If you have created a complex format, quickly transform it into a style by recording the format, using the style selection box.

❑ Define the Normal style with the font and size you want to use for all documents, and save the style to the default style sheet. Then base all the new styles you create on Normal. That way, you can redefine the font for an entire document just by redefining the Normal style for that document's style sheet.

❑ If you know that a style will always (or usually) be followed by a second style, use the Next Style box in the Define Styles window to name the second style. Word will apply the second style automatically after you apply the first style and press Return.

❑ To edit a style quickly, use the Format or Font menu, the ruler, or the keyboard commands. Then click the style selection box and the drop-down arrow. When the dialog box appears, click the Redefine Style Based on the Selection option.

❑ If you're using 6.5-inch line lengths, redefine the Header and Footer automatic styles with a centered tab at 3.25 inches and a flush-right tab at 6.5 inches. Save the redefined style to the default style sheet.

❏ To make footnotes more readable, add a blank line before each
paragraph of footnote text by modifying the Footnote Text automatic
style. Save the redefined style to the default style sheet.

❏ To copy a document style sheet, open a new document, choose Define
Styles, and choose the Open command. Choose the file that contains
the document style sheet you want to copy, and click OK.

8

Checking Spelling, Saving, and Printing

Few satisfactions in computing compare with creating a handsome Word document and seeing it come to life, page by page, on an ImageWriter or LaserWriter printer. Ordinarily, printing is a simple process; you just choose Print from the File menu and click OK. To make sure that your printed copy looks (and reads) its best, however, be sure to use Word's excellent spelling-checking program, the automatic-hyphenation utility, and the Print Preview and Page View commands for previewing print output. And before you print, be sure to explore the full range of Word's many printing options. You will find full coverage of these topics, as well as saving and backing up your document, in this chapter.

Checking Spelling

Business and professional writing require perfect spelling. Many people consider spelling errors or typos to be signs of limited intelligence, lack of professionalism, or carelessness. You cannot afford to make a negative impression, and with Word's spelling-checking feature, you can make sure that you don't. Run Word's spelling-checking program on *every* document that will leave your computer.

Caution: Like all computer spelling-checking programs, Word doesn't really check spelling. Word compares the words in your document, one by one, with correctly spelled words stored in the program's dictionaries. When Word cannot find a match, the program indicates that the word is unknown. A word categorized as unknown may actually be spelled correctly. In this case, you can add the word to the dictionary. Be aware that Word's spelling-checking program skips over a correctly spelled word used in the wrong context; do spell check your document but remember that there's no substitute for a final proofreading.

Word doesn't check the spelling of hidden text unless the text is displayed. To display hidden text, click Show Hidden Text in the Preferences dialog box, which you access from the Edit menu.

Starting the Spelling-Checking Program

You can check your entire document or just a portion (a word, sentence, paragraph, or block of text). You control the size of text to be checked by selecting it. If no text is selected, Word begins checking your document from the insertion point's location. Then, when the spelling-checking program reaches the end of your document, an alert box appears and asks whether you want to continue checking from the beginning of your document. If you click OK, Word continues from the beginning until it reaches the insertion point again. For this reason, you don't need to scroll to the beginning of your document before choosing the Spelling option. Even if you start in the middle or near the end, you can still check your entire document.

Remember, if you have selected some text, Word begins the check at the beginning of the selection and then checks only the selected portion. To check your entire document, therefore, make sure that you haven't selected a block of text.

⌘-L

To perform a spelling check, follow these steps:

1. To check a selection, select the text. To check your entire document, click the location at which you want the spelling check to start.

2. Choose Spelling from the Utilities menu or use the ⌘-L keyboard shortcut.

   If Word cannot find the spelling dictionary, a message box appears and asks you to locate the dictionary. If necessary, insert the disk containing the MS Dictionary file.

3. When the Spelling window appears (see fig. 8.1), click the Ignore Words in All Caps button to remove the X beside the option if you want to check the spelling of acronyms (such as NASA or ASCAP).

4. Click the Start Check button.

When Word finds an unknown word, you have the following options:

❏ Correct the word's spelling by typing the correct spelling at the Change To prompt. You can ask Word to check the spelling of the correction you have supplied.

❏ Ask Word to suggest a correct spelling.

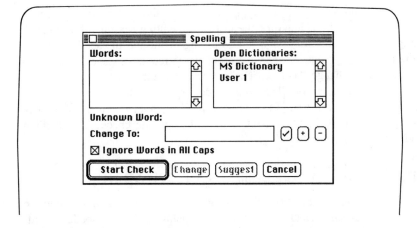

Fig. 8.1.

The Spelling window.

❑ Add the unknown word to the user dictionary, if it is spelled correctly, so that Word will no longer report the word as unknown.

❑ Ignore the word.

❑ Quit the spelling check by clicking the Cancel button.

In the sections that follow, these options are examined in detail.

Correcting a Word

When an unknown word is found, the Start Check button becomes No Change, which is the *default* option—the one Word uses if you press Return instead of clicking a button.

To correct an unknown word by retyping it, do the following:

1. Type the correct spelling in the Change To box. Alternatively, you can click Unknown Word to echo the unknown word immediately in the Change To box. Then edit the word.

2. When you are satisfied with the correction, click the ✔ button if you want Word to look up the correction.

    If the word is spelled correctly, Word highlights the Change To box and the word disappears from the Unknown Word message area. If the correction is misspelled, the misspelling appears in the Unknown Word message area.

3. To carry out the correction, click the Change button or press Return. To abandon the correction, click No Change.

Note: When you choose Change and type a correction, the spelling-checking program then remembers the change for the rest of the editing session. If you check spelling again in the same session without quitting Word and the spelling-checking program finds the same error, your previous correction appears as the proposed word in the Change To box. The same is true for words you ignore by clicking the No Change button. The program continues to ignore those words for the rest of the editing session. To clear this memory, hold down the Shift key when you pull down the Utilities menu to start the spelling check. The Spelling command changes to Reset Spelling.

Asking Word To Suggest a Correct Spelling

The spelling-checking program uses a sophisticated computer search technique to suggest—with surprising accuracy—the correct spelling of a misspelled word. When the program reports an unknown word, click Suggest. Word then displays a list of one or more potentially correct spellings in the Words list box (see fig. 8.2). If you see the correct spelling, highlight it; Word automatically echoes the highlighted word in the Change To box. Click Change to make the correction.

Fig. 8.2.

A list of potentially correct spellings.

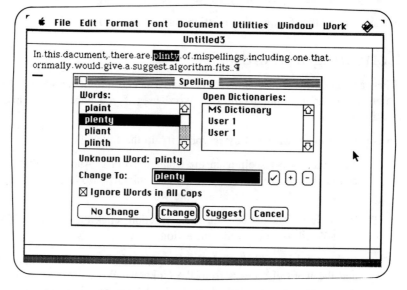

As figure 8.3 shows, the program may have difficulty with words beginning with transposed letters. If the suggestion isn't correct, type the correction in the Change To box and click Change. Sometimes Word cannot find a potentially correct spelling; in this case, a message box appears, alerting you that no correct spellings can be found. Click OK to continue and type the correct spelling.

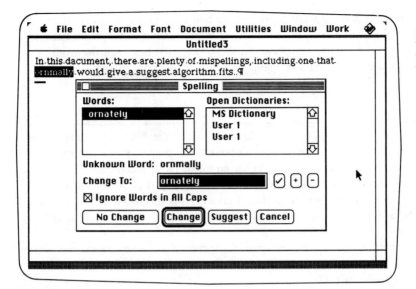

Fig. 8.3.

No correct spellings retrieved.

Adding Words to a User Dictionary

Word's main dictionary, MS Dictionary, is a *closed* file; you cannot add words to it. (MS Dictionary is stored in a special file format that enables extremely fast search-and-retrieval operations.) You can add words to user dictionaries, each of which can contain approximately 1,000 words without slowing Word's performance.

Why would you want to add words to a user dictionary? As you probably have discovered already, Word's main dictionary contains some place names and personal names, but it does not contain many of the proper nouns you will use (such as your organization's name, your boss's name, your surname, your street's name, and so on). Because these words aren't in the dictionary, Word reports them as unknown words—even when they're spelled correctly—which slows the spelling-checking process. To speed spelling correction, add these types of proper nouns to a user dictionary.

The first time you check spelling with Word, no user dictionary exists. When you click the add button (the + button in the Spelling window) to add a word, however, Word automatically creates a default user dictionary, called User 1. Word will use this dictionary automatically in subsequent editing sessions.

To add words to the User 1 dictionary, do the following:

1. When Word reports a correctly spelled word as unknown, click the + button. Word adds the word to the User 1 dictionary and echoes the word in the Words list box.

2. Double-click the word to make sure that it's spelled correctly. If the word is misspelled, select the word by clicking it in the Word list box. When the word appears in the Change To box, edit the word and click the + button again.

3. Click the Continue Checking button.

Because Word's spelling-checking program consults the User 1 dictionary every time you check spelling, add to this dictionary the proper nouns and other correctly spelled words you are likely to use in all or most documents. If a word is specialized, however, and likely to occur only in one kind of document (such as a quarterly report), create a custom user dictionary for this word. For more information on adding words to custom user dictionaries, see "Creating Custom User Dictionaries" in this chapter.

Ignoring a Word

If the spelling-checking program finds a correctly spelled word that you will not use in another document, you may want to click the No Change button instead of adding the word to a dictionary. (The No Change button takes the place of Start Check after you start the spell checking.) The program works most efficiently if you limit your user dictionary to about 1,000 words. The program will ignore all subsequent instances of that word in the document.

When you choose No Change, the spelling-checking program adds the word to a list of words to be ignored during the rest of the editing session. If you open a new document during that same session (without quitting Word), the program continues to ignore the word. To have the program forget its list of words to ignore, hold down the Shift key when you pull down the Utilities menu and choose the Reset Spelling option.

Creating Custom User Dictionaries

You can create more than one user dictionary, and you can set up the spelling-checking program so that Word uses two or more user dictionaries as it checks your document. As long as each dictionary contains fewer than approximately 1,000 words, the program's performance will not degrade appreciably.

Think of different ways you can divide your user dictionaries by subject. Here is an example:

General Correspondence   Contains the names of friends and family members with whom you correspond frequently, as well as important proper nouns in your personal life (street names, city names, and so on).

Business Correspondence   Contains the names of business associates, contacts, organizations, and companies; also contains important proper nouns in your business life (your boss's name, your boss's spouse's name, your boss's club, and your boss's favorite brand of Scotch, for example).

Technical/Legal   Contains terms, jargon, and proper nouns needed for spell checking technical or legal reports, proposals, and other documents.

Once you decide on a way to divide your user dictionaries, create new dictionaries as described in the following tutorial. You also will need to know how to open user dictionaries and save them after you add new words.

Word always consults the User 1 dictionary, even if you have created and opened additional user dictionaries. For this reason, use the User 1 dictionary to store the proper nouns you probably will use in *all* documents—your surname, your street name, and so on.

To create a new user dictionary and add words to it, follow these steps:

1. Choose Spelling from the Utilities menu (alternatively, press ⌘-L). Don't click the Start Check button.

2. Choose New from the File menu. Word creates a new user dictionary (called User followed by a number).

3. Click the new dictionary's name in the Open Dictionaries list box.

4. Type a word you want to add, such as your last name, in the Change To box and click the + button.

5. Continue adding proper nouns and other correctly spelled words to the user dictionary as described in step 4.

6. Choose Save As from the File menu.

7. When the Save As dialog box appears, type a name for the user dictionary in the Save Current Document As text box and click OK.

Note: If you're using a hard disk, always save your user dictionaries to the folder containing Microsoft Word. That way, you can be sure that you will not accidentally create more than one version of a user dictionary. To change folders, drag on the folder name in the Save As dialog box and choose Word's folder.

When you quit Word, the program keeps a record of the user dictionaries that were open when you chose the Quit option. The next time you use the spelling-checking program, you will find that the program opens all these dictionaries automatically. You can speed the spelling-checking process by closing the dictionaries you don't need.

To close a user dictionary, do the following:

1. Choose Spelling from the Utilities menu or choose ⌘-L. Don't click the Start Check button.

2. Select the user dictionary you want to close.

3. Choose Close from the File menu.

4. Click Cancel to return to your document.

If you closed a user dictionary in a previous section, you must open it if you want the program to use it.

To open a user dictionary, do the following:

1. Choose Spelling from the Utilities menu or choose ⌘-L. Don't click the Start Check button.

2. Choose Open from the File menu. If you don't see the dictionary in the list box, click the folder dropdown list box or the Drive button to explore other folders or disks. If you're using a hard disk and followed an earlier suggestion, your dictionaries should be in Word's folder.

3. Highlight the dictionary name and click Open.

If you accidentally add an incorrectly spelled Word to a user dictionary, the spelling-checking program will pass over the misspelled word without comment the next time you check spelling. Occasionally, therefore, you should check the words in your user dictionary. At that time, do the following:

❏ Remove words you probably will not use again. Although you can add 64,000 words to a user dictionary, the program's performance starts to degrade when you add more than about 1,000 words.

❏ Correct misspelled words you may have added accidentally to a user dictionary.

To check the words in your user dictionary, follow these steps:

1. Choose Spelling from the Utilities menu (or press ⌘-L) but don't click the Start Check button.

2. Open the dictionary if necessary.

3. Select the dictionary name. The dictionary's contents appear in the Words list box.

4. Scroll through the dictionary's contents by using the vertical scroll bar.

To correct a misspelled word you have stored in a user dictionary, follow these steps:

1. Highlight the name of the user dictionary in the Open Dictionaries list box.

2. In the Words list box, select the incorrectly spelled word. Word echoes the word in the Change To box.

3. Make the correction.

4. Click the + button.

Hyphenating Your Document

If you're using justified multiple columns (see Chapter 5) or right justification, you may find that Word leaves unsightly gaps at the ends of lines or between words (see fig. 8.4). You can prevent such gaps by choosing the Hyphenate command and inserting optional hyphens within lengthy words. Word can perform the job automatically or with confirmation before each insertion.

If you want to use the Hyphenate command, wait until you have made the final editing changes to your document. The hyphenation program goes through your document line by line, looking for words at the beginning of lines that can be hyphenated for improved document appearance. If you add text to or delete text from your document, the words at the beginnings of lines will differ (at least for the paragraphs in which you have made changes), and you probably will have to use the Hyphenate command again to improve the document's appearance. Save time by using Hyphenate just once, right before you print.

You can hyphenate your entire document or just part of it. To hyphenate part of your document, select the part you want to hyphenate before you choose the Hyphenate command. Also decide whether you want to hyphenate with or without confirmation.

Fig. 8.4.

*Document
requiring
hyphenation for
improved
appearance.*

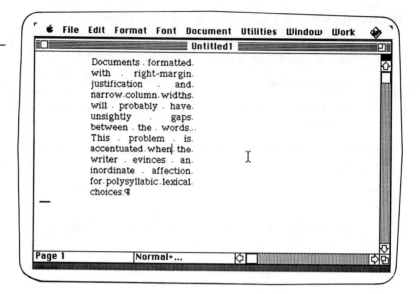

Caution: If you hyphenate without confirmation, bear in mind that Word may insert hyphens in a way that breaks the rules of many style books. Many stylebooks forbid hyphen breaks that leave two letters at the end of a line (as in *be-tween*), for example, but Word breaks words in this way.

To hyphenate your document, follow these steps:

1. Choose Hyphenate from the Utilities menu.

2. Click Start Hyphenation to hyphenate your document with confirmation for each hyphen placement. To hyphenate without confirmation, choose Hyphenate All. (If you select a block of text before choosing the Hyphenate command, the Hyphenate All button changes to Hyphenate Selection.)

   After you start hyphenating, the Start Hyphenation button becomes the No Change button.

3. Click Hyphenate Capitalized Words if you want Word to insert hyphens within words beginning with a capital letter.

   If you are hyphenating with confirmation, Word displays the word (with the proposed hyphen highlighted) in the Hyphenate text box (see fig. 8.5).

   The dotted line shows the maximum number of characters that can be accommodated on the line above the one on which the word is currently positioned. The hyphen break must occur to the left of this dotted line.

If the program has identified more than one possible location for hyphenation, you can choose among the ones that occur to the left of the dotted line (see fig. 8.6). To choose a hyphen break other than the one proposed, drag the highlighted hyphen.

4. Click Change to accept the hyphenation or No Change to skip this word and go on.

5. To undo hyphenation, choose Undo from the Edit menu immediately after using the Hyphenate command. If you chose to hyphenate with confirmation, Word undoes only the last hyphenation you confirmed. If you chose to hyphenate without confirmation, however, Word undoes all the hyphenations.

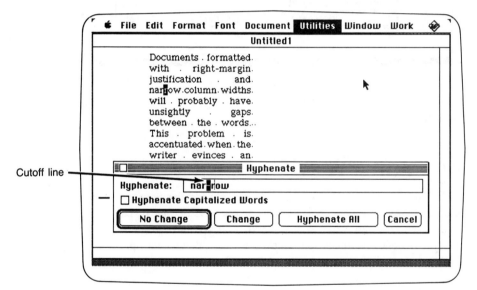

Fig. 8.5.

A word in the Hyphenate box with a proposed hyphen highlighted.

Cutoff line

To inspect the hyphen breaks Word inserted without confirmation, position the insertion point at the beginning of your document and choose the Find command, which you access from the Utilities menu. When the Find window appears, type ^- (a caret and a hyphen) in the Find What dialog box. (The ^ - code instructs Word to search for optional hyphens.) Then click Find. Repeat the search to inspect the next hyphen. Continue until you have checked all the hyphens Word inserted.

While preparing your document, performing a spelling check, and adding polishing touches such as hyphenating words to enhance the final appearance, you will want to save your work frequently on disk. Otherwise, you may lose hours of

Fig. 8.6.

*Choosing among
the possible
proposed hyphens.*

Cutoff line —

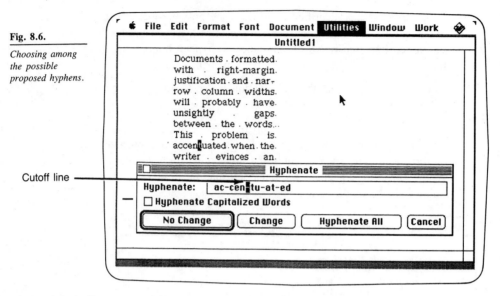

work if a power failure occurs. In the next section, you will examine Word's
saving features in detail.

Saving Your Work

Your document isn't stored safely on disk until you choose the Save command
from the File menu. As you work, choose Save frequently. Sooner or later, you
will experience a power failure while you're working. If you have just saved your
work, little harm is done; if you haven't, however, the power interruption may
cause many hours of work to be lost.

Saving Your Document the First Time

The first time you choose Save to save your document, Word displays the Save
As dialog box. Use this box to tell Word how and where to save your file.

To save your document the first time, do the following:

1. Choose Save from the File menu. Or you can use the ⌘-S keyboard
   shortcut.

⌘-S

2. When the Save dialog box appears (see fig. 8.7), type a name for
   your document in the Save Current Document As text box. You can
   use any combination of letters, numbers, or symbols except the
   colon (:).

Don't duplicate another file's name unless you want to overwrite the file's contents. Look in the list box to see which names you have already used. (You cannot select any of these files; thus, they are dimmed. You can, however, select the current disk or folder names, which are displayed above the file name list box.)

3. Choose the folder or disk in which you want the file saved. The current disk or folder name box shows the disk or folder that's currently selected; the file name list box shows the files in this disk or folder. To choose a folder you have stored within the current folder, select the name of the folder in the file name list box and double-click. To choose a folder at a higher level than the current folder, drag down the disk or folder name list box. To choose a disk other than the current disk, click the Drive button. To eject the disk currently in the drive, click Eject.

4. Click Save to save the file.

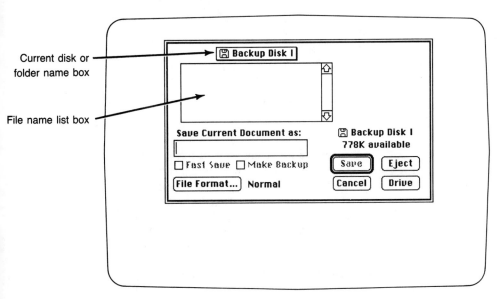

Current disk or folder name box

File name list box

Fig. 8.7.

The Save dialog box.

Saving Your Document Using Alternative File Formats

Word 4.0 uses its own, unique file format, which differs from that used by other programs—and even from that used by Word 3.0. If you want to exchange your work with someone using another Macintosh word processing program (such as MacWrite or Microsoft Write) or another version of Word (such as Word 1.0 or

3.0), click the File Format button in the Save dialog box. When the File Format dialog box appears (see fig. 8.8), choose one of the options listed in table 8.1.

Fig. 8.8.

The File Format dialog box.

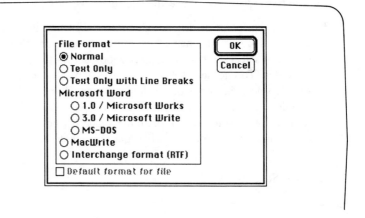

Table 8.1
Options in the File Format Dialog Box

Option	Function
Normal	Saves the document in the Word 4.0 default file format
Text Only	Saves the document without formatting. Lines that end with word-wrapped returns are stored as very long lines. If this option is unsuitable, choose Text Only with Line Breaks.
Text Only with Line Breaks	Saves the document without formatting. Choose this option to save your file as an ASCII text file for telecommunications or other purposes. Word places a hard line break (carriage return) in place of a word-wrapped return.
Microsoft Word 1.0/ Microsoft Works	Saves your document so that Word 1.0 and Microsoft Works can open it. Note that Word 4.0 features such as tables, positions, outlining, styles, hidden text, and colors are not transferred. To save your document for Microsoft Works Version 2.0, choose the Interchange Format (RTF) option.

Table 8.1—*Continued*

Option	Function
Microsoft Word 3.0/ Microsoft Write	Saves your document so that Word 3.0 and Microsoft Write can open it. Note that Word 4.0 features such as tables, positions, and colors are not transferred.
Microsoft Word MS-DOS	Saves your document so that most character and paragraph formatting can be read by the MS-DOS version of Microsoft Word 4.0. For Word 5.0 (MS-DOS version), choose the Interchange Format (RTF) option.
MacWrite	Saves your document so that MacWrite can read most of the character and paragraph formats. Note that Word 4.0 features such as tables, positions, outlining, styles, hidden text, and colors are not transferred.
Interchange Format (RTF)	Stores your document as an ASCII text file with embedded formatting commands. These commands conform to the Microsoft-IBM Rich Text Format (RTF) coding scheme, which some other programs can read.
Default Format for File	Makes the choice you have selected the default for this document. Note that this option is dimmed until you choose one of the other options in this dialog box.

Saving Your File Again

As you work, a wise idea is to save your file every 15 minutes as a general rule. By following this suggestion, you will be certain never to lose more than 15 minutes of work if the power ever fails.

To save your file again after saving it the first time, choose Save from the Edit menu or use the ⌘-S keyboard shortcut.

Understanding the Make Backup Option

Word users are sometimes confused by the Make Backup option in the Save As dialog box. This option doesn't make a backup copy of the most recent version of your file. On the contrary, this option renames the version of the document that's on disk (the version Word wrote the last time you saved the document). To understand the function of this option correctly, then, you should think of it as ''Keep Previous Version'' rather than ''Make Backup Copy.''

The best reason for using this option is to keep a copy of the previous version of your document, before you made editing changes. (Some writers like to keep all intermediate forms of their work to use if they decide to give up on subsequent changes.) If you save repeatedly in an editing session, however, the backup copy and the final copy on disk closely resemble each other. A much better idea, in sum, is to make backup copies of your work by using the Save As command, described in the following section.

Saving Your Document with a Different Name

Use the Save As command to save the current document with a different file name. You can use this technique to make a backup copy of your document. Perform this backup operation when you are finished with your editing session.

To make a backup copy of your document, follow these steps:

1. Save your document to its normal location by choosing Save or pressing ⌘-S.

2. Choose the Save As command from the File menu. Word puts the current file's name in the file name text box.

3. To save the document to a drive or folder other than the current drive or folder, click and drag on the folder name box to change folders or click the Drive button to change drives.

4. Click Save.

5. Choose Quit from the File menu.

Note: If you continue working after using Save As to copy your document to a new disk, Word assumes that when you choose Save again, you want to save the document on the new disk or in the new location specified when you chose Save As. So if you insert or delete text after using Save As, you must use Save As *again*, this time saving the file to the old disk (the one you used to store the main copy, not the backup copy). When the message box appears and asks whether you want to overwrite the copy of the file on the old disk, click OK.

After you have created, edited, formatted, and spell checked your document, you can preview how the document will look when printed, the topic of the next section. If you haven't yet installed your printer with the Chooser desk accessory, turn now to Appendix A, "Installing Word 4 and Configuring Your System," because Word cannot show you how your document will look when printed until you have chosen your printer.

Previewing Print Output

Why preview print output? Printing supplies (such as paper and ribbons) are expensive—especially if you're using a laser printer. Before you know it, your toner cartridge needs to be replaced, and to buy a new one, you will have to pay more than one hundred dollars. (You can save money by using recharged cartridges, in which there's an increasingly brisk market. Don't throw away your used toner cartridges! You can sell them to the companies that recharge these cartridges or get a discount on recharged cartridges.) You can save money and time by making sure that you have formatted your document correctly before printing.

An additional reason for using Word's Print Preview command is to fine-tune the position of page numbers, margins, page breaks, headers and footers, or text and graphics assigned to a fixed position. As you move these document elements on-screen, you get visual feedback, allowing you to make formatting choices whose visual effect you can gauge before committing ink to paper.

You can preview print output by using two commands:

⌘-I

❑ Print Preview presents an on-screen simulation of your document's printed appearance, showing two pages at a time (see fig. 8.9). Although you cannot edit while using Print Preview, you can adjust page breaks, headers, footers, page numbers, margins, and positions of "anchored" graphics. You also can click the print icon to print directly from the Preview mode.

❑ Page View, new to Word 4, presents an on-screen simulation of almost all document formats except line numbers (see fig. 8.10). You see margins, headers, footers, footnotes, page numbers, multiple columns, and other formats on-screen just the way they will print. What's more, you can edit text as you see these formats. The complexity of the on-screen image, however, results in slow scrolling, even on a Macintosh IIx or SE/30.

Fig. 8.9.

The Print Preview window.

Page number icon

Margins icon

One-page/two-page icon

Printer icon

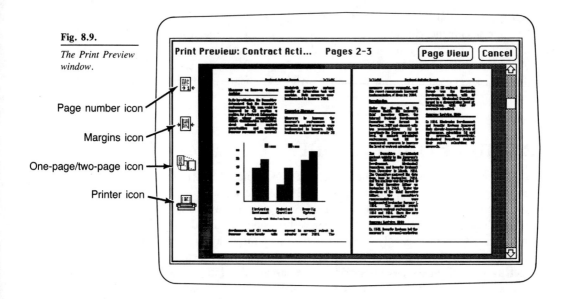

Fig. 8.10.

The Page View mode.

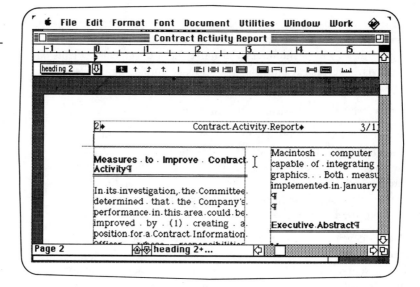

For maximum efficiency in previewing print output, use Print Preview to page through your document and inspect its formats. When you need to take a closer look, shift to Page View by clicking the Page View button in the Print Preview window, or by double-clicking anywhere on the document in Preview mode. Word displays a page view of the page. To continue scrolling through your document, shift back to Print Preview.

As you preview your document, ask yourself the following questions:

❑ Are page numbers turned on?

❑ Are the margins appropriate?

❑ Are the headers and footers properly situated within the top or bottom margins? If not, you can adjust the headers and footers after clicking the margins icon in the Print Preview window.

❑ Are any page breaks unsatisfactory? Are any headings, for example, situated at the bottom of the page with no text underneath?

❑ Are graphics positioned properly so that they're balanced on the page?

As you will learn in the following section, you can adjust all these document formats without leaving the Print Preview mode.

Examining Print Preview Features

When you choose Print Preview, your document appears in the Print Preview window (again see fig. 8.9). Here's an overview of the Print Preview features:

❑ *Page number icon.* Click this icon to insert an automatic page number anywhere on the page. After you click the icon, the pointer changes to the numeral 1, which you can drag to any location. As you drag, the top of the window shows the current location of the pointer. To position the page number automatically in the upper right corner of the page, double-click the icon. To adjust the page number's location after inserting it, choose the Section dialog box (from the Format menu) and change the measurements in the From Top and From Right boxes.

❑ *Margins icon.* When you click this icon, Word displays lines and boxes showing the current locations of margins, page breaks, headers, footers, and graphics. You can drag all these document elements to new locations on the page, and except for changes made to the location of graphics, the changes you make affect the entire document.

❑ *One page/two page icon.* Click this icon to display one page or two pages in the Print Preview window.

❑ *Printer icon*. Click this icon after you finish previewing your document and are ready to print.

❑ *Page View button*. Click this button if you want a closer look at the document formats you have chosen. You can edit in Page View mode.

Note: Word 3.0 users may be surprised to find the magnify icon missing in Print Preview. In Version 3.0, you can click this icon for a closer look at document formats. In Version 4, you can choose Page View to get a much closer look at your document, and you can edit as well as inspect and change the fonts, font sizes, and other formats you have chosen.

Using Print Preview

You can use Print Preview at any time before printing your document. Be sure to use this feature just before you print, however, to make sure that you have formatted your document correctly. You can choose the Print dialog box from within Print Preview, so you may want to think of Print Preview as a necessary prelude to printing.

To preview your document's print output, do the following:

1. If you want to preview your entire document starting at the beginning, position the insertion point on the first page of your document.

2. Choose the Print Preview option from the File menu or use the ⌘-I keyboard shortcut.

3. When the Print Preview window appears, click the up and down scroll arrows (or drag the scroll box) to scroll through your document.

If you see an unsatisfactory page break, click the margins icon, drag the dotted line up from the bottom margin, and double-click anywhere on the document. Likewise, if the margins or running heads are unsatisfactory, you can click the margins icon to make changes. When you click the margins icon, Word displays your current settings for margins, header and footer locations within the top and bottom margins, graphics locations, and page number location (see fig. 8.11). Each margin has a *drag box*, a solid black box, and the other formats are surrounded by boundaries. To reposition any of these formats, drag the boxes or boundaries. To fix the unsatisfactory page break, for example, click the margins icon and drag the dotted line up from the bottom margin. Word makes the change immediately by repaginating the document. To change the unsatisfactory margins or running heads, click the margins icon and drag the margin's drag box. To see the effect of the changes, click outside the page area.

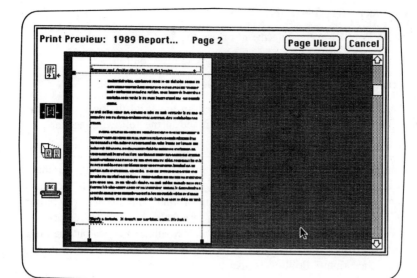

Fig. 8.11.

Print Preview after the margins icon has been selected.

Use the margins icon in Print Preview to adjust the margins of business letters before printing them. Often, you will find that your letter is just a little too long and that a couple lines of the closing wind up on the second page. Before printing your letter, widen the margins with the margins icon feature until the entire letter fits on one page. Check the letter's overall visual balance and alignment, too.

For a closer look at the formats you have chosen, click the Page View button if you're displaying just one page or double-click the page you want to view if you're displaying two pages. The current page displayed in the Print Preview window appears in the Page View window. After adjusting the formats, choose Print Preview from the File menu (or press ⌘-I) to return to Print Preview. The page you were examining in the Page View window reappears in the Print Preview window.

After you preview all the pages of your document, click the printer icon to display the Print dialog box. Printing your document is the topic of the next section.

Printing Your Document

After you check spelling and preview document formats to your satisfaction, you will be ready to print your document. Make sure that your printer is turned on, loaded with paper, and selected (on-line). Normally, printing is a simple, automatic process.

⌘-P

To print your document, follow these steps:

1. Choose Print from the File menu or use the ⌘-P keyboard shortcut.

2. When the Print dialog box appears, click the OK button.

3. To cancel printing at any time, press ⌘-period.

You can choose among many print options, in both the Print dialog box and the Page Setup dialog box. These options are examined in the following sections.

To avoid tying up your Macintosh while a lengthy document is printing, purchase a printer buffer or print spooler. A *printer buffer* is an accessory that contains memory chips. Connected between your Macintosh and your printer, the buffer has electronic characteristics exactly like your printer's, but the buffer accepts your Macintosh's output at a much faster rate. Your Macintosh sends out the print output as fast as possible, and then the buffer stores the output and doles it out, line by line, to the printer. Printing is speeded considerably.

If you have a hard disk and an ImageWriter, purchase print spooler software. A *print spooler* directs print output to your hard disk; once the output is stored on your hard disk, you can continue working with your Macintosh, and the spooler doles out the print output in the background without disturbing your work session. If you have a LaserWriter and MultiFinder, Apple's system software includes a spooler that does the job.

Choosing Print Options with the Print Dialog Box

The Print dialog box contains options for controlling the number of copies, the range of pages to be printed, the type of paper to be used, and (for the ImageWriter) the print quality. With the exception of Page Range, Section Range, and Copies, all the options you choose in the Print dialog box are saved with the document you're printing, and the options become the default for new documents.

Two Print dialog boxes are available: one for the ImageWriter and one for the LaserWriter (see figs. 8.12 and 8.13). After you choose your printer by using the Chooser desk accessory (see Appendix A), Word displays the correct Print dialog box automatically.

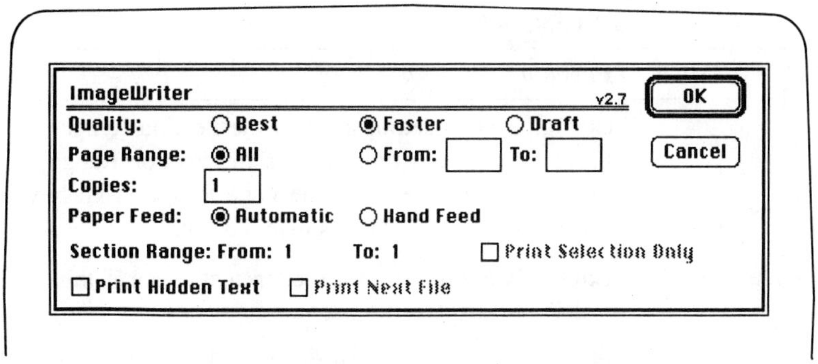

Fig. 8.12.

The Print dialog box for an ImageWriter printer.

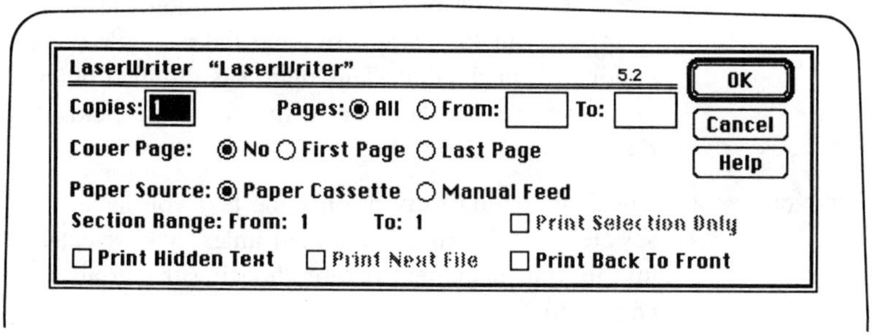

Fig. 8.13.

The Print dialog box for a LaserWriter printer.

Table 8.2 lists printing options available in the ImageWriter Print dialog box. Table 8.3 lists printing options available in the LaserWriter Print dialog box. The first six options listed in the tables are the same in both dialog boxes.

Table 8.2
Options in the ImageWriter Print Dialog Box

Option	Function
Copies	To print more than one copy, type the number in the Copies box.
Page Range	To print a range of pages, click From and type the beginning page number of the range. Then type the last page number in the To box. Leave the To box empty to print to the end of your document. To print just one page, type the same number in the From and To boxes.
Section Range	If your document has more than one section and you want to print a range of pages, type the section range in the Section Range boxes and the page numbers in the Page Range boxes. To print from page 15 of section 2 to page 34 of section 4, for

Table 8.2—*Continued*

Option	Function
	example, use a setting of 2 in the Section Range From box and a setting of 4 in the Section Range To box. Then type *15* in the Page Range From box and type *34* in the Page Range To box.
Print Hidden Text	Click this option to print hidden text, even if this text is not displayed on-screen.
Print Next File	If you entered a name in the Next File field of the Document dialog box, clicking this option causes Word to print the current file and the next file with continuous pagination. This option is dimmed unless you have specified a name in the Next File field of the Document dialog box.
Print Selection Only	Click this option to print only the text you have selected. This option is dimmed unless you selected text in your document before choosing the Print command.
Quality	Choose Draft to print at the highest speed but without the fonts you see on-screen (you will receive the ImageWriter's native dot-matrix fonts instead); choose Faster to print graphics output and formatting, and choose Best to print at the highest quality but slowest speed.
Paper Feed	Choose Automatic to use tractor-fed paper or paper supplied by an automatic sheet feeder. Choose Hand Feed for Word to pause at every page break so that you can position the next page manually.

Table 8.3
Options in the LaserWriter Print Dialog Box

Option	Function
Copies	To print more than one copy, type the number in the Copies box.
Pages	To print a range of pages, click From and type the beginning page number of the range. Then type the last page number in the To box. Leave the To box

Table 8.3—*Continued*

Option	Function
	empty to print to the end of your document. To print just one page, type the same number in the From and To boxes.
Section Range	If your document has more than one section and you want to print a range of pages, type the section range in the Section Range boxes and the page numbers in the Page Range boxes. To print from page 15 of section 2 to page 34 of section 4, for example, use a setting of 2 in the Section Range From box and a setting of 4 in the Section Range To box. Then type *15* in the Page Range From box and type *34* in the Page Range To box.
Print Hidden Text	Click this option to print hidden text, even if this text is not displayed on-screen.
Print Next File	If you entered a name in the Next File field of the Document dialog box, clicking this option causes Word to print the current file and the next file with continuous pagination. This option is dimmed unless you have specified a name in the Next File field of the Document dialog box.
Print Selection Only	Click this option to print only the text you have selected. This option is dimmed unless you selected text in your document before choosing the Print command.
Cover Page	This option prints a cover page that identifies the document (title, date, time, user name, and printer name). This option is most useful when several Macintoshes have been connected to a single laser printer with an AppleTalk network.
Paper Source	Choose Paper Cassette to supply paper automatically from the paper tray; choose Manual Feed to insert pages individually (such as envelopes).
Print Back To Front	Click this option to print your document from the last page to the first page. This option saves you the trouble of restacking the pages manually.

If you're using an ImageWriter, keep old ribbon cartridges handy to print drafts using the Faster option at the Quality field. For the final draft, use a new ribbon cartridge and choose the Best option at the Quality field.

Choosing Print Options with the Page Setup Dialog Box

With the Page Setup dialog box, you can choose additional print options, including paper type, paper orientation, and special printing effects. Like the Print dialog box, the Page Setup dialog box differs depending on which printer you choose (see figs. 8.14 and 8.15). The choices you make in the Page Setup dialog box are saved with the current document and become the default for new documents.

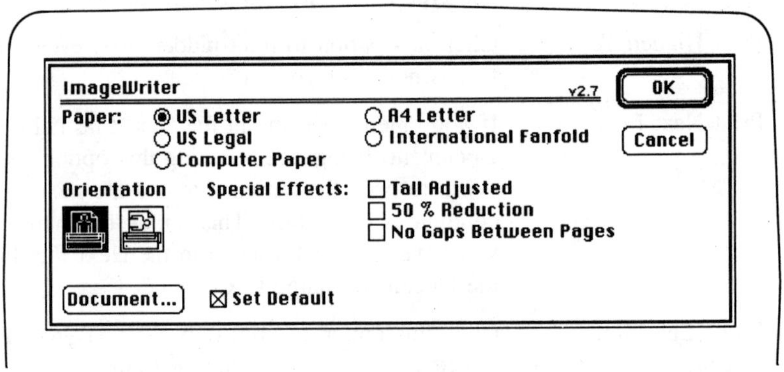

Fig. 8.14.

The Page Setup dialog box for an ImageWriter printer.

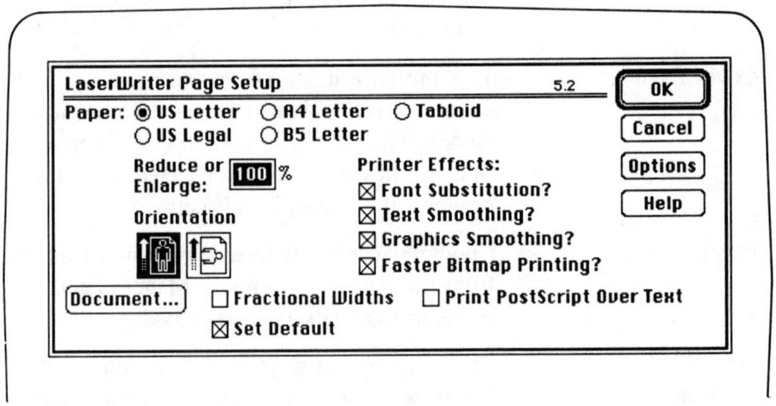

ImageWriter	v2.7	OK
Paper: ● US Letter	○ A4 Letter	
○ US Legal	○ International Fanfold	Cancel
○ Computer Paper		
Orientation **Special Effects:**	☐ Tall Adjusted	
	☐ 50 % Reduction	
	☐ No Gaps Between Pages	
Document... ☒ Set Default		

Fig. 8.15.

The Page Setup dialog box for a LaserWriter printer.

LaserWriter Page Setup		5.2	OK
Paper: ● US Letter	○ A4 Letter	○ Tabloid	Cancel
○ US Legal	○ B5 Letter		Options
Reduce or 100 %	**Printer Effects:**		Help
Enlarge:	☒ Font Substitution?		
Orientation	☒ Text Smoothing?		
	☒ Graphics Smoothing?		
	☒ Faster Bitmap Printing?		
Document... ☐ Fractional Widths	☐ Print PostScript Over Text		
☒ Set Default			

Note: Users of Version 3.0 will find that they no longer can set the margins from the Page Setup dialog box. To set margins and control other document formats, click the Document button or choose Document from the Format menu.

Table 8.4 lists the options available in the ImageWriter Page Setup dialog box, and table 8.5 lists the options available in the LaserWriter Page Setup dialog box. The first two options listed in the tables are the same in both dialog boxes.

Table 8.4
Options in the ImageWriter Page Setup Dialog Box

Option	Function
Paper	Choose among several standard paper sizes. To choose a custom size, choose Preferences from the Edit menu.
Orientation	Click the icon to print in Portrait mode (across the width of the page) or Landscape mode (across the length of the page).
Special Effects	Choose the Tall Adjusted option to correct the discrepancy between the 72-dpi (dots-per-inch) horizontal resolution of the Macintosh screen and the 80-dpi horizontal resolution of the ImageWriter. If you click this option, you can view a 6.5-inch line length on the Macintosh screen.
	Choose the 50% Reduction option to reduce the size of print output by 50 percent. To produce an exceptionally sharp printout, for example, reformat a document by using 24-point fonts and a 17-by-22-inch page size. Then click this option before printing.
	Choose the No Gaps Between Pages option to print continuous mailing labels.

Table 8.5
Options in the LaserWriter Page Setup Dialog Box

Option	Function
Paper	Choose among several standard paper sizes. To choose a custom size, choose Preferences from the Edit menu.
Reduce or Enlarge	You can choose a reduction or enlargement between 25 and 400 percent. To get razor-sharp printouts,

Table 8.5—*Continued*

Option	Function
	create a document by using large fonts and a large paper size and then reduce it.
Orientation	Click the icon to print in Portrait mode (across the width of the page) or Landscape mode (across the length of the page).
Printer Effects	Choose the Font Substitution option to substitute Times for New York, Helvetica for Geneva, and Courier for Monaco. This option is selected by default.
	Choose the Text Smoothing option to smooth the edges of bit-mapped fonts. This option is selected by default.
	Choose the Graphics Smoothing option to smooth the edges and contours of graphics that print with a "jagged" appearance. This option is selected by default.
	Choose the Faster Bitmap Printing option to speed the printing of bit-mapped fonts and graphics. Disable this option if the document doesn't print correctly. This option is selected by default.
Fractional Widths	Choose this option to improve spacing of printed text with certain fonts. If your document prints with poor letter spacing or word spacing, click this option and try again.
Print PostScript Over Text	Choose this option if you are using PostScript commands to print graphics (such as shaded boxes) on top of text.
Options	Click this button for several additional options (see fig. 8.16). Those that follow are of interest for word processing applications.
	Choose Precision Bitmap Alignment to align graphics and text properly. Word scales down the entire document by 4 percent.
	Choose Larger Print Area if your LaserWriter doesn't have sufficient memory to print a

Table 8.5—*Continued*

Option	Function
	complicated page. You will not be able to use as many downloadable fonts, however.
	Choose Unlimited Downloadable Fonts in a Document to remove the limitation on the number of downloadable fonts you can use with a given document. Printing will be slower, however.

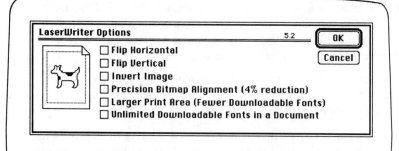

Fig. 8.16.

Additional Page Setup options available for the LaserWriter.

 # High-Productivity Techniques To Remember

❏ Word's spelling-checking program compares the words in your document with a dictionary of correctly spelled words. If the program reports an unknown word, it may be spelled correctly. If so, add the word to a user dictionary. Word cannot detect where you have used correctly spelled words in the wrong context, so a final, personal proofreading is a good idea.

❏ Add the proper nouns you are likely to use in all or most documents to the User 1 dictionary, which Word always consults. Add specialized words to a series of custom user dictionaries. Place no more than 1,000 words in each user dictionary.

❏ If your document has narrow columns or justified text, use the Hyphenate command just before the final printing. Because the hyphenation program violates common style guidelines for hyphenation, confirm each hyphen placement. Alternatively, disable confirmation and find all the optional hyphens by typing ^ - at the Find What box of the Find dialog box.

❏ Save your document frequently—about every 15 minutes. To make a backup copy of your document, choose Save at the end of your editing session. Then choose Save As to save your document to a different disk and choose Quit.

❏ Even if you're using an ImageWriter, previewing print output can save you money. Use Print Preview to check the margins, page breaks, page numbers, header and footer positions, graphics positions, and overall balance of text on the page. For a closer view of fonts and other formats, click the Page View button.

❏ Click the margins icon to adjust many document formats. Drag on the drag boxes to reposition margins. Drag from the bottom margin to change the page break. Drag on page numbers, graphics, and headers and footers to reposition them on the page.

❏ If you have forgotten to turn on page numbers, you can do so by clicking the page-number icon in Print Preview and dragging the number to a location on the page.

❏ If you're using a LaserWriter, you can speed printing by clicking Print Back To Front in the Print dialog box and Precision Bitmap Alignment in the Page Setup Options dialog box. To avoid printing delays because of insufficient printer memory, choose Larger Print Area in the Page Setup Options dialog box.

This chapter marks the end of Part II, ''Word 4 Fundamentals.'' Congratulations! You have learned enough about Word 4 to tackle virtually any business or professional word processing application. In Part III, ''Word 4's Features and Applications,'' you will learn more about special Word features.

Part III

Word 4's Features and Applications

Includes

Customizing Word 4's Menus and Keyboard

Organizing Your Document with Outlining

Creating and Using Glossaries

Creating Tables and Lists

Creating Business Forms

Page Layout Strategies with Text and Graphics

Adding an Index and Table of Contents

Creating Form Letters and Mailing Labels

223

9

Customizing Word 4's Menus and Keyboard

In Part II, you learned the fundamentals of Microsoft Word—and more than the fundamentals, because you learned how to put style sheet formatting to work for high-productivity applications. But in most of those chapters, you adapted to Word; you learned how to speak its language and work in its rhythms and patterns. In Part III of this book, you learn how to bend Word to your will. You start with one of Word 4's most amazing features: its capability to adapt to your preferences, not Microsoft's, for the organization of menus and keyboard shortcuts.

In this chapter, you learn how you can redesign the program so that it becomes exactly the program you want. If you wish, you even can make the program resemble MacWrite. The power users who read this book, however, will want to know how to harness the powerhouse that lies under the surface of this big, complex program, and this chapter is one of the most important avenues to this goal. You learn how to add productivity-enhancing commands to Word's pull-down menus, how to reconfigure the keyboard in a way that suits your professional and business writing needs, and how to create AutoMac III macros, which can make short work of procedures normally requiring dozens of keystrokes, mouse actions, and menu manipulations.

About the Preferences File

When you start Word for the first time, the program automatically creates a file called Word Settings (4) and stores it in your Macintosh's System folder. As you choose preferences, customize the menus, and create new keyboard shortcuts, Word stores your choices in this file.

Switching Configuration Files

You can create more than one configuration file and switch among them. To explore this feature of Word, try switching to the sample settings files provided on the Word Utilities 1 disk. These files, stored in a folder called Sample Settings Files, include MacWrite settings and Write Now settings. If you switch to the MacWrite settings file, Word's menus and keyboard resemble Mac-Write—although, as you will quickly discover, the program still works the way Word does, not the way MacWrite does, with respect to formatting. Even so, switching to the MacWrite or Write Now configuration files may prove helpful if you're familiar with one of these programs and want to learn Word without giving up your existing keyboard and menu knowledge.

To switch to a new configuration file, follow these steps:

1. Choose Commands from the Edit menu.

    Choose Full Menus if you don't see the Commands command. If you have already switched to a configuration that doesn't include the Commands command, press ⌘-Shift-Option-C.

    If you have chosen new preferences or created new keyboard shortcuts since you started Word, save them by clicking the Save As button in the Command dialog box. Accept the highlighted file name, and click Save.

2. In the Command dialog box, click the Open button (see fig. 9.1).

3. Choose the configuration file you want and click Open.

4. Click Cancel to close the Command dialog box.

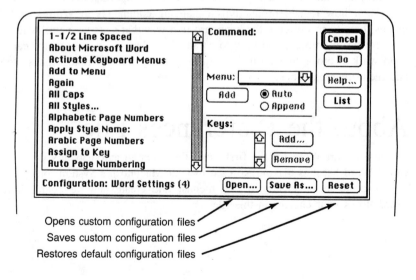

Fig. 9.1.

The Command dialog box.

Opens custom configuration files
Saves custom configuration files
Restores default configuration files

When you quit Word, the program notes the configuration file in effect at the time of quitting and saves any preferences or custom settings you chose during the editing session. When you start Word the next time, the program uses the configuration file in effect when you last chose Quit.

Creating a New Configuration File

If you're planning to embark on a major menu- and keyboard-customization project, as this chapter suggests, you will be wise to create a new configuration file to store your experiments in. That way, if you're not happy with the results after you have reconfigured the file, you can switch back to the original.

To create a new configuration file, follow these steps:

1. Choose Commands from the Edit menu.

   Choose Full Menus if you don't see the Commands command. If you have already switched to a configuration that doesn't include the Commands command, press ⌘-Shift-Option-C.

   If you have chosen new preferences or created new keyboard shortcuts since you started Word, save them by clicking the Save As button in the Command dialog box. Accept the highlighted file name, and click Save.

2. Click the Save As button.

3. In the Set Configuration As box, type a new file name (see fig. 9.2).

   For this chapter's experiments, type *Experimental Version*.

4. Click Save.

5. Click Cancel to close the Command dialog box.

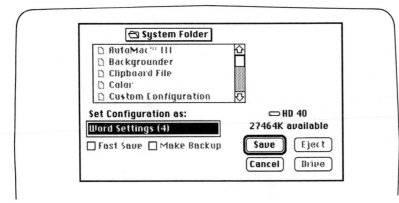

Fig. 9.2.

The Set Configuration As dialog box.

Erasing the Changes You Have Chosen in a Session

As you're experimenting, bear in mind that you can erase all the menu and keyboard customization choices you have made in the current editing session, thus restoring the configuration file to its state when you started the program.

To erase the changes you have made in a session, follow these steps:

1. Choose Commands from the Edit menu.

2. Click Reset.

3. When the alert box appears, click OK.

Restoring the Default Configuration

At any time, you can restore the defaults set by Microsoft for Full Menus. Use this option when, for any reason, you want to go back to the original version of Word, the one you saw when you first started the program.

To restore the default configuration file, follow this procedure:

1. Choose Commands from the Edit menu.

2. Hold down the Shift key and click Reset.

3. When the alert box appears, click OK.

Listing Key Assignments

As you customize Word's menus and keyboards, you will find it handy to create a list of your key assignments. Word automatically generates an up-to-date list for you. The list also shows current menu assignments.

To create a list of key assignments, do the following:

1. Choose Commands from the Edit menu.

2. Click List.

Word creates a table of all Word commands and their key assignments, and puts the table in a new, untitled document.

Customizing Word's Menus

If Word's pull-down menus aren't organized the way you want, don't despair: you easily can add or delete menu items. You can, for example, add to the first-level menus (such as the Format menu) commands that are buried in submenus (or even submenus of submenus, as is the Position dialog box). And if you don't admire the logic by which a given menu item has been placed in one pull-down menu, you can put the item in a different menu.

To customize Word's menus, you have two choices: you can use the ⌘-Option-Plus (and ⌘-Option-Minus) keyboard techniques, or you can use Word 4's new Command dialog box (Edit menu). Use the keyboard technique to add to primary-level menus items that are buried deep within submenus (or submenus of submenus). Use the Command dialog box to add to menus items that aren't available in any menu.

Adding Menu Items with the Keyboard

Use this technique to add an item buried within a submenu or dialog box so that the item is available on the top level of the pull-down menus. You can choose any menu option and items from dialog boxes (such as glossary entries from the Glossary list box). In addition, you can choose styles from the style selection box on the ruler and paragraph formats from the ruler. To add fonts and sizes to the Format menu, choose them in the Character dialog box. To add the date, time, and page number commands to the Document menu, click the icons in the Header window.

To add menu items with the keyboard, follow these steps:

1. Press ⌘-Option-Plus (on the keyboard, not the numeric keypad).

   The pointer becomes a big plus sign. To cancel, press Esc or ⌘-period.

2. Choose a command from the pull-down menus, a dialog box, the style selection box, or the ruler.

Word automatically adds the item to the appropriate menu. Character formats, paragraph formats, borders, ruler and spacing settings, section formats, and the Show Hidden Text option are added to the Format menu. The font and font size choices you make in the Character dialog box are added to the Font menu. Outlining options and header icons (date, page, and time) are added to the Document menu. Other choices, such as document names, glossary entries, and style names, are added to the Work menu. (If Word doesn't have a Work menu when you use this command, Word creates a Work menu automatically.)

Deleting Menu Items with the Keyboard

You can delete items from the pull-down menus—and it's a good idea to clean them up. For example, unless you're using your Macintosh in a network and using Microsoft Mail, you don't need the Open Mail and Send Mail commands in the File menu. (These commands are placed there in a rather obvious attempt to make us all aware of the commendable linkages between Word and Mail.) But there are other candidates, too. If you don't plan to create documents with indexes or tables of contents, for instance, you can delete the Insert Index Entry and Insert Toc Entry commands from the Document menu.

Don't worry about adverse consequences of deleting menu items—if you delete an item from a menu, you haven't sent the item off to a computer version of Nowhere. You can get the item back by using the Command dialog box. But don't delete Commands from the Edit menu! If you do, you cannot choose the Command dialog box from the menu.

To delete menu items with the keyboard, follow these steps:

1. Press ⌘-Option-Minus (on the keyboard, not the numeric keypad).

   The pointer becomes a big minus sign. To cancel, press Esc or ⌘-period.

2. Choose a command from the pull-down menus, a dialog box, the style selection box, or the ruler.

Adding Menu Items with the Command Dialog Box

The Command dialog box (Edit menu) provides tools for adding items to Word's menus. Using this dialog box has two major advantages over the keyboard technique: you can add items that aren't currently available in the menus, and you can choose the menu that Word places the command in.

The list box in the Command dialog box (again see fig. 9.1) includes every Word command, alphabetized by name (see table 9.1 for a complete list). Just browsing through table 9.1 will give you an excellent idea of Word 4's power and versatility! Look more carefully, however, for commands not presently assigned to menus or keys, that may prove useful to you in your work. To learn the function of any of these commands, select the command in the Command dialog box and click the Help button.

Table 9.1
Alphabetical List of Word Commands

About Microsoft Word	Insert Line Break	Outline
Activate Keyboard Menus	Insert New Paragraph	Outline Command Prefix
Add to Menu	Insert New Section	Outlining
Again	Insert Nonbreaking Hyphen	Page Break Before
All Caps	Insert Nonbreaking Space	Page Setup...
All Styles	Insert Optional Hyphen	Page View
Alphabetic Page Numbers	Insert Page Break	Paragraph Border:
Apply Style Name:	Insert Page Number	Paragraph Borders...
Arabic Page Numbers	Insert Rows	Paragraph...
Assign to Key	Insert Tab	Paste
Auto Page Numbering	Insert Table...	Paste Cells
Background Repagination	Insert Time	Paste Link
Backspace	Insert TOC Entry	Paste Special Character
Black	Insert ¶ Above Row	Plain For Style
Blue	Italic	Plain Text
Bold	Italic Cursor	Position...
Calculate	Justified	Preferences...
Cancel	Keep Lines Together	Print...
Cell Border:	Keep with Next ¶	Print Merge...
Cell Borders	Larger Font Size	Print Preview...
Cells	Line Numbers By Page	Promote Heading
Centered	Line Numbers By Section	Quit
Change	Line Numbers Continuous	Red
Change Font	List All Fonts	Redefine Style From
Change Ruler Scale	List header	Selection
Change Style	Load File into Memory	Remove From Menu
Character	Load Program into Memory	Renumber...
Clear	Lowercase Alphabetic Page	Repaginate Now
Close	Numbers	Reset Spelling...
Close Spacing	Lowercase Roman Page	Restart Page Numbering at 1
Collapse Selection	Numbers	Roman Page Numbers
Collapse Subtext	Magenta	Save
Columns:	Make Backup Files	Save As...
Commands...	Make Body Text	Screen Test
Condensed:	Merge Cells	Scroll Line Down
Context Sensitive Help	More Keyboard Prefix	Scroll Line Up
Copy	Move Down One Text Area	Scroll Screen Down
Copy as Picture	Move Heading Down	Scroll Screen Up
Copy Formats	Move Heading Up	Section Starts on Even Page
Copy Text	Move Left One Text Area	Section Starts on New
Cut	Move Right One Text Area	Column
Cyan	Move Text	Section...
Define All Styles...	Move to Bottom of Window	Section Starts on New Page
Define Styles...	Move to End of Document	Section Starts on Odd Page
Delete Cells, Shift Left	Move to End of Line	Section Starts with No Break
Delete Cells, Shift Up	Move to First Text Area	Select Whole Document
Delete Columns	Move to Last Text Area	Send Mail...
Delete Forward	Move to Next Cell	Shadow

Table 9.1—*Continued*

Delete Next Word	Move to Next Character	Short Menus
Delete Previous Word	Move to Next Line	Show All Headings
Delete Rows	Move to Next Page	Show Body Text
Delete...	Move to Next Paragraph	Show Clipboard
Demote Heading	Move to Next Sentence	Show Formatting
Document...	Move to Next Text Area	Show Heading 1
Dotted Underline	Move to Next Window	Show Heading 2
Double Space	Move to Next Word	Show Heading 3
Double Underline	Move to Previous Cell	Show Heading 4
Edit Link (Quickswitch)	Move to Previous Character	Show Heading 5
Expand Subtext	Move to Previous Line	Show Heading 6
Expanded:	Move to Previous Page	Show Heading 7
Extend to Character	Move to Previous Paragraph	Show Heading 8
Fast Save Enabled	Move to Previous Sentence	Show Heading 9
Find Again	Move to Previous Text Area	Show Hidden Text
Find Formats	Move to Previous Word	Show Menu Function Keys
Find...	Move to Start of Document	Show Styles on Ruler
First Line Indent	Move to Start of Line	Show Table Gridlines
First Page Special	Move to Top of Window	Show Text Boundaries
Flush Left	Move Up One Text Area	Show/Hide Ruler
Flush Right	Nest Paragraph	Show/Hide ¶
Font Name:	New	Side by Side
Font Size:	New Window	Single Line Spaced
Footer	New ¶ After Ins. Point	Small Caps
Footnote Cont. Notice...	New ¶ with Same Style	Smaller Font Size
Footnote Cont. Separator...	No Line Numbers	Smart Quotes
Footnote Separator...	No Line Numbers in	Sort
Footnote...	Paragraph	Sort Descending
Fractional Widths	Normal Paragraph	Spelling...
Full Repaginate Now	No Paragraph Border	Split Cell
Glossary Entry:	Normal Position	Split Window
Glossary...	Normal Spacing	Strikethru
Go Back	Numeric Lock	Styles...
Go To...	Open Any File...	Subscript:
Green	Open Documents in Page	Superscript:
Hanging Indent	View	Symbol Font
Help	Open Documents With Ruler	Table of Contents...
Hidden Text	Open Even Footer...	Table to Text...
Hyphenate...	Open Even Header...	Table...
Include Endnotes in Section	Open File Name:	Tabs...
Include RTF in Clipboard	Open First Footer...	Underline
Index...	Open First Header...	Undo
Insert Cells Down	Open Footer...	Unnest Paragraph
Insert Cells Right	Open Footnote Window	Update Link
Insert Columns	Open Header...	Use Picture Placeholders
Insert Date	Open Mail...	White
Insert Formula	Open Odd Footer...	Word Count...
Insert Glossary Text	Open Odd Header...	Word Underline
Insert Graphics	Open Spacing	Yellow
Insert Index Entry	Open...	Zoom Window

To add to Word's menus an item in the Command list box, follow these steps:

1. Choose Commands from the Edit menu.

2. In the list box, choose the item you want to add to a menu.

   Click Help to find out what a command does.

3. If the item you have selected is followed by a colon, you must choose from a dropdown list box, which appears automatically under the word Command in the center panel of the box (see fig. 9.3). Select the item you want from the list.

   In the Menu box, you see the name of the command's default menu, the one Word will place the command in if you accept the automatic placement.

4. To add the command to the default menu with automatic placement, click the Add button. Word selects the Auto option automatically and groups the command with others that have similar functions. To append the item to the menu so that the item appears at the end of the menu, click the Append button and then click the Add button.

   If you want to add the command to a different menu, click the Menu box's drag-down arrow and choose the menu from the list. Word will append the command to the menu.

5. Repeat steps 2 through 4 to add additional items to menus.

6. Click the Cancel button to close the Command dialog box.

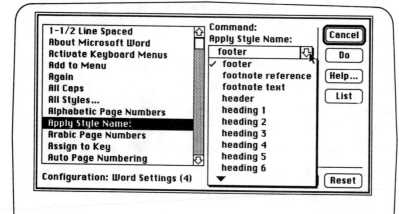

Fig. 9.3.

The dropdown list box for choosing command options from the Command dialog box.

Many commands in the Command list box aren't available on the pull-down menus, although the commands are assigned to the default keyboard shortcuts. (See table 9.2 in this chapter for a complete alphabetized list of these keyboard assignments.) A few aren't assigned to menus or keyboard shortcuts, and two are particularly useful:

❏ *Open Documents with Ruler*. Word adds this command to the Format menu if you choose the Auto option, and groups the command with the Ruler command. When Open Documents with Ruler is on (checked in the menu), Word opens all documents with the ruler in view. (You can still hide it by pressing ⌘-R or choosing Hide Ruler from the Format menu.)

❏ *Fast Save Enabled*. Word adds this command to the Edit menu if you choose the Auto option, and groups the command with commands at the bottom of the menu. When Fast Save Enabled is on (checked in the menu), Word saves documents by using the Fast Save option, which updates the file only by noting the changes you have made.

Reorganizing Word's Command Menus

If you think that you can improve on Microsoft's default menus by reorganizing them, you can delete a command from one menu and add it to another. For instance, you can delete Find, Find All, and Change from the Utilities menu and add these commands to the Edit menu. The only drawback to this technique is that when you move a command in this way, you must append it to its new menu. You cannot take advantage of the automatic command grouping that occurs when you add an item to its default menu after clicking the Auto button in the Command dialog box.

To reorganize Word's default command menus, use this procedure:

1. Choose Commands from the Edit menu.

2. In the list box, choose the item you want to delete from one menu and add to another. (Click Help to find out what a command does.)

3. Click the Remove button to remove the item from its current menu.

4. Click the Append button.

5. Pull down the Menu list and choose the menu to which you want to assign the command.

6. Click the Add button.

7. Repeat steps 2 through 6 for additional commands you want to move from one menu to another.

To see at a glance how Word automatically differentiates the commands by menu, choose Commands. Then hold down the Option key while you click Reset. Word will add all the commands to the pull-down menus. (You wouldn't want to work with the program this way—there are far too many commands!) To restore the pull-down menus as you have set them in your configuration file, click Reset again.

Customizing Word's Keyboard

In *The Psychology of Everyday Things*, an important book on the principles of good design, Donald A. Norman waits until page 182 before praising the Apple Macintosh for its design excellence. (As you read the book, you keep thinking, "He must love the Macintosh—everything he's saying applies to the Macintosh's user-friendly design." And in fact, he wrote the book on a Macintosh.) But Norman reserves one criticism: the computer "fails badly" in that it uses obscure key combinations to accomplish some tasks.

Any Word user reading this passage will probably conclude that Norman must have been using Microsoft Word, for the program has often been criticized for its welter of obscure and non-mnemonic (and therefore not easily memorized) key combinations. How on earth is one supposed to remember, for instance, that ⌘-Option-[(left bracket) scrolls the screen one line up, but ⌘-Option-] (right bracket) zooms the window?

To be fair to Microsoft, the Macintosh was designed with the idea that people would (and should) use the mouse for most command, editing, and formatting operations. But business and professional users, who are often competent typists, expressed misgivings about taking their hands away from the keyboard so often and criticized the Macintosh for not offering keyboard equivalents for mouse actions. Sensitive to this criticism, and hoping to develop the business market for its Macintosh version of Word, Microsoft apparently made a management decision that every mouse command would have a keyboard equivalent, even if that decision meant creating an impossibly complex wilderness of keyboard commands. And so that's just what Microsoft did (see table 9.3)—and one result was criticism like that voiced by Norman. But one has to admit that the programmers have mapped almost all the mouse commands onto the keyboard!

In response to criticism of its keyboard assignments, the Word 4 design team has said, essentially, "If you're so smart, configure the keyboard yourself." And you can do precisely that by using the Commands command (Edit menu), which is new to Word 4.

Should you reconfigure your keyboard? Can you really do a better job of configuration than the master programmers at Microsoft? By all means, and here's why. Unlike Microsoft's programmers, who were under orders from Microsoft to create what was essentially a marketing plus (''There's a keyboard equivalent for every mouse procedure!''), you need not create a key equivalent for every mouse action. If you're like most Word users, you probably like using the mouse for some actions (such as selecting text or scrolling) and don't like the mouse as much for other procedures (such as deleting the character to the right of the insertion point). You can reconfigure the keyboard with a manageable number of keyboard shortcuts (about two dozen), which duplicate the mouse actions for which you really want keyboard shortcuts.

Assuming that you like to use the mouse for some actions and not others, here's how to proceed:

1. As you work, make a list of all the mouse actions and procedures with which you're comfortable (and don't want keyboard equivalents).

2. Make a second list of the mouse actions or procedures you don't like, and add to the list any keyboard shortcuts you find yourself using regularly.

3. Create a systematic keyboard layout for all the actions or procedures that you listed in step 2, and don't hesitate to wipe out existing (default) keyboard assignments for anything you listed in step 1.

How do you create a systematic keyboard layout? Programmers use four techniques to arrange keys on a computer keyboard:

❑ *The Mnemonic Approach.* In this approach, the key letters remind you of their function. Some default key assignments are mnemonic (such as ⌘-S for Save and ⌘-P for Print), but unfortunately, mnemonic key assignments are in the minority.

❑ *The Mnemonic Approach with Intensification.* A big drawback to the mnemonic approach is that often two or more commands begin with the same letter, like Print and Print Preview. One way around this problem is to create additional commands using a second command letter. A command using just one command key (such as ⌘-P) gives the ''mild'' command, an everyday command that won't harm your document or set off a lengthy process. A command using two command keys (such as ⌘-Shift-P) is more ''drastic,'' in that it has broader, more dangerous, or more time-consuming effects. With this approach, you use ⌘-P for Print Preview and ⌘-Shift-P for Print. Word uses this approach sometimes; for instance, ⌘-C is Copy, but ⌘-Option-C sets up a copy procedure in which you select text to be copied and identify the place to which you want the text copied.

❑ *The Command Differentiation Approach*. With this approach, commands are sorted into categories, and each kind of command starts with its own command letter or letters. Word uses this approach in differentiating editing commands (⌘-Option) from formatting commands (⌘-Shift). You can use this technique in tandem with mnemonic or other approaches.

❑ *The Finger Geometry Approach*. In this approach, the key letters aren't mnemonic, but they're arranged so that they're next to one another on the keyboard or otherwise arranged for convenient keyboard selection. In the default keyboard layout, for instance, ⌘-Option-J moves the insertion point one word left, and ⌘-Option-K moves the insertion point one character left; ⌘-Option-L moves the insertion point one character right, and—you guessed it—⌘-Option-semicolon moves the insertion point one word right. All four keys are lined up in a row on the keyboard.

With these concepts in mind, you can see right away one of the big problems with Word's default keyboard assignments. They combine all these approaches, creating no small confusion because one principle cross-cuts the others with illogical results. For instance, ⌘-X (Cut), ⌘-C (Copy), and ⌘-V (Paste) combine the finger geometry approach with the mnemonic approach—but only partly. As a result, the poor user may try to think of Paste as "Vaste." (Don't laugh! Many Word users find themselves making weird accommodations of this sort.) And because these are editing commands, shouldn't they be ⌘-Option keys? What a mess!

The moral of the story: Pick one, or at the most two, of the four keyboard mapping techniques. At the extreme, use three. But for heaven's sake, don't pick all four (unless you're under orders from management)!

Table 9.2 lists a keyboard mapping that employs the mnemonic approach with intensification. This approach won't be right for all users, because every user will probably come up with a highly personal list of mouse actions and procedures he or she wants to assign to the keyboard.

Table 9.2
Suggested Keyboard Assignment
Mnemonic Approach with Intensification

Keyboard Command	Command Given
⌘-B	Bold
⌘-Shift-B	Borders
⌘-C	Copy
⌘-Shift-C	Copy and Paste
⌘-D	Delete Word Right

Table **9.2**—*Continued*

⌘-E	Extend Selection
⌘-F	Find
⌘-Option-F	Change
⌘-G	Glossary
⌘-H	Hanging Indentation
⌘-Shift-H	Help
⌘-I	Italic
⌘-J	Justification
⌘-K	But
⌘-L	Flush Left
⌘-M	Menus
⌘-N	Nest Paragraph
⌘-O	Open Spacing
⌘-Shift-O	Open File
⌘-P	Print Preview
⌘-Shift-P	Print
⌘-Q	Quit
⌘-R	Show Ruler/Hide Ruler
⌘-S	Save
⌘-Shift-S	Save As
⌘-T	Table
⌘-U	Undo
⌘-V	Page View

Power User Tip

With the ⌘ and ⌘-Shift keys used as table 9.2 suggests, you can use ⌘-Option (or if you have a Macintosh SE or II, the Control key) for other differentiated functions. Use ⌘-Option, for instance, to assign styles to keys. Continue with the mnemonic principle: ⌘-Option-N, for instance, to apply the Normal style and ⌘-Option-1 to assign Heading Level 1.

Word's Default ⌘-Key Assignments

Before reconfiguring your keyboard, you will find it helpful to consider what you're giving up when you redefine a key. (When you use the Commands command, you are asked to confirm the redefinition of an existing key if the key you have chosen is already defined.) To prepare for the job of redefining the keyboard, however, use table 9.3 to mark the keyboard assignments that you want to preserve.

Note that Word's default keyboard assignments are differentiated by command function:

❏ ⌘. Chooses a command, using (as far as possible) the standard Macintosh nomenclature (⌘-X for Cut, ⌘-S for Save, and so on).

❏ ⌘-Option. Chooses an editing command, such as scrolling the screen or deleting text.

❏ ⌘-Shift. Chooses formatting commands, such as italic, boldface, or flush-right paragraphs.

Table 9.3 organizes the commands this way so that you can see the pattern.

Table 9.3
⌘ Key Assignments in Alphabetical Order
(Default Version of Word 4)

Key	Menu Command
Command Keys (Giving Commands)	
⌘-A	Again
⌘-B	Page View
⌘-C	Copy
⌘-D	Character
⌘-E	Footnote
⌘-equals	Calculate
⌘-F	Find
⌘-G	Go To
⌘-H	Change
⌘-I	Print Preview
⌘-J	Repaginate Now
⌘-K	Glossary
⌘-L	Spelling
⌘-M	Paragraph
⌘-N	New
⌘-O	Open
⌘-P	Print
⌘-Q	Quit
⌘-R	Show Ruler/Hide Ruler
⌘-S	Save
⌘-T	Define Styles
⌘-U	Outlining
⌘-V	Paste
⌘-W	Close

Table 9.3—*Continued*

⌘-X	Cut
⌘-Y	Show/Hide
⌘-Z	Undo

⌘-*Option Keys (Editing)*

⌘-Option-/ (slash)	Scroll Line Down
⌘-Option-;	Move to Word Right
⌘-Option-[(left bracket)	Scroll Line Up
⌘-Option-\ (backslash)	Formula
⌘-Option-]	Zoom Window
⌘-Option-B	Move to Next Paragraph
⌘-Option-Backspace	Delete Word Left
⌘-Option-C	Copy Text
⌘-Option-D	Copy as Picture
⌘-Option-F	Delete Character Forward
⌘-Option-G	Delete Next Word
⌘-Option-H	Extend Selection to Character
⌘-Option-J	Move to Word Left
⌘-Option-K	Move to Character Left
⌘-Option-L	Move to Character Right
⌘-Option-M	Select Whole Document
⌘-Option- −	Remove from Menu
⌘-Option-P	Scroll Screen Up
⌘-Option- +	Add to Menu
⌘-Option-Q	Paste Special Character
⌘-Option-R	Find Formats
⌘-Option-Return	New Paragraph After Insertion Point
⌘-Option-S	Split Window
⌘-Option-Space bar	New Paragraph Above Row
⌘-Option-V	Copy Formats
⌘-Option-W	Move to Next Window
⌘-Option-X	Move Text
⌘-Option-Y	Move to Previous Paragraph

⌘-*Shift Keys (Formatting)*

⌘-Shift-/ (slash)	Strike through
⌘-Shift-<	Smaller Font Size
⌘-Shift->	Larger Font Size
⌘-Shift-[	Double Underline
⌘-Shift-B	Bold
⌘-Shift-C	Centered Alignment

Table 9.3—*Continued*

⌘-Shift-D	Outline
⌘-Shift-F	First Line Indent
⌘-Shift-H	Small Caps
⌘-Shift-I	Italic
⌘-Shift-J	Justified alignment
⌘-Shift-K	All Caps
⌘-Shift-L	Flush Left
⌘-Shift-M	Unnest Paragraph
⌘-Shift- −	Subscript
⌘-Shift-N	Nest Paragraph
⌘-Shift-O	Open Spacing
⌘-Shift- +	Superscript
⌘-Shift-Q	Symbol Font
⌘-Shift-R	Flush Right
⌘-Shift-S	Change Style
⌘-Shift-T	Hanging Indent
⌘-Shift-U	Underline
⌘-Shift-W	Shadow
⌘-Shift-W	Word Underline
⌘-Shift-X	Hidden
⌘-Shift-Y	Double Space

Function Keys (Apple Extended Keyboard Only)

F1	Undo
F2	Cut
F3	Copy
F5	New
F6	Open
F7	Save
F8	Print
F9	Plain For Style
F13	Page View
F14	Character dialog box
F15	Spelling
⌘-F14	Document dialog box
⌘-F15	Renumber
Option-F2	Edit Link
Option-F3	Update Link
Option-F4	Paste Link
Option-F13	Print Preview
Option-F14	Section dialog box
Option-F15	Word Count

Table 9.3—*Continued*

Shift-F5	New Window
Shift-F6	Open Any File
Shift-F7	Save As
Shift-F8	Page Setup
Shift-F9	Plain Text
Shift-F13	Outlining
Shift-F14	Paragraph dialog box
Shift-F15	Hyphenate

Deciding Which Keyboard Shortcuts To Omit

From the user's point of view, a well-designed keyboard layout for Microsoft Word *minimizes* the number of keyboard shortcuts. After all, who wants to memorize 150 key assignments? Look for ways you can access commands quickly using routes other than ⌘-key shortcuts. As you see in this section, omitting most of the keyboard commands Microsoft assigned to the ⌘ key alone (⌘-A, ⌘-B, and so on) has merit.

Most of the commands beginning with the ⌘ key access primary items from the pull-down menus (such as Print, Save, and Outlining). Another, and probably better, way exists to access menu commands by using the keyboard. When you press the period key on the numeric keypad, you can select menu commands by using the arrow keys or by typing the command's first letter. See Chapter 3, "Writing and Editing Strategies," for information on this technique.

To take full advantage of the keyboard menu selection technique, redefine the Activate Keyboard Menus command as ⌘-M. (The Activate Keyboard Menus command is assigned by default to the numeric keypad's period key). The ⌘-M assignment makes it easy to access the pull-down menus; your fingers don't have to leave the keyboard to find the keypad period key. For information on redefining the keyboard, see "Assigning Keyboard Shortcuts with the Command Dialog Box," in this chapter.

Guidelines for Creating Keyboard Shortcuts

You must use the ⌘ key in every keyboard shortcut you create. (The only exception occurs when you assign a shortcut to a function key on the Apple Extended keyboard.) In addition to the ⌘ key, you may use the following keys to construct keyboard commands:

❏ Shift
❏ Option
❏ Control (Macintosh SE and II keyboards only)
❏ Letter or number keys on the keyboard

You may use up to four keys to define a keyboard shortcut. Remember, though, that a keyboard shortcut isn't much of a shortcut if you have to press four keys to use it! Examples of valid keyboard-shortcut assignments include the following:

⌘-Shift-P
⌘-Control-B
⌘-Option-X
⌘-Control-Option-7

You can assign more than one keyboard shortcut to a menu item or command. For instance, you can assign both ⌘-P and ⌘-Option-P to the Print command.

Remember the advantages of command differentiation when you choose keyboard shortcut assignments. You may, for instance, create one mnemonic set of commands for editing using the ⌘-Shift key combination and create another set for entering styles using ⌘-Control.

Power
User
Tip

Assigning Keyboard Shortcuts with the Keyboard

If the command you want to assign is on a pull-down menu or the dropdown Style menu in the ruler's style selection box, you can use ⌘-Option-Plus (the numeric keypad plus key) to assign it. However, if you redefine the keyboard this way, the new function-key assignment you choose does not show up on the pull-down menus, so this technique is not recommended (unless you seldom use menus). If you want the new key assignment to appear on the pull-down menus, redefine the keyboard by using the Command dialog box, as described in "Assigning Keyboard Shortcuts with the Command Dialog Box."

To assign a keyboard shortcut with ⌘-Option-Plus, do the following steps:

1. Press ⌘-Option-Keypad Plus. The pointer becomes a ⌘ symbol. To cancel, press Esc or ⌘-period.

2. Use the ⌘ symbol to choose the menu item you want.

3. When the alert box appears asking you to press the key combination you want to assign to the selected command, press the desired keys.

   To assign the selected command to the key sequence ⌘-Control-B, for instance, press these keys, just as if you were giving the command at the keyboard.

4. If the key is already assigned, an alert box warns you that you will erase the existing key definition. To erase the existing definition, click OK.

Assigning Keyboard Shortcuts with the Command Dialog Box

Two big advantages accrue to those who assign keyboard shortcuts with the Command dialog box from the Edit menu. Using the Command dialog box, you can choose from many commands not on the menus. You also can delete existing keyboard assignments when you assign new ones. The happy result of using the Command dialog box (as opposed to ⌘-Option-Keypad Plus) is that you see the shortcut you assign on the pull-down menus (if the command you selected is on a menu). If you assign ⌘-B to the Bold command, for instance, and delete the current assignment (⌘-Shift-B), ⌘-B appears on the Format menu next to the Bold command.

When you choose Commands from the Edit menu, you see a list box showing all the commands you can give with Microsoft Word (refer to fig. 9.1). You can use this list box, as explained earlier in this chapter, to add items to Word's menus. You also can use this list box to redefine Word's keyboard, as described in this section.

To assign a command to Word's keyboard by using the Command dialog box, follow these steps:

1. Choose Commands from the Edit menu. If this command does not appear on the menu, choose Full Menus from the Edit menu and try again. You may also press ⌘-Shift-Option-C. The Command dialog box appears.

2. Scroll the list box to choose the command you want to assign to a shortcut. If you're not sure what a command does, click the Help button.

3. When you have highlighted the command you want to assign to a keyboard shortcut, look at the Keys dropdown list box. The Keys dropdown list box lists all keyboard shortcuts already assigned to the selected command. If you see one or more existing key assignments there, highlight them and delete them by clicking Remove.

4. Click Add.

5. When the Key Assignment dialog box appears, press the key combination you want to use, just as if you were giving the command. To assign the command to ⌘-Option-R, for example, press those keys.

6. If you see an alert box warning you that the shortcut keys are already assigned, think twice about reassigning them. If you're sure that you want to redefine the shortcut keys, click OK.

7. Click Cancel to close the Command dialog box.

Note: When you click cancel, you don't lose the assignments you have made. Cancel just closes the box.

Customizing Word's Keyboard with AutoMac III

Word's keyboard-customization features are fine for assigning single commands to keys, but you cannot assign more than one command to a key. That's too bad, because often you may find it convenient to give several commands at once. Suppose, for instance, that you create a nice style sheet for letters, another nice one for reports, and yet another one for memos. You cannot save all the styles to the default style sheet because they conflict—the Normal style, which sets the default character style, is Helvetica for the letters style sheet and Times for the report style sheet. Every time you write one of these documents, you go through the rather tedious procedure of opening a new document, choosing Define Styles, clicking the Open button, naming the document that contains the style sheet you want, and clicking OK.

Thanks to Microsoft's packaging of AutoMac III with Word 4, you now can automate procedures of this sort quite easily. AutoMac III gives you the tools needed to create *macros*. Macros are recorded commands, mouse actions, and keystrokes. To create a macro, go through the procedure you want to record, pressing keys, moving the mouse, and choosing commands as you please. Once you record an AutoMac macro, you can play it back anytime you want, right in the middle of a Word session. The macro plays back at top speed—an impressive sight, especially on one of the faster Macintosh systems, but always faster than you could perform the action by hand. You can even assign an AutoMac macro to a keyboard shortcut.

Note: This section isn't designed to teach you everything about AutoMac III, but the tutorial to follow illustrates several highly useful techniques, such as creating macros that display dialog boxes and pause for user input. With a little experimentation, you can adapt the macro techniques in this tutorial to serve a variety of automation objectives.

Installing AutoMac III

To install AutoMac III on your hard disk system, follow these steps:

1. Insert Word Utilities Disk 2 in the external drive.

2. Double-click the AutoMac III folder.

3. Drag the AutoMac III icon to the System folder.

4. Restart your computer by choosing Restart from the special menu.

Tutorial: Creating an AutoMac III Macro

This section presents a tutorial you can follow to create a macro and addresses a problem you will run into once you have created complex style sheets. If you want to use one of these style sheets for a new document, you must deliberately add the style sheet to the document by choosing Define Styles and then Open. Because this procedure is both tedious and repeated many times (every time you open a new document), it is an excellent candidate for automation with a macro. The entire macro is activated by pressing ⌘-Shift-S.

1. After opening Word 4, click the AutoMac icon (the little letter a in the left corner of the menu bar).

2. When the AutoMac III dialog box appears, as shown in figure 9.4, click the Record button.

3. When the Record New Macro dialog box appears, as shown in figure 9.5, click the command key boxes you want to use to access the macro and type a character in the Key box. To assign the macro to ⌘-Shift-S, click the ⌘ and Shift boxes and type *S* in the Key box.

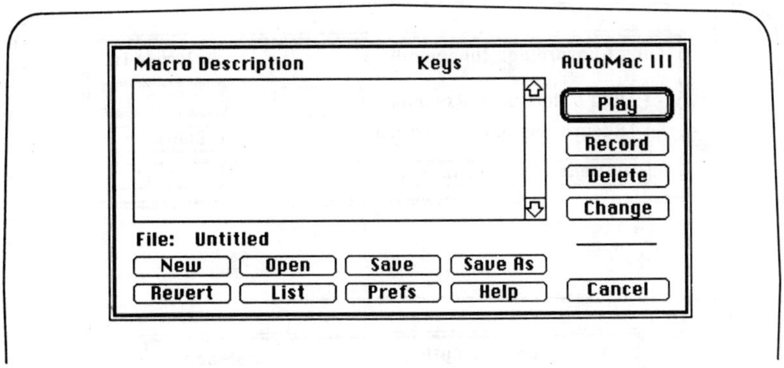

Fig. 9.4.

The AutoMac III dialog box.

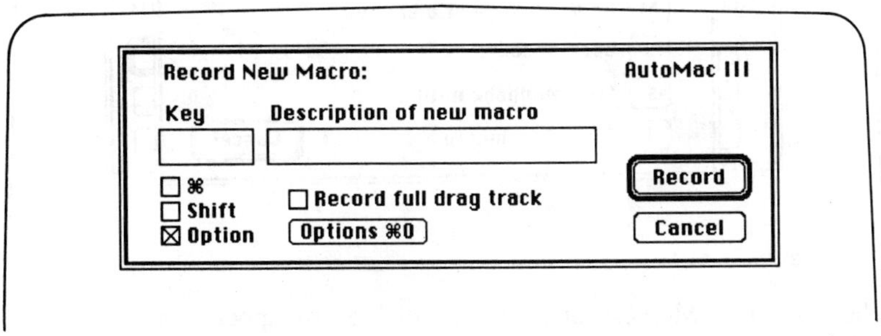

Fig. 9.5.

The Record New Macro dialog box.

4. Type in the text box *Attach style sheet to new document* to name your macro.

5. Click Record.

   From now on, AutoMac will record all your actions so that you can play them back whenever you want.

6. Choose Define Styles from the Format menu. This command is the first action you want your macro to take.

7. Choose Open from the File menu.

8. When the Open dialog box appears, click the AutoMac icon (the little a). By clicking the little a, you interrupt the recording. Now you will make the macro display an alert box and pause for your input.

9. When the End of Recording dialog box appears, as shown in figure 9.6, click the Misc button. You are not going to end the recording yet.

10. When the Misc Recording Options dialog box appears, as shown in figure 9.7, click the M button to add a message to your macro.

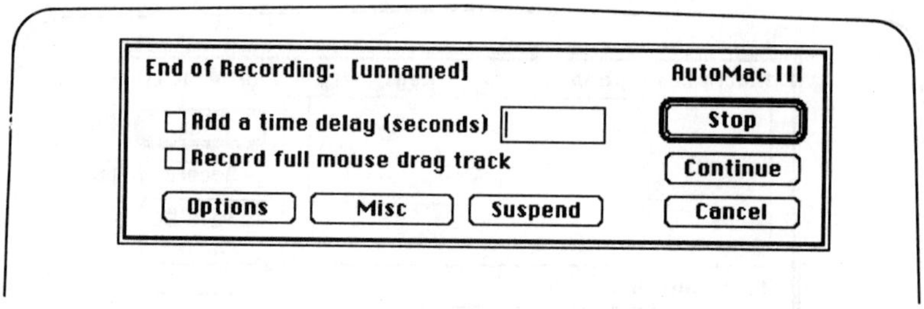

Fig. 9.6.

The End of Recording dialog box.

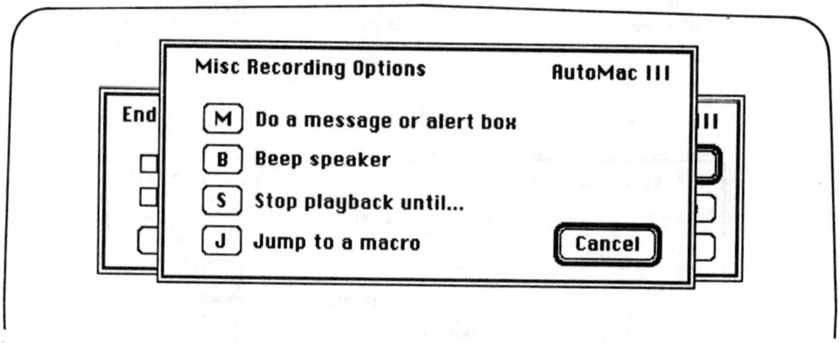

End of Recording: [unnamed]   **AutoMac III**

☐ Add a time delay (seconds) |

☐ Record full mouse drag track

[Options]   [Misc]   [Suspend]

[Stop]
[Continue]
[Cancel]

Fig. 9.7.

The Misc Recording Options dialog box.

Misc Recording Options   **AutoMac III**

[M] Do a message or alert box

[B] Beep speaker

[S] Stop playback until...

[J] Jump to a macro

[Cancel]

11. When the Do a Message or Alert Box dialog box appears, as shown in figure 9.8, type *Choose the document that contains the style sheet you want and press Return when done.* This message will appear in a dialog box when you execute the macro.

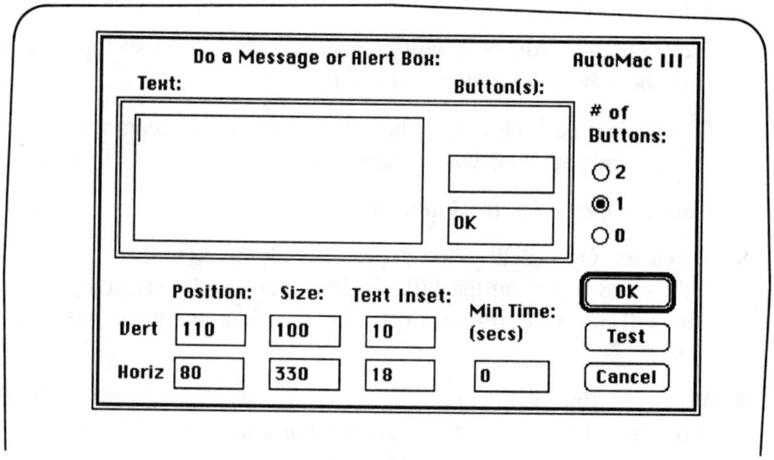

Fig. 9.8.

The Do a Message or Alert Box dialog box.

Do a Message or Alert Box: **AutoMac III**

Text: Button(s):   # of Buttons:

                                              ○ 2
                                              ◉ 1
                          OK   ○ 0

                    Position: Size: Text Inset: Min Time: [OK]
Vert   110   100   10   (secs)   [Test]
Horiz 80   330   18   0   [Cancel]

12. Click OK.

13. When the End of Recording dialog box appears again, click the Misc button.

14. When the Misc Recording Options box reappears, click the S button. This option allows you to tell the macro to pause for user input.

15. When the When Playing the Macro, STOP at This Point Until dialog box appears, as shown in figure 9.9, click Return or Enter Key Is Pressed. Then click OK. Now you're returning to recording. At this point, the user would have chosen a file and pressed Enter, so you should continue recording the steps you want the macro to execute automatically.

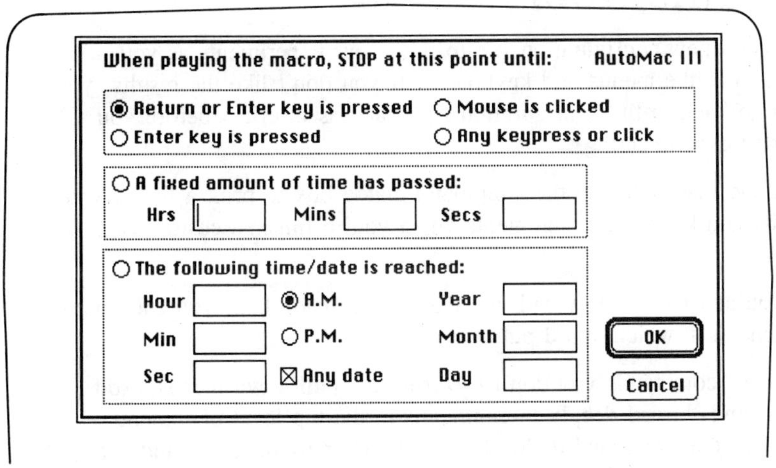

Fig. 9.9.

The When Playing this Macro, STOP dialog box.

16. Click Open in the Open dialog box.

17. Click Cancel in the Define Styles dialog box.

18. Click the AutoMac icon, the little a. This step stops the recording again.

19. When the End of Recording menu appears, click Stop. To use this macro, you simply press ⌘-Shift-S when you start a new file. The macro opens the Define Styles dialog box and then chooses the Open command. Next, a dialog box appears asking you to choose a document from the list. After you choose the document and press Return, the macro adds the document's style sheet to your new document, and returns control to you.

Much more can be said about the AutoMac III options so briefly covered here. AutoMac is beyond the scope of this introductory-level book. This tutorial, however, should help you get started with recording macros.

Caution: When you create AutoMac III macros, be very careful to avoid creating a macro that will wipe out your work. Never include destructive commands in macros. If you're writing a macro in which you delete text or a file, make the macro pause so that you can perform the action yourself. When you test the macros you create, always save your work and experiment with an unwanted document!

High-Productivity Techniques To Remember

❑ Create a new configuration file to hold your experiments as you customize the menus and keyboards. If you don't like the results, you can go back to the configuration file that was in effect before you started experimenting.

❑ Use the List button in the Command dialog box to print a list of your menu and keyboard assignments when you're finished customizing Word.

❑ If you add menu items with the Command dialog box, you can control the menu in which Word puts them.

❑ Remove commands you don't use from the pull-down menus. Add commands buried deeply in submenus to the top level of a menu. Explore the Command dialog box to discover useful commands not present on the menus.

❑ Develop a plan for reconfiguring your keyboard. Assign commands mnemonically and use intensification or differentiation to create two or three maps, each for a distinct purpose. Because you can use the keypad period key to choose commands from menus, you can dispense with Word's default ⌘-key shortcuts (such as ⌘-A and ⌘-P), which aren't assigned mnemonically.

❑ If you create keyboard shortcuts with the Command dialog box (instead of using the keyboard technique), you can delete existing assignments. In addition, *your* keyboard assignments show up on the pull-down menus.

❑ To create a command or keyboard shortcut that enters two or more commands in a series, create an AutoMac III macro. Creating a macro that pauses for user input and presents dialog boxes is easy. Be sure to test your macro on an unwanted document!

10

Organizing Your Document with Outlining

n Chapter 2, you learned that the most beneficial aspect of Word's outlining feature isn't the help it can give you in *planning* your document (although the outlining feature is useful for this purpose). Even more beneficial, however, is the help the outlining feature can give you in managing and reorganizing long documents. A Word outline isn't a separate document, something apart from the actual document you're creating; a Word outline is another way of viewing the same document you're creating in Galley view. The Outline view shows your document's overall structure and plan. What's more, by rearranging headings on the outline, you can restructure your document as well.

When you combine outlining with the automatic heading styles, the result is an excellent productivity-enhancing feature for business and professional writing—a feature that has no real parallel in other word processing programs. If you write long reports, articles, or dissertations with chapter or section headings and subheadings, read on! Continuing the Part III theme of making Word your own, this chapter shows you how to set up outlining and heading styles to suit your business and professional writing needs.

Understanding a few key terms will help you grasp Word's outlining capabilities. For ordinary (paper) outlines, you arrange headings and subheadings by indenting them. Word's outlines are arranged the same way. The first-level headings are called Level 1, second-level headings are called Level 2, and so on. In a Word outline, however, changing outline levels is much easier; you can *promote* an outline heading (move it up one logical level, such as from Level 2 to Level 1), and you also can *demote* an outline heading. Furthermore, you can restructure your outline by moving headings up or down on-screen, one line at a time. If too many subheadings exist for you to keep the entire outline in view, you can *collapse* (hide) all the subheadings under a heading; when you want to see them again, you can *expand* the subheadings. You also can display headings and subheadings throughout your outline down to a level you specify (such as Level 2 or Level 3). And you can hide or display *body text*, the text making up the paragraphs of your document.

If you ever have used a computer outlining program before, you will recognize all these features. What makes Word's outlining feature stand out, however, is its seamless integration with your document. As you make changes in your outline, the changes are reflected in your document. And as you make changes in your document's headings and subheadings, the changes are reflected automatically in your outline! At all times, therefore, you can switch to Outline view for an almost instantaneous view of your document's overall structure. And as writing experts know, having a solid overall structure is one of the best ways to ensure high quality in the reports, articles, and other long documents you create.

Outlining was introduced in Word Version 3.0. In Version 4, experienced users will find that manipulating outlines with the mouse is much easier. Adjacent to every heading and subheading is an outline selection icon, which you can drag to promote, demote, or move outline headings. You will find that creating and restructuring an outline require considerably less fussing with the keyboard.

Creating an Outline

The first step in creating an outline is to switch to the Outline view. When the Outlining window appears, you see a new menu bar with icons that perform special functions in the Outline view. In this view, you can enter headings and subheadings, demoting and promoting them to the levels you prefer.

Switching to Outline View

To explore outlining, start by creating an outline in a new, blank document. Starting this way is less confusing because you don't have to deal with body text. You will learn about outlining an existing document later in this chapter.

To switch to Outline view, do the following:

1. Start Word and display a new document. Alternatively, choose New from the File menu.

⌘-U

2. Choose Outlining from the Document menu or choose the ⌘-U keyboard shortcut.

You use the same commands—Outlining or ⌘-U—to return to Galley view when you're finished in Outline view.

Understanding the Outline Menu Bar

After you choose Outlining from the Document menu, you see a new, blank window with the Outlining menu bar (see fig. 10.1). Table 10.1 gives an overview of this menu bar's features.

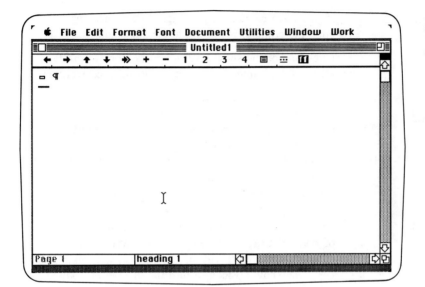

Fig. 10.1.

The Outlining menu bar.

Table 10.1
Features on the Outlining Menu Bar

Icon	Function
←	Click the promote arrow icon to move the selected heading one logical level up (for example, from Level 2 to Level 1).
→	Click the demote arrow icon to move the selected heading one logical level down (for example, from Level 1 to Level 2).
↑ ↓	Click the move-up and move-down arrow icons to move the selected heading up or down one line at a time in the outline.
↠	Click the demote to body text arrow icon to transform an outline heading into body text.

Table 10.1—*Continued*

Icon	Function
+	If you have collapsed the subheadings under a heading, click the expand icon to display the subheadings.
—	If you have created subheadings under a heading, click the collapse icon to hide the subheadings.
1 2 3 4	Click one of the show level numbers icons to display all the subheadings in the outline down to a level you specify.
▤	Click the show all icon to toggle between two views of the outline. The first view displays no body text; only headings and subheadings are displayed. The second view displays body text. Click the show/hide body text icon to control the display of body text (whether all body text is displayed or just the first line of each paragraph).
⁞	Click the show/hide body text icon to display all lines of body text or just the first line followed by an ellipsis. Note that this icon's name is misleading. Click the show all icon to turn the display of body text on and off; click this icon (as the ellipsis actually suggests) to control *how* body text is displayed—that is, whether all lines are displayed or just the first line of the paragraph.
ff	Click the show/hide formatting icon to display heading and other formats or to display all text in a plain style.
▬ ✛	The outline selection icon (the outlined dash if no subheadings are beneath the heading and the outlined plus sign if subheadings are beneath the heading) gives you a way to drag the heading (to promote, demote, or move it) and also to select the heading.

The menu bar is useful, but bear in mind that you can duplicate all its functions in Version 4 by using some handy mouse procedures. Just by dragging on the outline selection icon (the outlined dash or plus sign next to each heading or subheading), you can promote, demote, and move headings easily. Double-click the icon to collapse or expand a heading. Click the heading once to select the entire heading, all subheadings beneath it, and all body text beneath it.

As you work in Outline view, watch the status line; the style indicator shows the heading level you have chosen; Word automatically assigns the predefined heading styles as you type outline headings. The first-level heading is assigned to the Heading 1 style, the second-level heading to Heading 2, and so on.

Creating Headings and Subheadings

When you type in Outline view, Word enters the lines you type as outline headings, not as body text paragraphs. Here's a quick guide to creating an outline for document planning purposes:

1. Begin typing your outline by entering the title on the first line. Before you type anything under this heading, the first line is preceded by an outlined dash. This icon indicates that this line contains an outline heading, but no subheadings are beneath it.

2. After you type the first-level heading, press Return. Word moves the insertion point to the next line, and you see another outline heading icon.

3. Drag the second line's outline selection icon. Click the demote arrow. Alternatively, press the right-arrow key.

   Note that the outline heading icon on line 1 changes to an outlined plus sign. This symbol tells you that this heading now has subheadings. That's obvious right now, but after you collapse subheadings, you will have no other way to see that subheadings are hidden under a heading.

4. Type the second-level heading.

5. Continue by typing additional second-level headings. To type a third-level heading, press Return and click the demote arrow (or press the right-arrow key). To return to a second-level heading, press Return and click the promote arrow (or press the left-arrow key). Figure 10.2 shows an outline with many levels of headings.

6. To insert additional headings anywhere in your outline, *do not* insert a line as you normally do in a document, by positioning the cursor at the end of a line and pressing Return. If you insert a line this way after you have hidden some subheadings, you will separate the subheadings from their main heading! To guard against this error, develop the habit of inserting a line by positioning the insertion point at the *beginning* of the line (but without highlighting the line or any characters) and pressing Return.

Fig. 10.2.

*An outline with
five levels of
headings.*

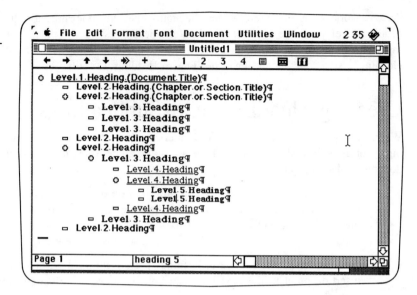

As you create, edit, and restructure your outline, bear in mind the many keyboard shortcuts you can use (see table 10.2). You may find some of these shortcuts helpful. Word 4's new mouse features for outlining, however, make the mouse much more useful than most of these commands for promoting, demoting, and moving outline headings. The ⌘-Option-T commands in table 10.2 were designed for users of the original Macintosh keyboard, which doesn't have a numeric keypad.

Returning to the Galley View

After you have roughed out the overall plan for your document, return to Galley view (choose Outlining again or press ⌘-U) to see how your headings look. As you can see in figure 10.3, Word's predefined styles for the heading levels are—in a word—unimaginative. You surely will want to redefine these styles. You can do so directly by using the ruler and other direct formatting commands (see fig. 10.4), but the best procedure is to redefine the heading styles by using the Define Styles dialog box (see Chapter 7 for more information on defining styles). When you redefine these styles, be sure to use the Keep with Next option (and add blank lines by using the After box in the spacing options group) so that Word will not leave any heading alone at the bottom of a page.

Table 10.2
Keyboard Shortcuts in Outline View

Outlining Command	Keyboard Shortcut	⌘-Option-T Command
Promote heading	←	K or Keypad 4
Demote heading	→	L or Keypad 6
Move heading up	↑	O or Keypad 8
Move heading down	↓	, or Keypad 2
Demote to body text	⌘-→	>
Expand subheadings	Keypad +	$
Collapse subheadings	Keypad −	−
Display to level		1, 2, 3, 4 (keyboard)
Display all	Keypad *	A
Display first line only	Keypad =	B
Display formatting	Keypad /	F

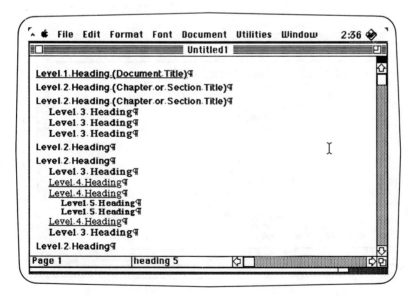

Fig. 10.3.

Outline headings in Galley view (Word's predefined styles).

Don't worry about losing the outline's pattern of indentations when you redefine the styles. Even after you center the Heading 1 format and remove the indenta-

Fig. 10.4.

Outline headings in Galley view (redefined styles).

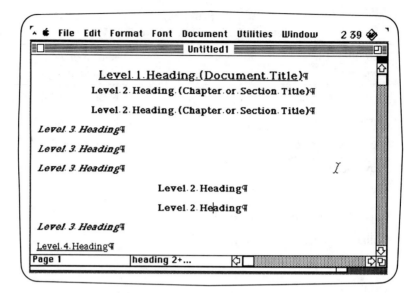

tions from the other heading styles, the indentation logic is preserved when you choose Outlining again (see fig. 10.5).

Fig. 10.5.

Formatted headings in Outline view.

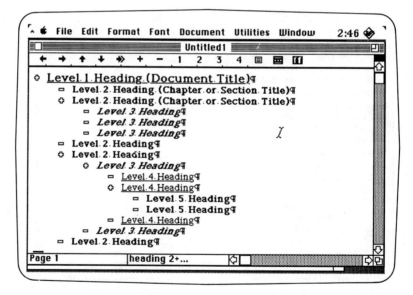

Return to Galley view and add body text underneath the headings, as shown in figure 10.6. To create a new paragraph for body text, place the insertion point at the end of the heading and press Return. (You learned earlier that you *shouldn't* do this procedure in Outline view, but it's OK in Galley view.)

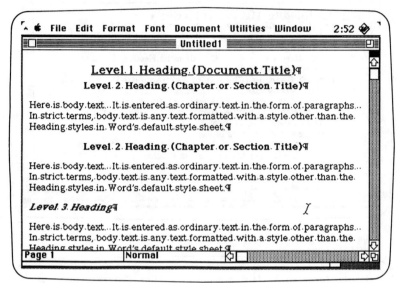

Fig. 10.6.

Adding body text to your outline.

When you return to Outline view after adding body text, you see the body text on-screen (see fig. 10.7). To hide the body text, you can click the misleadingly named hide body text icon on the menu bar, which reduces the display of body text to the first line of each body text paragraph (see fig. 10.8). Hiding all the body text by clicking the hide all icon is a much better idea. After you hide the body text, the headings with hidden body text are displayed with fuzzy gray underlining (see fig. 10.9).

Collapsing and Expanding Headings

Once you create an outline with many levels of subheadings, the outline can become long and start to defeat its purpose of giving you a way to view your document's overall structure. For this reason, collapsing or hiding subheadings is useful. You can collapse all the subheadings under a specific heading, or if you prefer, you can collapse all the subheadings in your outline down to a level you specify. After you collapse subheadings, you can expand them again when you need to view the subheadings.

Fig. 10.7.

The outline after body text is added.

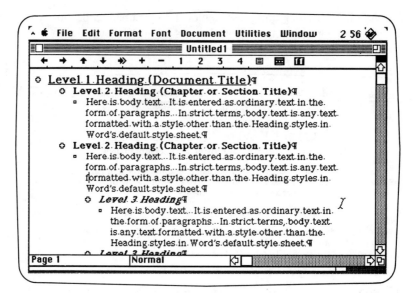

Fig. 10.8.

Displaying only the first line of each paragraph of body text.

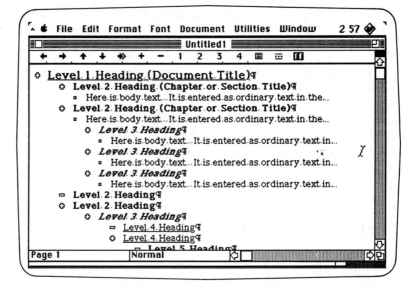

To collapse the subheadings under one heading, double-click the outline selection icon next to the heading. Alternatively, select the entire heading and click the collapse icon (the minus sign) on the Outlining menu bar.

To collapse all the subheadings down to a level you specify, click one of the show level numbers icons on the menu bar. If you want to display down to a

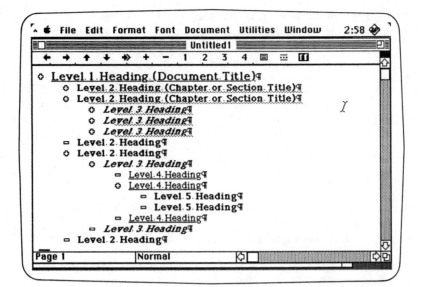

Fig. 10.9.

*All body text
hidden.*

number that's not on the menu, press ⌘-Option-T and then press a number between 1 and 9 on the keyboard (not the numeric keypad).

To expand the subheadings under a heading, double-click the outline selection icon next to the heading. To expand all the subheadings throughout the entire outline, click the show all icon on the menu bar.

Restructuring the Outline

When you restructure an outline by moving headings, Word moves the body text, too. For this reason, you can restructure a huge document in seconds just by dragging headings around in Outline view. To make sure that you select all the body text under a heading, however, you must make sure that you select the heading and all the body text by clicking the outline selection icon.

To move a heading and its body text up or down in the outline, follow these steps:

1. Click the outline selection icon next to the heading you want to move. If you're moving a heading with many subheadings, double-click the heading before selecting it to collapse it. Collapsing the heading leaves more room on-screen for viewing the heading's destination.

2. Drag the selection to its new location. As you drag the selection, you see a dotted line indicating the pointer's current location. When

you have moved the heading to the location you want, release the mouse button. If you prefer, you can click the move-up or move-down arrow icon on the menu bar instead. You also can press the up arrow or down arrow on the keyboard.

You also can move a heading by selecting it and choosing Cut from the Edit menu. Move the insertion point where you want the heading to appear and choose Paste from the Edit menu. This technique is best when you're restructuring a long outline.

To change the level of a heading, do the following:

1. Click the outline selection icon to select the heading.

2. Drag the heading right to demote it or left to promote it. You also can click the demote or promote arrow icon or press the right- or left-arrow key on the keyboard.

In some cases, you may decide to turn an outline heading into body text. To do so, select the heading and click the demote to body text arrow icon.

Managing a Long Document with Outlining

When you're creating a long document, bear in mind the advantages of switching to Outline view to get a quick view of your document's structure. To hide body text and collapse subheadings quickly, click one of the show level numbers icons (such as 2 or 3).

You also can use the Outline view to move quickly through a document. Instead of scrolling page by page through a long document, switch to Outline view. Position the heading or subheading you want at the top of the screen and switch back to Galley view.

Outlining an Existing Document

If you have created a document already without beginning with an outline, you can easily add headings to the document so that you can take full advantage of outlining. In Galley view, just enter headings and subheadings formatted with one of the heading styles in Word's default style sheet. To apply the heading styles if you haven't used them before, hold down the Shift key when you choose Define Styles or drag down the style selection box. You will see all the default styles from which you can choose the heading levels you want. After you apply the styles to headings in your document, the headings will appear automatically in your outline as outline headings.

Numbering Outlines

If you prefer a numbered outline, you easily can add numbers or letters by selecting the entire outline and choosing Renumber from the Utilities menu (see fig. 10.10). Using the default settings, Word numbers the outline as shown in figure 10.11. If you don't like the results, select the outline again, choose Renumber, click the Remove button, and click OK.

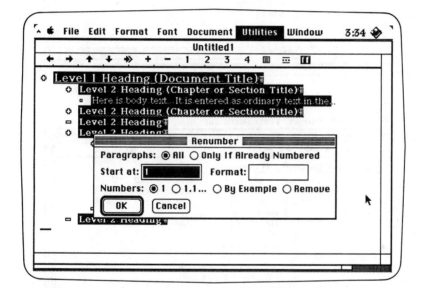

Fig. 10.10.

The Renumber dialog box.

You're not limited to the default numbering format. If you type a format in the Format text box in the Renumber dialog box, Word will use that format in numbering your outline. Suppose, for example, that you type

> I.A.1.a.i.(a).(i)

in the Format text box and then click OK. You see the results shown in figure 10.12.

The Renumber command is flexible and useful, but be sure to experiment with it before using Renumber on an outline of critical value. Remember that you can remove the numbers Renumber inserts just by using the command again and clicking the Remove button.

Fig. 10.11.

Outline numbered with default settings.

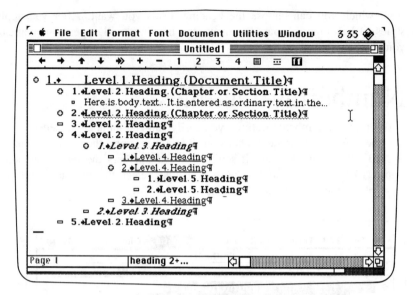

Fig. 10.12.

Outline numbered with standard outline numbering format.

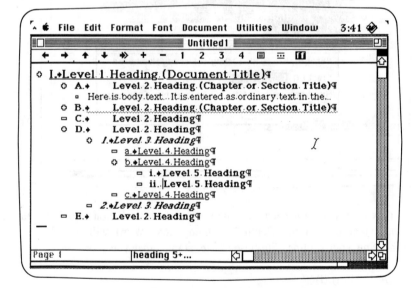

Printing Your Outline

Having a printout of your outline can be handy. Printing your outline will give you another way of keeping your document's structure in mind. You can tape the printed outline to the wall adjacent to your computer.

The procedure for printing is simple. To print your outline, do the following:

1. Collapse headings and body text to a level you specify by clicking one of the show level numbers icons. Word prints only what is displayed, no matter how much body text or other material is collapsed.

2. Choose Print from the File menu.

High-Productivity Techniques To Remember

❑ The icons on the menu bar are useful, but most of the icons have powerful analogues in mouse techniques. Just by dragging on the outline selection icon (the outlined dash or plus sign next to each heading or subheading), you can promote, demote, and move headings easily. Double-click the icon to collapse or expand a heading. Click the heading once to select the entire heading, all subheadings beneath it, and all body text beneath it.

❑ To add a line within an outline, position the insertion point before the first character of a heading. Then press Return.

❑ Before you move a heading (with its linked subheadings and body text), be sure to click the outline selection icon so that the subheadings and body text will move also.

❑ To move around rapidly in a large document, switch to Outline view and position at the top of the screen the heading to which you want to move. Then switch back to Galley view.

❑ To outline an existing document, add headings and subheadings to your document in Galley view and format them by using the heading styles. The headings and subheadings will appear as outline headings when you switch to Outline view.

11

Creating and Using Glossaries

If you have to say the same thing over and over—and if whether you say it right matters—Word's glossaries are for you. Using Word's glossaries, you can store carefully worded passages of text, ranging from a few words to dozens of pages. These glossaries are accessible just by pulling down a menu and choosing the glossary's name from a list box. With this technique, an attorney can store and retrieve standardized passages for documents, such as wills or contracts; or a small-business owner can create and retrieve paragraphs that respond to typical questions people ask in letters of inquiry so that answering a letter takes only a matter of seconds. Glossaries are, in short, another of Word's many features for high-productivity writing. If you're not already using glossaries, you're missing out on ways to save time and money.

The name *glossary* isn't very descriptive. The term dates back to the days when this feature really was used to store a glossary of words, terms, and phrases. Back in the days when computer memory was very limited (64K was considered wildly luxurious), there were sharp limits on how much text you could store in a glossary entry. So writers used this feature to store only single words or—at most—a four- or five-word phrase. If you had to type *autochthonous processes of spontaneous generation* over and over, the better method was to store the glossary item so that you could retrieve it just by typing *apsg* and entering a keyboard command.

You still can use Word's glossaries to store terms and phrases, but with storage space limited only by the size of your disk, there's nothing to stop you from storing longer passages of text, such as paragraphs in legal contracts. What's more, you can store graphics in Word's glossaries—a capability that is a far cry from this feature's original application. What's more, Word's glossaries retain the formats you have applied to the text you store in them.

In short, this feature is far more useful now than it was in the early days of personal computing, and the feature really ought to be known by some new name, such as "cubbyholes." But computer nomenclature doesn't change rapidly, so we're stuck with glossaries for now, just as we're still stuck with the key name Return (short for carriage return—a throwback to the typewriter keyboard).

In this chapter, you learn how to create glossary entries, how to retrieve them, and how to save them to disk. You learn, too, how to manage glossary files. (You can create more than one and open and close them as you please.) You also learn how to set up glossaries to streamline the task of answering routine inquiry letters in a business context.

About Glossaries

Each glossary item you create and store becomes a glossary entry in a glossary file. A *glossary entry* is a named unit of text (or a graphic). You can place dozens or even hundreds of glossary entries in each glossary file. You're limited only by the size of your disk. After creating the entry, you see its name in the Glossary window's list box (accessed by choosing Glossary from the Edit menu). To insert the glossary entry into your document, you choose the entry's name from the list and click the Glossary window's Insert button.

You can create more than one glossary file. By default, Word uses a glossary file called the Standard Glossary. When you open the Glossary window, you use the Save As command to create and name a new glossary file, and you use the Open command (File menu) to open a glossary other than the Standard Glossary. A good reason for creating more than one glossary file is to keep glossary entries segregated according to the type of document for which they're used. For instance, you can create one glossary of entries for letters, another for memos, and a third for reports. If you plan to create just a few glossary entries, however, you can use the Standard Glossary to store all your entries.

The Standard Glossary contains 13 predefined glossary entries, all of which have special uses:

❑ *date - now - abbreviated*. Enters the current date in abbreviated form (Sat, Apr 1, 1989)

❑ *date - now - long*. Enters the current date in long form (Saturday, April 1, 1989)

❑ *date - now - short*. Enters the current date in short form (4/1/89)

❑ *date - print - abbreviated*. Prints the date at the time of printing, in abbreviated form (Sat, Apr 1, 1989)

❏ *date - print - long*. Prints the date at the time of printing, in long form (Saturday, April 1, 1989)

❏ *date - print - short*. Prints the date at the time of printing, in short form (4/1/89)

❏ *index*. Enters the proper index code as hidden text

❏ *page number*. Same result as clicking the page number icon in the Header or Footer window: inserts a special symbol that displays the document's current page number

❏ *print merge*. Inserts the special symbols used to create Print Merge instructions

❏ *time - now*. Inserts the current time (10:51 AM)

❏ *time - now - with seconds*. Inserts the current time with seconds (10:51:46 AM)

❏ *time - print*. Inserts the time at the time of printing (10:51 AM)

❏ *time - print - with seconds*. Inserts the time at the time of printing, with seconds (10:51:46 AM)

When you create a new glossary file, Word copies all these default glossary entries to the new file. All glossary files always contain the default glossary entries, and you cannot delete these entries. To help you distinguish the default glossary entries from the ones you create, the names of the default entries are preceded by a bullet in the Glossary window's list box.

Creating and Managing Glossary Entries

To create a glossary entry, you select the text or graphic and choose Glossary from the Edit menu. After creating a glossary entry, you can insert it, edit it, rename it, or delete it.

Creating Glossary Entries

You can copy any amount of text—from one character to many pages—to a glossary. You also can copy a graphic. When you create the glossary entry, Word copies all the character formats you have chosen for the selection. If you include a paragraph mark or marks in the selection, Word also stores the paragraph formats.

To create a glossary entry, follow these steps:

1. Select the text or graphic you want to store in a glossary.

   If you want to include paragraph formats in the glossary, be sure to include the paragraph's trailing paragraph mark in the selection.

2. Choose Glossary from the Edit menu.

   In the Glossary window, New is selected in the list box (see fig. 11.1).

Fig. 11.1.

The Glossary window with New selected in the list box.

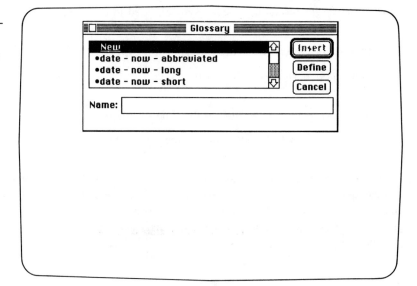

3. Type a glossary entry name in the Name box.

   You can use up to 32 characters, including spaces, to name glossary entries.

4. Click the Define button.

5. Click Cancel.

Power User Tip

If you create a glossary entry that has been formatted with styles, watch out for a trap. If you insert the entry into a document that has a different style sheet, and Word cannot find the style name, you will lose the format. If you create a glossary entry formatted with a style named Bulleted List, for example, and insert this entry into a document whose style sheet doesn't contain Bulleted List, you lose the formatting.

Inserting Glossary Entries

Once you have created a glossary entry, you can insert it into your text by using the menus or the keyboard.

To insert a glossary entry with the menu, follow these steps:

1. Place the insertion point where you want the glossary entry to appear.

2. Choose Glossary from the Edit menu or use the ⌘-K keyboard shortcut.

3. Choose the entry you want from the Glossary window's list box.

   When you select an item in the list box, Word displays the entry's first line at the bottom of the list box (see fig. 11.2).

4. Click Insert. Word inserts the glossary entry at the insertion point's location.

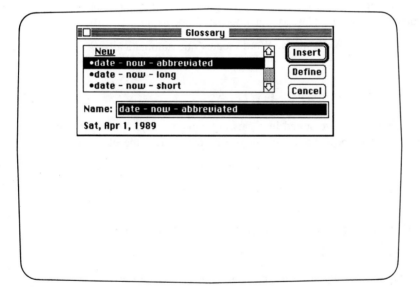

Fig. 11.2.

First line of glossary entry displayed at bottom of the Glossary window.

If you neglected to place the insertion point where you want the glossary entry to appear, choose Copy from the Edit menu to copy the entry to the clipboard. Then click Cancel.

To insert a glossary entry with the keyboard, follow these steps:

1. Position the insertion point where you want the glossary entry to appear.

2. Press ⌘-Delete or ⌘-Backspace.

3. When the lower left corner of the status line displays the message Name, type the full name of the glossary entry and press Return.

   Word inserts the glossary entry at the insertion point's location.

To cancel, press Esc or ⌘-Backspace.

After you insert a glossary entry, you can cancel the insertion by choosing Undo immediately.

If you find yourself choosing a glossary entry frequently, add it to the Work menu. Here's how:

1. Press ⌘-Option-Plus (use the plus key on the keyboard, not the numeric keypad).

2. Choose Glossary from the Edit menu.

3. In the Glossary list box, choose the glossary entry you want. Word automatically adds the glossary entry to the Work menu.

If you don't have a Work menu, Word creates one automatically.

Editing Glossary Entries

Editing the text you have stored in a glossary entry is easy. You insert the entry, edit the text, and repeat the procedure you used to define the glossary entry.

1. Choose Glossary from the Edit menu or press ⌘-K.

2. In the list box, choose the glossary entry you want to edit and click Insert.

3. Edit and format the entry as you edit any document text.

4. Select the entry.

5. Choose Glossary from the Edit menu or press ⌘-K.

6. In the list box, choose the glossary entry's name and click Define.

7. Click Cancel to close the Glossary window.

Renaming a Glossary Entry

If you have already created a glossary entry and want to rename it, the procedure is simple:

1. Choose Glossary from the File menu (or press ⌘-K).

2. When the Glossary window appears, select the glossary name in the list box.

3. Select the name in the Name box and edit the name as you please.

4. Click Define.

Deleting Glossary Entries

After you have created many glossary entries, you surely will find that some of them are no longer useful. Perhaps you created the glossary entry for a special one-time purpose, or perhaps you have found another, easier way of accomplishing the same task. Whatever the reason, deleting such entries is a good idea. By doing so, you make finding the entries in the list box easier.

To delete glossary entries, follow these steps:

1. Choose Glossary from the Edit menu (or press ⌘-K).

2. In the list box, choose the glossary entry you want to delete.

3. Choose Cut from the Edit menu.

   When the alert box appears, click Yes.

Managing Glossary Files

As with all Word files, the changes you make to a glossary file aren't saved to disk unless you deliberately save them. If you don't save your glossary file before choosing Quit, an alert box appears asking whether you want to save the changes to the glossary. To save the changes, click Yes when the alert box appears. To abandon the changes, click No. To cancel the Quit command and return to Word, click Cancel.

To save your changes to the standard glossary file before you choose Quit, follow these steps:

1. Choose Glossary from the Edit menu (or press ⌘-K).

2. Choose Save from the File menu.

3. Click the Save button.

4. Click the Cancel button in the Glossary dialog box.

To save your new glossary file, follow these steps:

1. Choose Glossary from the Edit menu (or press ⌘-K).

2. Choose New from the File menu. When the alert box appears, click OK to delete all the nonstandard glossary entries in the file.

Word creates a new glossary file containing nothing but the default glossary entries.

Remember that you must save the new glossary file to disk. If you forget to save the file before quitting Word, an alert box appears warning you to save your changes.

When you choose Quit, Word updates the Word Preferences file by noting which glossary you are using when you choose Quit. The next time you start Word, it uses this glossary as the default glossary. If you want to open a different glossary, you can do so by using the Open command.

To open a different glossary, follow these steps:

1. Choose Glossary from the Edit menu (or press ⌘-K).

2. Choose Open from the File menu.

    Word displays a list of glossary files (but not document or other files) in the Open list box.

3. Choose the glossary you want to use and click Open.

If you have created several glossary files, you may want to take advantage of a special (and little-known) Word feature: the program will print your glossary files in a special format. The glossary names are boldfaced and printed flush left, and the text or graphics stored in the glossary files are printed with a half-inch indent.

To print a glossary, follow these steps:

1. Choose Glossary from the Edit menu (or press ⌘-K).

2. Choose Print from the File menu.

After you have created two or more glossary files, you may find it convenient to copy an entry from one glossary file to another. Suppose, for example, that you created a letterhead glossary and stored it in a glossary file called Correspondence Glossary. It is so nice, though, you would like to have it in your standard glossary, so you want to copy it. Here's how:

1. Choose Glossary from the Edit menu (or press ⌘-K) and highlight the entry you want to copy.

2. Choose Copy from the Edit menu.

3. Choose Open from the File menu.

4. Highlight the name of the glossary file to which you want to copy the entry and click Open.

5. Choose Paste.

6. Click the Cancel button.

Applying Glossaries: A Boilerplate System for Business Inquiry and Order Letters

Businesses are besieged by mail—a good part of it junk. But buried amidst the junk are pearls and diamonds: inquiry and order letters from customers. In order for a business to create and sustain a clientele, every letter must be treated with care and competence. The highest standards of business communication require that almost every letter receive a personal reply, or at least a personalized one, in which the inquiry or order letter's specific requests are answered point by point. (Nothing is more frustrating for customers than to receive in reply a form letter that does not answer their questions.)

Businesses that receive many inquiry letters cannot always afford to answer each one personally. With Word's glossaries, however, you easily can create a boiler-plate system for answering inquiry letters—a system that will shorten the work involved in answering them. The term *boilerplate* refers to standard passages of text. These passages can be used to answer customer inquiries or complaints. Even though each letter should receive a tailored, personalized reply, using standardized boilerplate passages is still a good idea—and for several reasons. Why reinvent the wheel? If you have created a paragraph that responds to a customer inquiry in a way which builds up the company's image and pleases the customer, why write the answer differently in the future? What's more, passages about legal matters, such as warranties or liability, should be standardized after the passages have been inspected by legal staff; you don't want unintentionally to stimulate future litigation by casually adding a loosely worded clause to a first-class letter (which is, after all, admissible in a court of law as evidence of a contract).

This boilerplate system is founded on a simple principle: although each inquiry letter is unique and requires a unique response, you keep getting the same kinds of questions, over and over. The problem is that each inquiry letter requires a tailored response, one that addresses precisely the concerns the customer raises (but no others). The solution is to create a series of glossaries, each containing a standardized response to typical questions, such as "What is the warranty on your products? What kind of support do you give after the sale? Can I return a product after I buy it?"

The following list suggests a few glossary passages that a small direct-mail software firm might develop. As additional questions come up, more glossary entries can be created.

❏ *Ship*. All NexusLogic products are shipped within 24 hours of your order via SuperFast Express Second-Day Air service!

❏ *Support*. Help is just a toll-free call away when you choose NexusLogic Software. Our highly trained and patient technical support staff members are available from 7 a.m. to 7 p.m. (Pacific Standard Time), and they are ready to help with all your questions.

❏ *Return*. All NexusLogic products come with an unconditional 30-day guarantee. If for any reason you're not satisfied with a NexusLogic product, just return it within 30 days for a no-questions-asked cheerful refund. All we ask is that you return all the packaging, disks, documentation, and warranty certificates in new condition.

❏ *Wrnty*. All NexusLogic products are covered by a 30-day unconditional guarantee. In addition, NexusLogic disks are covered by an additional 1-year limited warranty against defects in manufacture. If a NexusLogic disk fails during this time, just give us a ring to get a replacement within three business days!

Suppose that a customer writes an inquiry letter, asking the following:

I'm thinking about buying NexusLogic File, your relational database manager, but I would like to know whether I can return the product if it doesn't meet my needs. Also, how long will it take to get to me after I order it?

To respond to this letter, you create the letter by opening a file containing your firm's letterhead. After typing the return address, you choose the Return and Ship glossary entries (in that order because that's the order the customer used in asking the questions). After adding an extra line or two to personalize the letter, you print it and it's ready to go (see fig. 11.3).

High-Productivity Techniques To Remember

❏ A glossary file is a collection of glossary entries, each of which has a name. A glossary entry can contain text, graphics, or both.

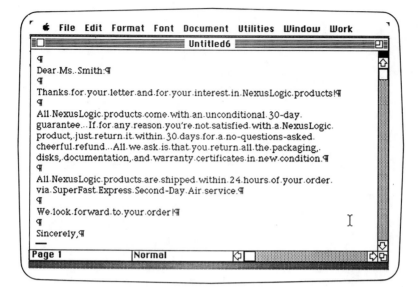

Fig. 11.3.

Personalized boilerplate letter constructed from glossaries.

❏ When you open Word, the program uses the Standard Glossary by default. After you create new glossary files, the program opens with the glossary you were using when you chose Quit.

❏ Every glossary file contains date and time entries, which insert the date or time now or at the time of printing.

❏ If you use some entries frequently, place them on the Work menu for super-fast access.

❏ When you create a glossary entry, Word copies with the text all the character formats. Paragraph formats aren't copied, however, unless you include the trailing paragraph mark or marks in the selection. If you format the selection with a style, the style formatting won't appear in a new document unless that document's style sheet contains a style with the same name.

❏ If you add entries to a glossary, you must save the glossary before quitting. If you create entries you don't want to save, however, you can abandon them simply by clicking No when the alert box appears after you choose Quit.

❏ Use glossaries to construct a system for dealing with inquiry or order letters. Once you have worked out a good paragraph of text that responds to a specific customer question, copy the paragraph to a glossary. The next time you write a response letter, construct it by combining glossary entries and adding a few personalizing touches.

CHAPTER 12

Creating Tables and Lists

Business and professional writers frequently type tables and lists, and these tasks can be tedious. Word 4, however, includes some wonderful features that make these tiresome jobs much easier. Chief among these features is the new Insert Table command, which is so revolutionary that it will take some getting used to. But after you have tried Insert Table, you're sure to say, "Of course! Why didn't someone think of this before?"

About Word's Tables

New to Word 4 is a set of tools for creating, editing, and formatting tables. In fact, this feature is so new—and so innovative—that you will need some time to learn about it. Using this command is nothing like creating a table by setting tabs on the ruler. More akin to Word's tables are the editing and formatting capabilities of a good spreadsheet program. The analogy is, as you will see, particularly apt because a Word table consists of rows, columns, and cells, just as you see them in a spreadsheet (see fig. 12.1). When you insert a table, you decide how many rows and columns you want, and Word creates the table automatically. The program surrounds each cell with nonprinting grid lines, and each cell contains an *end-of-cell marker*, a bullet dot.

The remarkable thing about a Word table is that each cell is expandable. When you type more text than the cell can accommodate, Word expands the cell and wraps the excess text down to the next line (see fig. 12.2). The other cells in that row also expand. This feature alone makes tables exceptionally easy to create, edit, and format—even complex multicolumn tables. When you create a table with ruler tabs, you run into difficulties if you don't have enough room for an

279

Fig. 12.1.

A Word table with nonprinting grid lines.

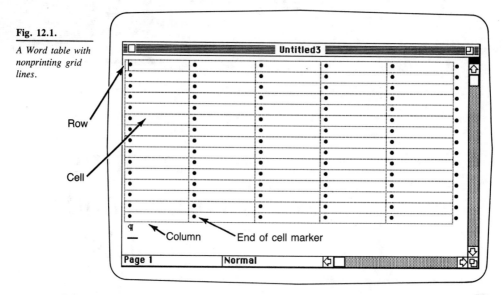

Row

Cell

Column   End of cell marker

item. You have to start a new line, and you are in for a certain amount of fussing with the keyboard and mouse to get all the text aligned correctly. It's much easier to create a table with the Insert Table command.

Fig. 12.2.

Cells expand automatically to accommodate text.

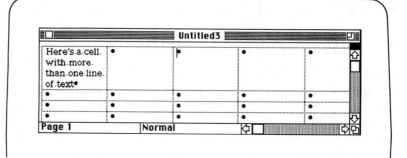

Word's tables have an advantage for another reason. Tab marks are just like any other character in that you can delete them, thus disrupting the alignment of text in your table. You cannot, however, accidentally delete a table's end-of-cell markers or grid lines. If you select a cell and choose Cut, Word erases the text or numbers in the cell—but not the cell grid lines or the end-of-cell marker. For this reason, you can edit a Word table without fear of accidentally erasing tab characters and ruining the column layout.

A Word table looks like a spreadsheet, but Word tables are much more flexible. You're not locked into a rigid matrix of rows and columns. Because Word treats each row independently, you can create a table in which some rows have four columns and others have two (or six).

You will find it helpful to think of tables in terms of the following procedures:

❏ *Creating tables.* You begin by choosing the Insert Table command in the Document menu. Word inserts the matrix of rows and columns.

❏ *Editing tables.* As you add text to the table, you will probably find that you need to add rows or columns or to move columns. All these editing procedures are exceptionally easy once you have created the table. To insert and delete rows, columns, and cells, you use the Table command in the Edit menu. To move and copy rows, columns, and cells, you use the Cut, Copy, and Paste commands in the Edit menu.

❏ *Formatting tables.* You can change the appearance of the table easily. You can change column width, row height, and text alignment within columns. You can add borders so that the cell boundaries will print if you want.

The following sections discuss these procedures in detail.

If you had the misfortune (!) to fuss with side-by-side paragraphs in earlier versions of Word, you will be delighted to learn that this feature has been entirely replaced by the Insert Table command (Document menu). By creating a table with this command, you easily can create side-by-side paragraphs (paragraphs formatted so that they will always print next to each other).

Creating a Table

To create a table, you choose the Table command from the Document menu. This command's dialog box provides text boxes in which you specify how many columns and rows the table should have.

If you're not exactly sure how many rows and columns you need, don't worry—you can easily add more later (or delete them if you don't need them).

If you're starting a new table from scratch, you begin by creating a blank matrix of rows and columns, as explained in the next section. If you have already created a table by setting tabs on the ruler, however, you needn't start from scratch. You easily can convert the existing table to the new table format, as the section following the next one explains.

Creating a New Table

Before creating your table, decide whether you want to display the grid lines—the lines that mark cell boundaries, rows, and columns. These grid lines don't print (unless you choose to print them, as explained elsewhere in this chapter). You control the grid lines by clicking the Show Table Grid Lines box in the Preferences dialog box (Edit menu). By default, grid lines are visible. You will find them handy in visualizing your table's overall form.

You also should decide whether you want to see the end-of-cell markers, the bullet characters that Word places in each cell. When the markers are displayed, you can easily see the alignment options you have chosen—if you have formatted a column with centered alignment, for instance, all the bullets are centered. To display these markers, choose Show in the Edit menu.

To create a table, follow these steps:

1. Position the insertion point where you want the table to appear.

2. Choose Insert Table from the Document menu.

3. When the Insert Table dialog box appears, type the number of columns you want in the Columns box (see fig. 12.3). Then type the number of rows you want in the Rows box.

   If you're not exactly sure how many rows or columns you need, don't worry—you can add or delete rows and columns later.

   After you type the number of rows and columns you want, Word calculates the column width automatically, assuming that each column is the same width. You can adjust column widths as you please later. To specify a column width (and override the automatic column width calculation), type a number in the Column Width box.

4. Click OK.

Word creates the table and enters the grid pattern in your document (see fig. 12.4).

Fig. 12.3.

The Insert Table dialog box.

```
              Insert Table
    Number of Columns: [2    ]     [  OK  ]
    Number of Rows:    [5    ]     [ Cancel ]
    Column Width:      [3.25in]    [ Format... ]
    ┌Convert From──────────────────────────┐
    │ ○ Paragraphs      ○ Comma Delimited   │
    │ ○ Tab Delimited   ○ Side by Side Only │
    └───────────────────────────────────────┘
```

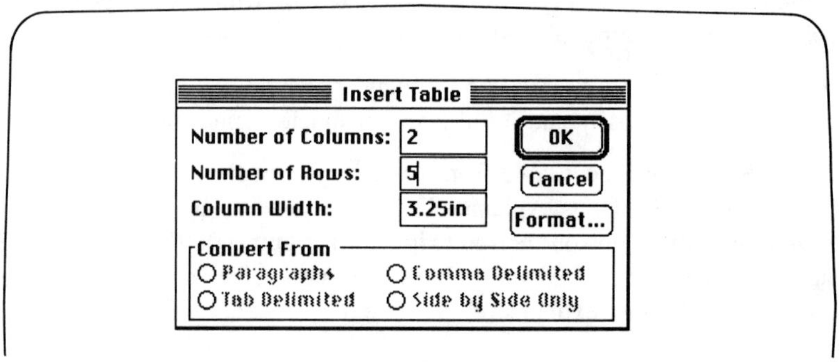

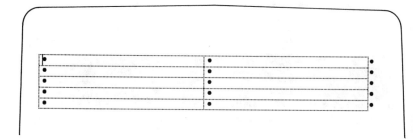

Fig. 12.4.

A blank two-column table.

Creating a Table from Existing Text

If you have already created a table with tabs, converting the table to Word's new table format is easy.

To convert an existing tab-formatted table to a Word table, follow these steps:

1. Select the entire table.

2. Choose Insert Table from the Document menu.

3. When the Insert Table dialog box appears, note that Word proposes to base the conversion on the tabs and suggests a column width (see fig. 12.5).

    You can adjust the column-width setting if you want.

    Click OK to accept these proposed settings.

4. Word displays the table in the new cellular format (see fig. 12.6).

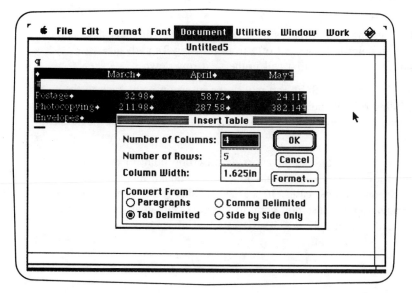

Fig. 12.5.

Converting an existing table to the new format.

Fig. 12.6.

Existing table in new table format.

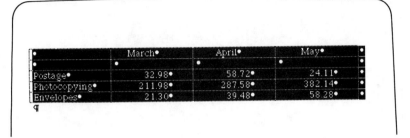

Using the Keyboard and Selecting Text within a Table

Once you have created the table and placed the insertion point in the table, you will find that the function of the Return and Tab keys has changed, so take some time now to learn how to navigate within the table. You also will need to learn a few additional selection techniques.

Using the Keyboard within a Table

Note that several keys have unique functions within a table:

❏ *Return*. Pressing this key does not start a new row. On the contrary, the Return key starts a new paragraph *within the cell*. Do not press Return unless you want to start a new paragraph inside the selected cell.

❏ *Tab*. Pressing Tab advances the insertion point to the next cell. If the insertion point is at the end of a row, pressing Tab advances the insertion point to the first cell in the next row down.

❏ *Shift-Tab*. Pressing Shift-Tab moves the insertion point back to the preceding cell. If the insertion point is at the beginning of a row, pressing Shift-Tab moves the insertion point to the last cell of the next row up.

❏ *Option-Tab*. Option-Tab advances the insertion point to the next tab stop in a cell. You can set tabs in a cell, although this step is unnecessary in most cases. If you do set tabs, remember that pressing Tab advances the insertion point to the next cell—that result is why you need Option-Tab, which advances the insertion point to the next tab stop *within* a cell.

Selecting Rows and Columns

All the normal Word selection procedures operate within tables. In addition, each column has its own selection bar, which runs down the column just to the left of the column's left border. Table 12.1 summarizes the methods of using the mouse to select text in a table.

Table 12.1
Using the Mouse To Select Text in a Table

To Select	Mouse Action
A cell's entire contents	Click the cell selection bar
A row of a table	Double-click the cell's selection bar next to the row you want to select
A column of a table	Click and drag in the column's selection bar. Alternatively, hold down the Option key and click any cell in the column.
An entire table	Hold down the Option key and double-click anywhere in the table

Controlling Alignment within Cells

To control alignment within the table's cells, you can use paragraph alignment or tabs. You choose paragraph alignment options (such as clicking an alignment icon on the ruler) for flush-left, centered, or flush-right alignments. To align numbers by the decimal point, select the entire column and set a decimal tab in the column's center.

Editing the Table Matrix

When you enter data into your table, use ordinary Word techniques to insert, modify, or delete text and numbers in the cells. To edit the matrix of rows and columns, however, you need special techniques. These techniques include commands for inserting and deleting rows and columns and for copying or moving cells.

Inserting Rows and Columns

To insert a row or column, follow these steps:

1. Position the insertion point in the row *below* the new row's location (or if you're inserting a column, in the column to the *left* of the new column's location).

   To insert more than one row or column, select two or more rows or columns.

2. Choose Table from the Edit menu.

3. When the Table dialog box appears (see fig. 12.7), click Row or Column. When you click Row or Column, the options in the Shift Cells group change automatically.

4. Click Insert.

Fig. 12.7.

The Table dialog box (Edit menu).

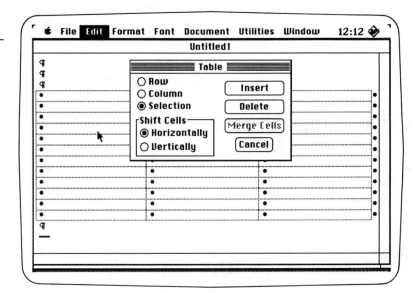

To add rows to the end of a table, do the following:

1. Position the insertion point just before the last end-of-cell marker in the table.

2. Press Tab.

Word appends a new row to the end of the table.

Deleting Rows and Columns

To prevent you from accidentally deleting rows or columns as you edit, you cannot delete cells by pressing Delete or choosing Cut after selecting the cells. You must use the Table command in the Edit menu to delete rows or columns.

To delete a row or column, follow these steps:

1. Place the insertion point in the row or column to be deleted.

   To delete more than one row or column, select two or more rows or columns.

2. Choose Table from the Edit menu.

3. Click Row or Column, depending on what you have selected.

4. Click Delete.

Inserting and Deleting Cells by Selection

Because Word treats the rows of a table independently, you can expand a row by adding additional cells. You also can push the cells of a column down (without affecting adjacent columns) by inserting cells within a column. The key to both techniques is first to select the cell or cells (instead of just placing the insertion point in a row or column).

To insert cells by selection, follow these steps:

1. Select the cell or cells *below* or to the *right* of the place where you want to insert new cells.

2. Choose Table from the Edit menu.

3. When the Table dialog box appears, click the selection button.

4. To shift the selected cells down, click the Vertically button. To shift the selected cells right, click the Horizontally button.

5. Click insert.

In figure 12.8, note the selected cells. After clicking the Vertically option and clicking Insert, Word shifts the cells down (fig. 12.9) and adds two rows. If you use the command again with the same selection but choose the Horizontally option, Word shifts the cells right as shown in figure 12.10.

Fig. 12.8.

Inserting cells with the Table dialog box.

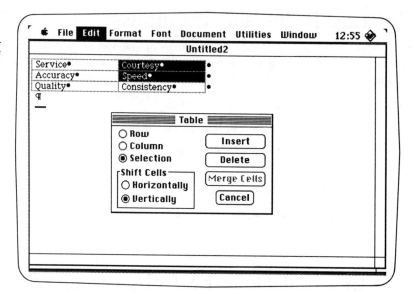

Fig. 12.9.

The table after inserting cells vertically.

Fig. 12.10.

The table after inserting cells horizontally.

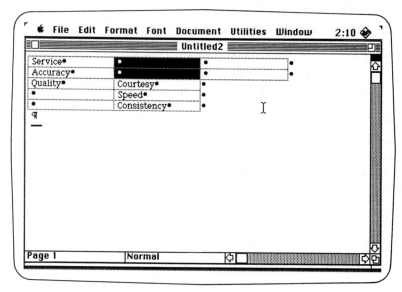

and Moving Cell Contents

reated a table, you can copy and move cell contents within the
you move text. Note, however, that when you cut cell contents,
ove the cell itself; that is, Word doesn't move the cell bound-
ut a whole column or row, the cells remain. If you want just to
r row, don't bother choosing Cut from the Edit menu. Instead,
the Edit menu and click Delete.

rk through these steps:

y, add columns or rows so that you have room for the
vant to copy.

rows, columns, or cells you want to copy.

py from the Edit menu.

s the cell contents to the clipboard.

ells into which you want to paste the clipboard contents.

e Cells from the Edit menu.

w these steps:

add columns or rows so that you have room for the
nt to move.

2. Select the rows, columns, or cells you want to move.

3. Choose Cut from the Edit menu.

   Word copies the cell contents to the clipboard. Note Word does *not*
   delete the rows and columns from which you cut the cell contents.

4. Select the cells to which you want to paste the clipboard contents.

5. Choose Paste Cells from the Edit menu.

Reorganizing a Table by Sorting

Once you have entered data, you may find that you regret the order in which you
have entered it. One solution is to move rows up or down (as just explained). If
you want to sort your table alphabetically or numerically, however, don't do the
job manually—use the Sort command in the Utilities menu.

When you sort a table, you sort by row or by column. When you sort by row,
Word places the selected rows in ascending order, going by the first characters in
the first cell in each row. When you sort by column, however, Word uses the first

characters of the column you have selected to order the rows. Note, though, that the cells in each row are kept together. The only difference between the two techniques is that when you sort by row, the first characters in the row determine the sort order; when you sort by column, the first characters in the column you select determine the sort order.

To sort your table, follow these steps:

1. Select the text you want to sort.

   To sort by row, select the rows. To sort by column, select the column by holding down the Option key and clicking the column.

2. Choose Sort from the Utilities menu.

To cancel the sort, choose Undo from the Edit menu immediately.

To sort a list in descending order, hold down the Shift key and choose Sort from the Utilities menu. The Sort command changes to Sort Descending.

Merging and Splitting Cells

Sometimes you may find it useful to merge two cells into one. For example, in a complex table, a *decked head* is useful for organizing data (see fig. 12.11—the cell containing the title *Expenses* is a decked head). The decked head spans the column headings (also called box heads) and clarifies the table's content. To create a decked head, you merge two cells so that they become one larger cell. If you find the effects displeasing, you can split the cells you have merged.

To merge cells, follow these steps:

1. Select the cells to be merged.

   When you have selected two or more cells horizontally, the Merge Cells button is no longer dimmed.

2. Choose Table from the Edit menu.

3. Click the Merge Cells button.

You cannot split a cell unless you have previously merged it. To split a merged cell, follow these steps:

1. Select the merged cell you want to split.

2. Choose Table from the Edit menu.

   The dialog box now displays a Split Cell button.

3. Click the Split Cell button.

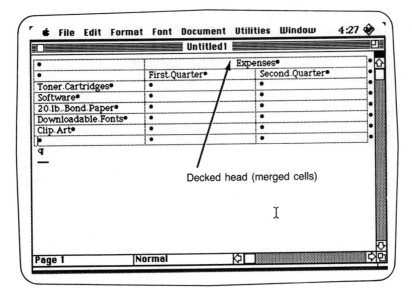

Fig. 12.11.

Merged cells create a table's box head.

Converting Rows into Text

If you have created too many rows for your table, or if you want to transform the table to text for some reason, you can do so with the Table to Text command in the Document menu.

To transform a table into text, follow this procedure:

1. Select the row or rows you want to convert into text.

2. Choose Table to Text from the Document menu.

3. When the Table to Text dialog box appears, click the option for text conversion (see fig. 12.12).

   Click Paragraph if you want to convert the cells to separate paragraphs. Click Tab Delimited if you want to preserve the columnar alignment of the text. Click Comma Delimited if you want to separate the cell contents by commas. (You might choose this option if you were creating text to be used by Print Merge. For more information on Print Merge, see Chapter 16, ''Creating Form Letters and Mailing Labels.'')

4. Click OK.

Fig. 12.12.

Converting a table to text.

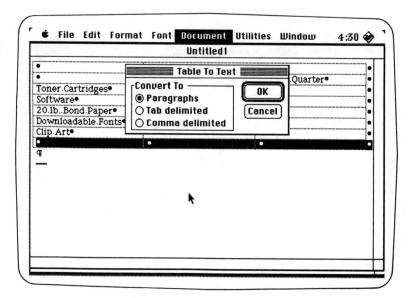

If you have added a table at the beginning of your document, you cannot enter a blank paragraph mark before the table by pressing Return. To enter a blank paragraph mark before a table, place the insertion point before the first end-of-cell mark and press ⌘-Option-space bar.

Formatting a Table

Once you have created a table by using the Insert Table command, you can control its appearance. You can adjust column widths, change the row height, and control the table's alignment on the page.

Adjusting Column Widths

When you create a table, Word automatically calculates column widths so that all the columns are the same. Often, however, you need to reduce or increase the size of one or more columns. This procedure is easy with the Ruler or the Cells command (Format menu). The Ruler command is better for changing the column width for a single selected cell or column.

As you will see when you try this technique, the ruler's function changes when you have selected a cell or cells in a table. The ruler shows you one of two views of the cell contents:

❑ *Default view*. The ruler displays the indents you have chosen (if any) for the text within the cell or cells you have selected (see fig. 12.13). If you drag the indent marks, you change the indents for the text within the selected cell, but you don't change the cell's boundaries.

❑ *Ruler view after clicking the scale icon*. The ruler displays the location of the cell boundaries (see fig. 12.14), marked with column markers (which resemble an uppercase T). If you drag the column markers, you change the width of the column. Note that you alter the width of only the cells you select. To select the whole column, hold down the Option key and click anywhere in the column.

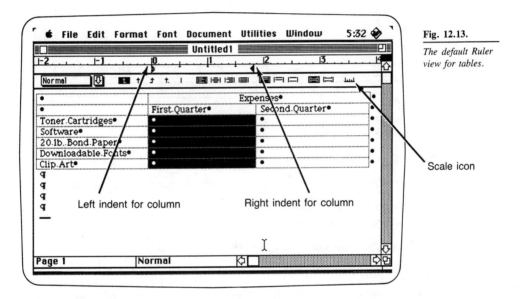

Fig. 12.13.

The default Ruler view for tables.

You also can adjust column widths by using the the Cells command, which has the advantage of letting you change column widths for the entire table, if you want, in addition to formatting just a single cell or column.

To adjust cell or column width with the ruler, follow these steps:

1. Select the cells or columns whose widths you want to change.

   To select an entire column, hold down the Option key and click anywhere in the column.

2. Click the ruler scale icon so that the column border symbols are displayed.

   If the ruler isn't displayed, choose Show Ruler from the Format menu or press ⌘-R.

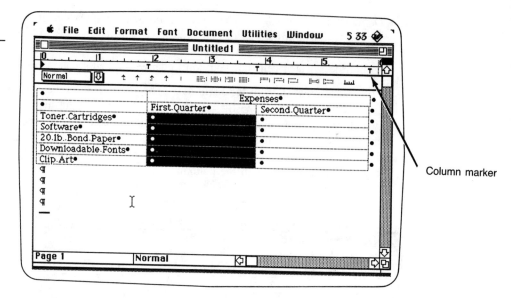

Column marker

3. Drag the column border symbols to the correct positions.

To adjust cell or column width with the Cells command, follow these steps:

1. Select the cells or the columns whose widths you want to change.

   To select an entire column, hold down the Option key and click anywhere in the column.

2. Choose the Cells command from the Format menu.

3. Type a measurement in the Space Between Columns box.

4. Click Selection to change the column width in just the cells you selected. Click Whole Table to change the column width for the entire table.

5. Click OK.

Changing Row Alignment

The Cells command (Format menu) provides a way to specify within the page's margins the alignment of selected rows (or the entire table). You can align the rows flush left, centered, or flush right. Note that these options do not refer to the text within the cells, which you align by using ordinary alignment techniques (such as clicking a ruler icon, using keyboard shortcuts, or choosing the Paragraph command from the Format menu).

To align rows within the margins, follow these steps:

1. Select the rows you want to align.

2. Choose Cells from the Format menu.

3. In the Align Rows box, click Left, Center, or Right.

4. Click Selection to format just the rows you have selected, or click Whole Table.

5. Click OK.

Using Borders

The cell grid lines you see on the screen won't print. But you can use the Cell Borders dialog box to add the borders you want.

The Cell Borders dialog box (see fig. 12.15) closely resembles the Paragraph Borders dialog box, but the boxes have some differences:

❑ *Selected Cells As Block.* Click this button to place borders around a block of cells (that is, don't place borders *within* the block). If you select eight cells in a column, for instance, and then click a box around the diagram in the Cell Borders dialog box, Word draws a box around the block (but no lines appear within the block).

❑ *Every Cell in Selection.* Click this button to add the borders you have chosen to each cell in the selection. If you click a right border, for instance, Word adds a rule to the right border of every cell you have selected.

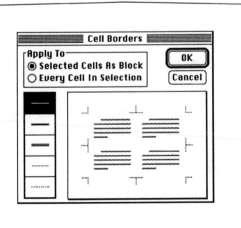

Fig. 12.15.

The Cell Borders dialog box.

To add borders to your table, do the following:

1. Select the cells to which you want to add borders.

2. Choose Cells from the Format menu.

3. When the Cells dialog box appears, click the Borders button.

4. When the Cell Borders dialog box appears, click Selected Cells As Block to place borders around (but not within) the selection. Click Every Cell in Selection to add borders within all the cells you have selected.

5. Click the border style you want (single, thick, double, dotted, and hairline, from top to bottom).

6. Click between the border guides to select the borders you want.

7. Click OK.

8. In the Cells dialog box, click Apply to apply the borders without closing the box or OK to close the box and return to your document.

To add a box quickly around all the cells as a block, double-click the border guides just *outside* the page displayed in the border box. To add a box around all the cells and to turn on all grid lines within the cells, double-click the borders guides *inside* the page.

To remove borders from cells, use the Cell Borders dialog box again and click off the borders you have added. When you see the Cell Borders dialog box, click the border guides again to turn off the borders.

Using Math

Word is no spreadsheet program, but you still can perform useful calculations (such as adding a column or row of numbers in a table). If you must do more extensive computations, create and analyze the data with a spreadsheet program, such as Excel, and transfer the data to Word by using the techniques discussed in "Importing Data from Spreadsheets," in this chapter.

Using the Calculate Command

You can perform calculations at any time by typing an arithmetic expression anywhere in your document, selecting the expression, and using the Calculate command (Utilities menu). The result appears on the status line. Word also places the result in the clipboard, from which you can insert the result by choosing Paste.

To create the expression, type numbers and use the operators listed in Table 12.2. If you include any text in the expression, Word ignores the text.

When Word evaluates arithmetic expressions, it proceeds from left to right without preference for one operator over another. You cannot use parentheses to override the left-to-right order of calculation; parentheses are always interpreted as an indication of a negative number (and thus subtracted).

Table 12.2
Arithmetic Operators for Use with the Calculate Command

Operator	Function
+ (or space)	Addition
− (or parentheses around number)	Subtraction
*	Multiplication
/	Division
÷	Calculates percentage (when typed after a number)

Performing Calculations on a Table

Because Word assumes addition when no other operator is used, you can quickly add up a column or row of figures in a table simply by selecting the row or column and choosing the Calculate command. If you include a figure in parentheses, Word treats the number as a negative number and subtracts it from the total.

If you're selecting a column of numbers in an ordinary table (one created with tabs), hold down the Option key and drag to select a rectangular column on the screen. If you're selecting a column of numbers in a table created with the Table command, hold down Option and click the column to select all the column.

Importing Data from Spreadsheets

Because the Macintosh was designed for easy data interchange, you easily can import data from any spreadsheet program into Word through the clipboard. You simply choose Copy or Cut in the spreadsheet program in order to place the data into the clipboard; then exit the spreadsheet program. After starting Word, you choose Paste, and presto! The data appears, formatted with tab stops to separate the columns of data. You can transform the data into a Word table by selecting the data and choosing Insert Table from the Document menu.

Importing spreadsheet data this way is easy, but this method has one major drawback. Once you have imported the data, you must update the Word table manually if you later change the spreadsheet. If you have Excel, MultiFinder, and at least two megabytes of RAM, however, you can take advantage of a unique Word feature called QuickSwitch. QuickSwitch enables you to import an Excel spreadsheet (or part of one) with an *active* link between the spreadsheet and the Word document. If you make changes to the spreadsheet after importing the data, you can update the Word version of the spreadsheet instantly just by choosing the Update Link command.

This chapter isn't the place for a review of the techniques you use to start your Macintosh with MultiFinder (instead of the ordinary Finder); nor are the techniques you use to start and switch among programs discussed here. Our concern is with the specifics of using QuickSwitch with Excel and Word. For information on Multifinder, see the manuals that came with your Macintosh.

Importing Data from Excel to Word with QuickSwitch

To copy data from Microsoft Excel (Version 1.5 or higher) to Word with Quick-Switch, follow these steps:

1. Before copying the data, save your spreadsheet to disk.

2. Select in Excel the cells that you want to copy into a Word document.

3. Choose Copy from Excel's Edit menu.

4. Switch to Microsoft Word by clicking the program icon in the upper right corner or choosing the application name from the Apple menu.

5. Position the insertion point where you want the data to appear.

6. Choose Paste Link from the Edit menu.

   Word inserts a paragraph of hidden text. This paragraph contains information that tells Word where to find the file from which you inserted the data.

7. Choose Insert Table from the Document menu to format the data as a Word table.

Updating Data with QuickSwitch

If you want to change the data in an Excel spreadsheet you have already imported into Word, you have two choices:

❏ *Update Link*. Choose this option in Word to update data you have *already* changed in your Excel spreadsheet. Word imports the data again, replacing the old Word table with the new version.

❏ *Edit Link*. Choose this option in Word to open the Excel spreadsheet and change the data. When you have changed the data, Word updates the table in your Word document.

To update a table after you have made the changes to your Excel spreadsheet (Version 1.5 or later), follow these steps:

1. Select the Excel data you want to update. You can select part of the table or all of it.

2. Choose Update Link from the Edit menu.

Word starts Excel if it isn't already open and opens the spreadsheet containing the data (if the spreadsheet isn't open). Word then updates the linked information.

To make the changes to your Excel spreadsheet and update the changes to Word, do the following:

1. Select the Excel data you want to update. You can select part of the table or all of it.

2. Hold down the .Shift key and choose Edit Link from the Edit menu.

   If you don't hold down the Shift key, you won't see the Edit Link option.

   If Excel and your document aren't open already, Word starts Excel and opens your document.

3. Edit or recalculate the Excel spreadsheet.

4. Press ⌘-, [comma] (the QuickSwitch command) to update the Word table and return to Word.

If you want to return to Word without updating the Word table, use one of the MultiFinder techniques for switching programs (such as clicking the program icon in the upper right corner).

Creating, Numbering, and Sorting Lists

Business and professional memos, letters, and reports contain lists of every conceivable kind: price lists, parts lists, specification lists, item lists, and on and on. If your boss is a little paranoid, you may even find yourself typing an enemies list. Scholars, for their part, list bibliographic citations, interview subjects, inventories of archaeological artifacts, and journals that have rejected their articles. There's no way around it—sooner or later, you will create a list yourself. If you're using Word, happily, you can automate the task substantially by taking full advantage of this program's capability to format, number, and sort lists with automated precision.

Creating a List

The easiest way to create a list is to type a series of paragraphs with a special format, such as a hanging indent. Make each item in the list a separate paragraph. That way, you can number and sort the list automatically.

Creating a Multiple-Column List

Many lists, such as parts lists and glossaries (lists of terms and their definitions), require a multiple-column format. The best way to create a multiple-column list is to create a table by using the Insert Table command (see fig. 12.16). Creating a table with this command is very easy. Because each cell is "infinitely" expandable, when you add text, Word wraps the text down to the next line in the cell automatically (and expands the adjacent cell to match the size of the cell in which you're typing). You can add borders by choosing Cells from the Format menu and clicking the Borders button.

Fig. 12.16.

Two-column table created with the Insert Table command.

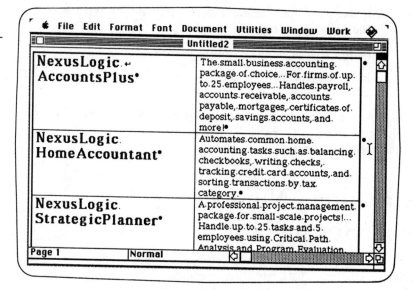

Sorting a List

Don't worry about putting your list in alphabetical order. Let Word do the alphabetizing for you. If you choose the Sort command from the Utilities menu, Word sorts in ascending order the paragraphs or table rows you have selected.

Unlike most programs, Word doesn't sort in strict ASCII order—which is good, because the order of ASCII characters doesn't match the guidelines that most style handbooks follow in recommending sorting order. For example, Word ignores punctuation marks—such as quotation marks, spaces, and tabs—when sorting text. And when you're sorting numbers, 2,519 comes before 25,190, which isn't the case in many programs.

To sort a list, following these steps:

1. Select all the items in the list.

2. Choose Sort from the Utilities menu.

To sort a list in descending order, hold down the Shift key before choosing Sort from the Utilities menu.

Numbering a List

If you have created a list with ordinary paragraphs, you can quickly add numbers to the items with the Renumber command (Utilities menu).

To number the items in a list created with paragraphs, do the following:

1. Select all the items in the list.

2. Choose Renumber from the Utilities menu.

3. When the Renumber dialog box appears, click OK (see fig. 12.17).

To cancel the numbering, choose Undo from the Edit menu immediately.

If you have created a list with a Word table, you must manually insert a dummy number at the beginning of each row. Type *1* followed by a period and a space at the beginning of each row. When you see the Renumber dialog box, click the Only if Already Numbered button.

Fig. 12.17.

*The Renumber
dialog box.*

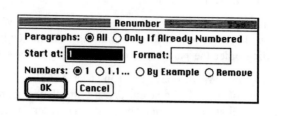

High-Productivity Techniques To Remember

❏ Don't create tables by setting tabs; use the Insert Table command instead. It's much easier to create a table with the Insert Table command.

❏ Learn the mouse commands for selecting cells, rows, and columns. Once you have learned them, you will find it easy to edit your tables.

❏ Choose Table from the Edit menu to edit the table matrix. You can insert or delete cells, rows, or columns as you want.

❏ To edit the cell contents (without affecting the matrix), use the Copy, Cut, and Paste commands in the Edit menu.

❏ To create headings that span two or more columns, learn how to merge cells.

❏ Click the scale icon on the Ruler to display the Column menu. Select the column and drag the marker to change column boundaries quickly.

❏ If you have Excel and at least 2MB of RAM, by all means investigate the QuickSwitch techniques that allow you to create an active link between an Excel spreadsheet and a table in a Word document. If you change the spreadsheet, you can update the Word table just by choosing one command.

❏ Use the Insert Table command to create a two-column list. This command replaces the side-by-side paragraph commands used in earlier versions of Word.

CHAPTER 13

Creating Business Forms

Every organization uses forms of one sort or another, and for good reason: they're essential tools for making sure that you get the information you need. Whether you're going through employment applications, quarterly reports, or time sheets, every form must contain all the information your organization requires. A well-designed form, one that prompts you for all the required information, is a real asset in a business or professional setting.

You can create two different kinds of forms with Word: forms you print and reproduce in quantity, and on-screen forms, which you fill in as you sit at your Macintosh. The forms you print and reproduce, such as employment application forms or order forms, take the place of forms you would otherwise have to pay a print shop to design. With Word's desktop publishing capabilities, however, you no longer need to hand over substantial sums to layout artists. You can easily design a professional-looking form with Word. And if you do, you can save your organization a tidy sum of money. What's more, if the form needs revision, you can make the necessary changes with Word in a matter of minutes, thus saving the trouble and time of contacting the printer again for yet another expensive go-round with the layout artist.

On-screen forms have their place, too, in your strategy to improve your business productivity. These forms are especially useful for invoices, period reports, or other applications in which you're the person who's filling in the form. As you will see, you can use Word's Print Merge instructions to set up a system that makes filling in such forms virtually automatic.

Creating your own business forms with Word is one of this book's biggest money- and time-saving applications. The key to creating business forms with Word is to make full use of Word 4's new Table commands, introduced in Chapter 12, "Creating Tables and Lists." To illustrate the use of these commands for creating business forms, this chapter presents an extended tutorial. The form you will create is shown in figure 13.1. To illustrate Word's many applications for the creation of on-screen forms, you also will learn how to create a form that bills clients for the time you spend providing professional services.

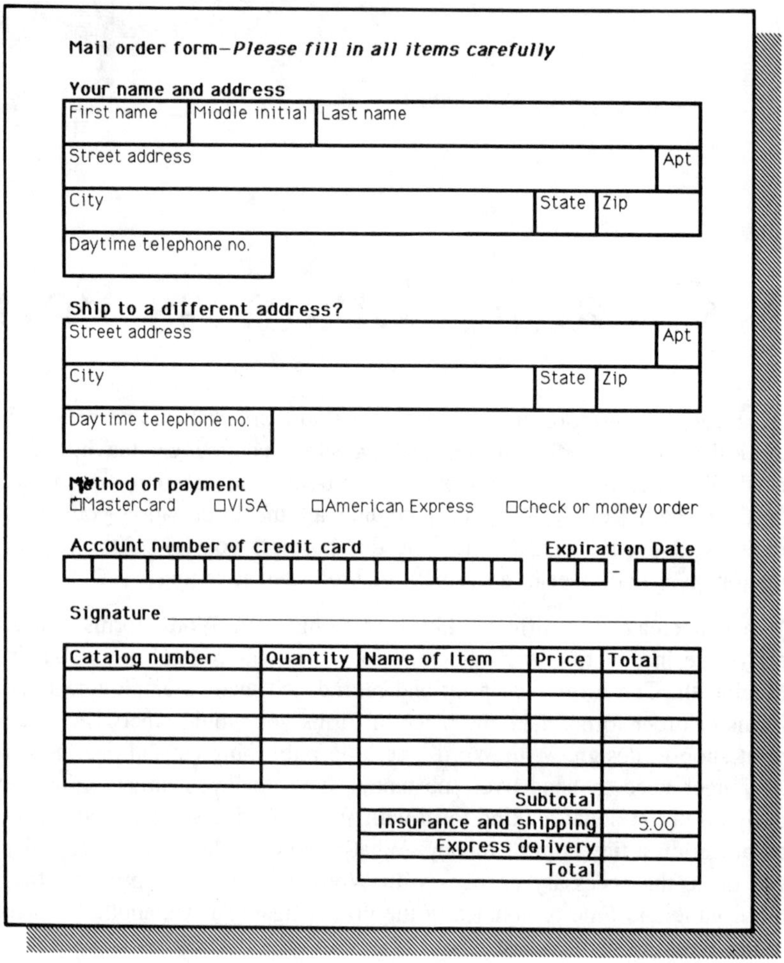

Fig. 13.1.

Form created with Word's Table commands.

Mail order form–*Please fill in all items carefully*

Your name and address

First name	Middle initial	Last name

Street address		Apt

City	State	Zip

Daytime telephone no.

Ship to a different address?

Street address		Apt

City	State	Zip

Daytime telephone no.

Method of payment
☐MasterCard   ☐VISA   ☐American Express   ☐Check or money order

Account number of credit card   **Expiration Date**

☐☐☐☐☐☐☐☐☐☐☐☐☐☐   ☐☐ - ☐☐

Signature _____

Catalog number	Quantity	Name of Item	Price	Total
		Subtotal		
		Insurance and shipping		5.00
		Express delivery		
		Total		

Tutorial: Designing a Business Form

In this tutorial, you will learn how to create a business form you can print and duplicate; it's designed to be filled in by hand. If you have your own application in mind, you can adapt the tutorial to your needs as you go along. If not, following the tutorial will teach you all the techniques you need to produce professional-looking business forms in short order.

To start this tutorial, open a new Word document.

1. Type *Mail Order Form* and press Return twice.

2. Choose Insert Table from the Document menu.

3. When the Insert Table dialog box appears, type *3* in the Number of Columns box and *4* in the Number of Rows box.

4. Click OK. Word enters the table.

5. Click the scale icon on the ruler to show the cell boundary markers (see fig. 13.2).

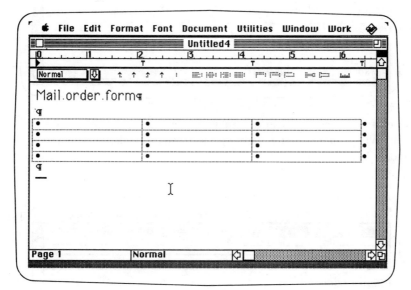

Fig. 13.2.

Cell boundary markers (T symbols on the ruler).

6. Type the headings shown in figure 13.3. Press Return after typing each heading to double-space the cells as shown.

7. If the ruler isn't displayed, choose Show Ruler from the Format menu or press ⌘-R.

Your form is coming along nicely, but you don't need all the blank cells.

1. Select one of the empty, unwanted cells.

2. Choose Table from the Edit menu.

3. Click the Selection button in the Table dialog box.

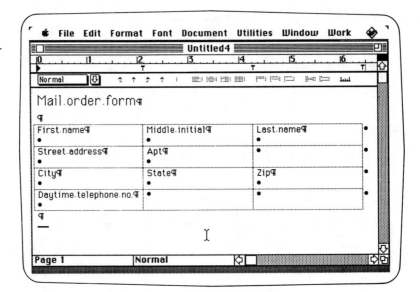

Fig. 13.3.

*Adding headings
to the form.*

4. Click the Delete button in the Table dialog box. Word deletes the cell. When you're finished deleting the unwanted cells, your table should look like figure 13.4.

Fig. 13.4.

*Table after
deleting unneeded
cells.*

Now it's time to add borders.

1. Move the mouse pointer to the selection bar next to the first row and double-click. Hold down the button after the second click and drag down to select the whole table.

2. Choose Cells from the Format menu.

3. When the Cells dialog box appears, click the Border button.

4. When the Cell Borders dialog box appears, click Every Cell in Selection under Apply To.

5. Click the thick line option.

6. Click all four borders of the boundary icon.

7. Click OK in the Cell Borders dialog box.

8. Click OK in the Cell dialog box. Word applies the borders as shown in figure 13.5.

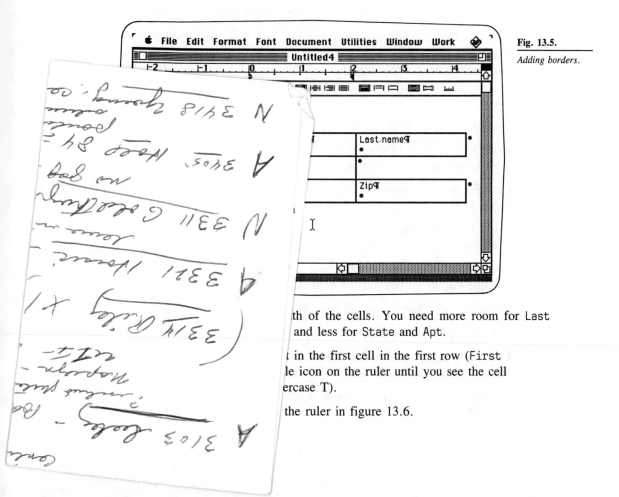

Fig. 13.5.

Adding borders.

th of the cells. You need more room for Last and less for State and Apt.

t in the first cell in the first row (First le icon on the ruler until you see the cell ercase T).

the ruler in figure 13.6.

Fig. 13.6.

Sizing cells by dragging the cell boundary markers.

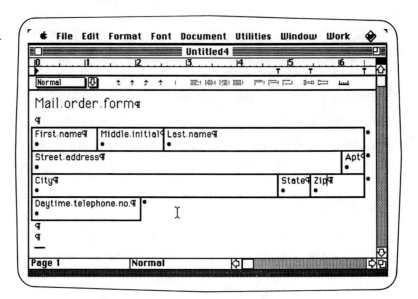

2. Click the first T on the ruler and drag left until you have reduced the size of the first cell to about 1.3 inches. Watch the lower left corner of the status line as you drag the boundary markers; you will see a measurement showing where you have positioned the marker on the ruler.

3. Select the Middle initial cell and shrink it the same way.

4. Expand the Last name scale to the right margin (the dotted line on the ruler) by dragging the T marker right.

5. Continue in this way until you have sized all the cells as shown in figure 13.6.

Now that you have sized the cells, you can copy part of this table for the next section of the form.

1. Double-click in the selection bar next to the second row of the table (the one that starts with Street address).

2. Drag down to select the rest of the table.

3. Choose Copy from the Edit menu.

4. Place the insertion point below the table. Press Return two times, if necessary, to create blank lines under the table.

5. Choose Paste cells from the Edit menu. Word inserts the table at the position of the insertion point.

6. Add the headings shown in figure 13.7 (Your name and address and Ship to a different address?).

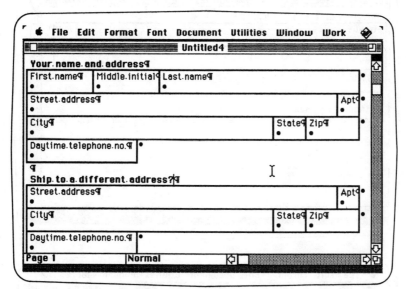

Fig. 13.7.

Adding additional headings.

7. Now type the heading *Method of payment.*

8. To enter the check boxes as shown in figure 13.8, use the Key Caps desk accessory to find a key that enters a blank box. If you're using Geneva, press Option-H or Option-K to enter the boxes.

9. Type the headings with the check boxes.

Next, you create the boxes for credit card numbers and a signature line.

1. Press Return twice to create blank lines. Position the insertion point on the second blank line and choose Insert Table from the Document menu.

2. When the Insert Table dialog box appears, type *22* in the Number of Columns box and click OK. Word enters a table with one row and 22 columns.

3. Select the first 16 columns and use the Cell Borders dialog box to add thick borders around these cells. Then skip a cell and add borders to the next two cells. Finally, add borders to the last two cells in the row, as shown in figure 13.9.

4. Press Return twice, type *Signature*, and hold down the underline key to create the signature line.

Fig. 13.8.

*Adding check
boxes.*

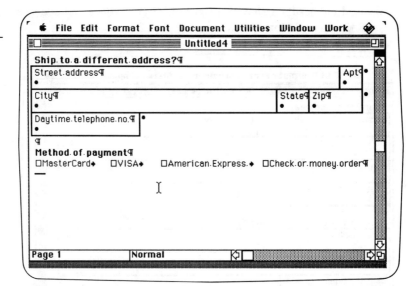

Fig. 13.8.

*Adding check
boxes.*

Fig. 13.9.

*Adding borders to
the 22-column
table.*

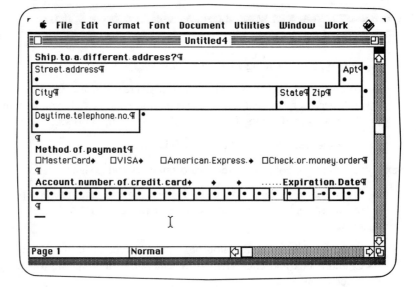

Your next step is to create the spaces for order information.

1. Press Return twice and choose Insert Table from the Document menu.

2. Type *5* in the Number of Columns box and *10* in the Number of Rows box. Click OK. Word enters the table.

3. Place the insertion point in the first cell of the first row, hold down the Option key, and click the mouse button. You have selected the column.

4. Click the scale icon on the ruler, if necessary, to display the boundary markers, and drag the column marker to the 2-inch mark on the ruler.

5. Continue sizing the columns in this way and type the headings as shown in figure 13.10.

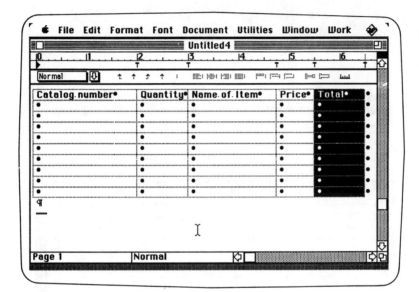

Fig. 13.10.

Adding more headings.

Now you will delete four of the columns from the last four rows.

6. In the last four rows, select the cells as shown in figure 13.11.

7. Choose Table from the Edit menu.

8. Click the Selection button. Then click the Delete button.

9. Select the last four rows of the first column and adjust their size and position as shown in figure 13.12.

10. To add the headings to the last four rows as shown in figure 13.12, drag down the first column in these rows. Then click the scale icon in the ruler until the paragraph alignment icons appear. Click the flush right icon. Then type the headings. To enter the shipping charge, select the cell and click a decimal tab stop in the center of the column on the ruler.

Fig. 13.11.

Selecting cells for deletion.

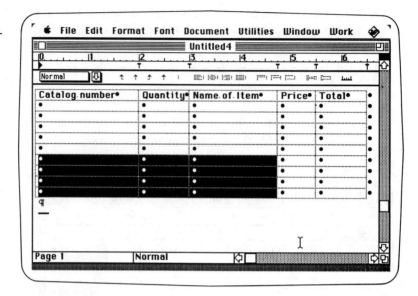

Fig. 13.12.

Positioning the last four rows.

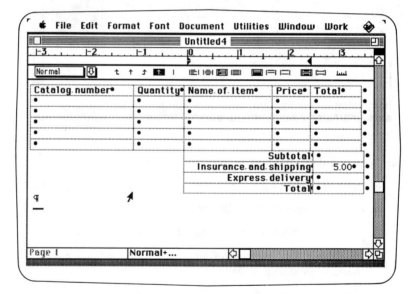

11. Double-click in the selection bar next to the first row of the table and drag down to select all the cells. Then use the Cell Borders command to add thick borders to all cells, as shown in figure 13.13.

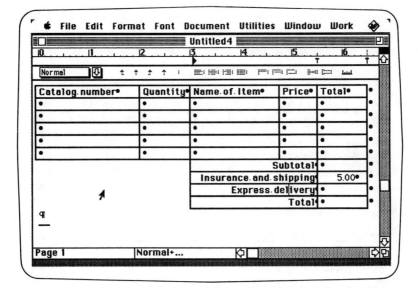

Fig. 13.13.

Adding more borders.

That's it! You have created in a matter of minutes a form that would have cost at least $100 to have professionally typeset. And what's more, if you need to change the form, you can do it in minutes without a time-consuming (and costly) trip to the printer.

Creating On-Screen Forms

The tutorial you just completed shows you how to create forms you can print and then reproduce in quantity. These forms are for other people to fill in—people such as your clients, customers, or employees. To save time with the forms you fill in yourself, you can use on-screen forms: forms you fill in as you sit at your Macintosh and then print in their completed version.

The application described in this section is of greatest value to you when you automate a form that you must complete periodically, such as a weekly time sheet, an invoice, or a quarterly report. Such forms aren't reproduced in quantity; at most, you will make only two or three copies of them. What's important is remembering to fill in all the necessary information! To help you do so, this application uses the ASK instruction from Word's armada of Print Merge commands, which are normally employed for form letter applications (see Chapter 16 for more information on form letters). However, you can use this Print Merge technique for producing just one copy of a completed form.

The next chapter discusses two techniques you can use to improve the appearance of business forms: graphics and absolutely positioned design elements. Using these techniques, you can add a company logo to a business form as shown in figure 13.14.

Fig. 13.14.

Adding a logo.

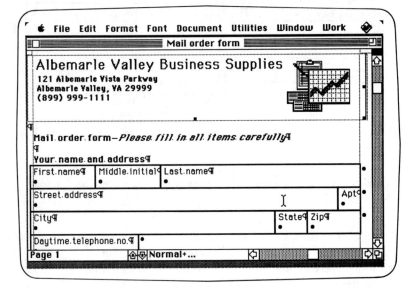

As you will see, you can use ASK instructions to display a series of on-screen dialog boxes, each of which prompts you to supply an item of information that's needed to fill in the form. From the information you supply, Word automatically completes the form. You can print the form right away, or if you want, Word will display the filled-in form in a new document in which you can perform calculations or add additional text.

Using the ASK instruction

With a little experimentation, you can see for yourself how the ASK instruction works. Try the following tutorial to get an idea of how to use the ASK instruction:

1. In a new Word document, press Option-backslash to enter a left chevron.

   Don't use less-than or greater-than symbols to create the chevrons. You must use the special symbol Word inserts when you press Option-backslash.

2. Type *ASK yourname = ?Hi! What's your name?*

3. Press Shift-Option-backslash to enter a right chevron. The whole ASK instruction should be surrounded with chevrons, like this:

   «ASK yourname=?Hi! What's your name?»

4. Press Return twice.

5. Type the variable name (*yourname*) surrounded by chevrons, like this

   «your name»

   You can create variable names of up to 65 characters in length.

6. Choose Print Merge from the File menu and click the Print button.

   You will see the dialog box shown in figure 13.15.

7. Click Stop Merge.

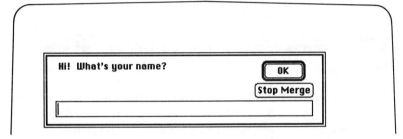

Fig. 13.15.

The dialog box you see after clicking the Print button.

That's the basic idea. As you can see, creating an ASK application is quite easy, so you can put this feature to work for you on a regular basis. In the next section, you will learn how to create an application that uses many ASK instructions.

If you're planning to experiment with ASK instructions, take advantage of a Glossary entry called Print Merge. This entry places the two chevrons in your document with the insertion point positioned between them. Add the entry to the Work menu by pressing ⌘-Option-Plus (on the keyboard, not the keypad), choosing Glossary, and choosing the Print Merge entry in the Glossary dialog box.

Power
User
Tip

Setting Up a Client Billing System with ASK Instructions

If you create a document with many ASK instructions (see fig. 13.16), you see a series of dialog boxes, not just one, when you choose Print Merge. These boxes query you, one after the other, for information to be entered on the form. In this way, you can set up an application that automates the procedure you follow when you fill in a form.

Fig. 13.16.

ASK instructions in an on-screen form.

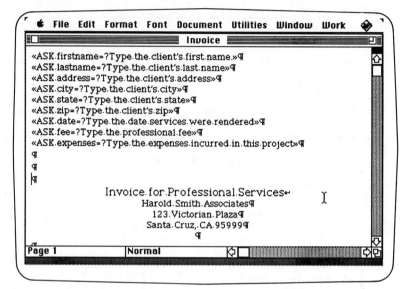

Each of the variable names mentioned in the ASK instructions appears on the form (see fig. 13.17). Note that each is surrounded by chevrons. Without the chevrons, Word cannot distinguish the variable names from other words on the form.

Fig. 13.17.

Form with variable names.

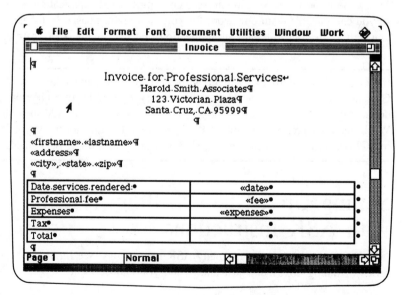

When you choose the Print Merge command to print this form, Word presents the ASK dialog boxes and automatically inserts the information you type in place of the variable names. In other words, Word fills in the form from the information you type in dialog boxes. You don't need to move the cursor or concentrate on what information is needed—Word prompts you to supply all the information by showing you the series of dialog boxes.

In this example, you print the form by choosing the New Document option in the Print Merge dialog box. This option tells Word to ''print'' the form to a file rather than send it to the printer. You can modify this file as you please, adding additional text or (as is required in this case) performing calculations and adding totals.

You will learn more about Print Merge and its many applications in Chapter 16. For now, it's time to survey one of Word's most remarkable features—its capability to integrate text and graphics on the same screen.

High-Productivity Techniques To Remember

❏ To create business forms quickly, use Word 4's new Table commands. You create the form by entering tables, adjusting the cells and columns, and adding borders.

❏ When you start the form, use a rough approximation of the number of rows and columns you need. You can always edit the table after you create it.

❏ To adjust column boundaries horizontally, display the ruler and click the scale icon until you see the T symbols. Select the cell or column and drag the T symbols.

❏ To add borders to the table, choose Cells in the Edit menu and click the Borders button.

❏ Use paragraph alignment options and tabs to format text within cells.

❏ Enhance your forms by adding graphics (see Chapter 14 for more information on importing graphics into Word documents).

❏ If you must complete the same form on a regular basis, consider automating the procedure by using ASK instructions. Create a list of ASK instructions that prompt you for all the information you need to enter on the form.

14

Page Layout Strategies with Text and Graphics

Although Microsoft Word isn't a desktop publishing program in the strict sense of the term, most users have found previous versions of the program more than adequate for a wide variety of desktop publishing applications, such as creating newsletters, price lists, instruction manuals, brochures, and guidebooks. With Version 4, the addition of an extremely important new feature, the Position command, makes the program far more than merely "adequate" for desktop publishing applications. With the Position command, you can "anchor" paragraphs of text or graphics on the page, so that text "floats" around the anchored frame. Just what this means will be clearer to you after you have experimented with the Position command, but suffice it to say that with the addition of this new feature, the increasingly murky boundary between desktop publishing and word processing software has become even less distinct.

Imagine a program that includes all the text-creation and text-editing features we have already discussed, including Word's incredible outlining capabilities. With these features, you can create, edit, and reorganize the text in your document until it meets the highest standards of professional and business communications. Now imagine taking that text, the text you have polished using Word's many tools, and expressing it in a page design that fully captures the spirit of your communicative intentions. Whether you're designing something as mundane as a price list or as important as an employee newsletter, you're very likely to find that Word has all the tools you need to do the job with professional-looking results.

Word's multiple-column, graphics, and positioning features are exceptionally easy to use. So if you have ever contemplated creating a well-designed newsletter, brochure, or flier, by all means explore the techniques discussed in this chapter.

319

Creating Columns and Newsletters

Word does an excellent job of arranging text in snaking columns, in which text runs down the page to the bottom and then "snakes" over and up to the top of the next column.

Most of this section focuses on these snaking columns, the column format of choice for newsletters, brochures, and most other multiple-column applications. Word's facilities for creating, formatting, and printing snaking columns are excellent. You can blend single- and multiple-column text on one page with a minimum of effort. Thanks to Word's new Page View mode, you can view multiple-column text and edit at the same time. And with the Border command, you can add thin lines (rules) to delineate the columns, creating an effect that's perfect for newsletters.

You also can create side-by-side paragraphs with Word; in this format, paragraphs are always linked so that the one always appears adjacent to the next. Side-by-side paragraphs are appropriate for lists, such as parts lists. In previous versions of Word, creating side-by-side paragraphs was quite time-consuming; you had to adjust paragraph indents to get the paragraphs to print correctly. With Version 4, however, creating side-by-side paragraphs with Word's new Table commands is very easy. You will learn how to create side-by-side paragraphs at the end of this section.

Creating Multiple-Column Text

Multiple-column text is a section format. To create multiple-column text, therefore, you use the Section command. If your document has only one section, the column format you choose in the Section dialog box affects your whole document. If you have divided your document into two or more sections by creating section breaks, however, you can blend single-column and multiple-column formats as you please.

To blend single- and multiple-column text in one document, you press ⌘-Enter to create a section break, thus dividing the single-column and multiple-column sections from each other, and you format the multiple-column section with the Section command.

Because the number of section breaks you create is unlimited, you can change column formats as many times as you want within a document, and you can use more than one column format on a page.

To create multiple-column text, follow these steps:

1. Choose Section from the Format menu.

2. When the Section dialog box appears (see fig. 14.1), type the number of columns you want in the Number box.

   If you want, change the default spacing between columns (0.5 inch).

3. Click OK.

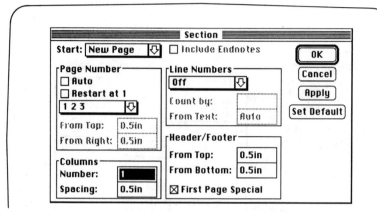

Fig. 14.1.

The Section dialog box.

Blending Single- and Multiple-Column Text in a Document

Changing column formats is easy, but you need to watch out for a potential trap. When you press ⌘-Enter to create a section break, Word may insert an unwanted page break at the section break. To blend single- and multiple-column text on a page, therefore, you must format the new section so that Word doesn't start a new page where the section break is located.

Why does Word sometimes create a page break when you enter a section break? When Word creates the new section, it copies the section formats currently in effect. If those formats are the default ones, then each new section will start with a page break.

To enter a section break without entering a page break, follow these steps:

1. Position the cursor where you want the section break to occur.

2. Press ⌘-Enter.

   Word enters a double-dotted line to mark the location of the section break.

3. Place the insertion point below the section break.

4. Choose Section from the Format menu.

5. Click the arrow on the Start dropdown box and choose the No Break option (see fig. 14.2).

6. Type the number of columns you want in the Columns box.

7. Click OK.

Fig. 14.2.

Choosing the No Break option in the Start dropdown box.

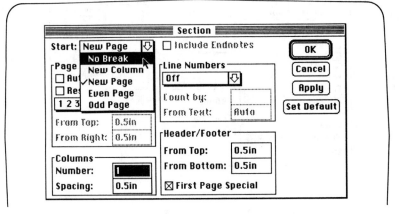

Blank lines at the tops and bottoms of columns can produce an unattractive effect, making the columns look unbalanced. To prevent blank lines, do not click the open space icon on the ruler or add blank lines before or after paragraph formats when you use the Paragraph dialog box. Enter blank lines by pressing Enter. That way, you can easily delete any blank lines that appear at the top or bottom of a column.

If you're using Widow Control (on by default), Word may insert a blank line at the top or bottom of a column to prevent widows and orphans. To disable Widow Control, click the Widow Control box in the Document dialog box so that the X disappears.

Automatic Column Balancing

When you end a multiple-column section by inserting a section break and formatting the new section with a different column format, Word groups all the columns of the previous format at the top of the page. This feature is called column balancing. In figure 14.3, for example, a two-column format is ended by a single column, which contains a bar (imported as a graphic from SuperPaint). Inserting the single-column format caused Word to group the two-column paragraphs above the bar, producing the results shown in the figure.

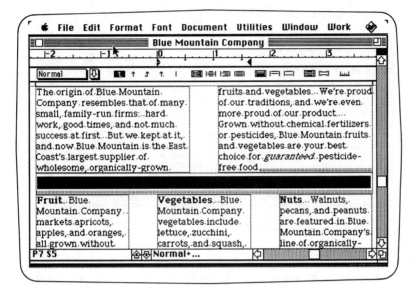

Fig. 14.3.

Automatic column balancing produced by changing column formats.

Adding a Banner over Columns

A banner is a headline or title that spans two or more columns (see fig. 14.4). You can enter a banner easily by inserting a single-column section for the banner above the multiple-column text. In figure 14.4, note the section break (the double-dotted line) that divides the single-column banner section from the multiple-column text section.

To add a banner over multiple-column text, follow this procedure:

1. Type the banner text and choose alignment options to format it as you please.

2. Press Return to start a new paragraph.

3. Press ⌘-Enter to create a section break.

4. Place the insertion point below the section break.

5. Choose Section from the Format menu, click the arrow on the Start dropdown box, and choose the No Break option.

6. Type the number of columns you want in the Columns box.

7. Click OK.

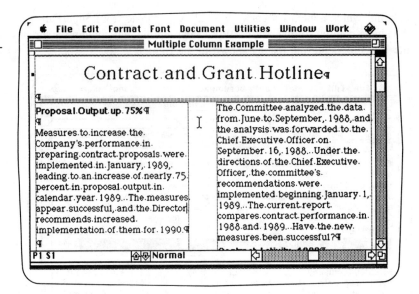

Fig. 14.4.

A banner (headline) spanning multiple-column text.

With Word's new Position command, you can create a banner that spans only two columns in a three-column format (see fig. 14.5). When you anchor the paragraph, you specify a column width equal to the width of the columns you want to span. For more information on the Position command, see ''Anchoring Text and Graphics on the Page'' later in this chapter.

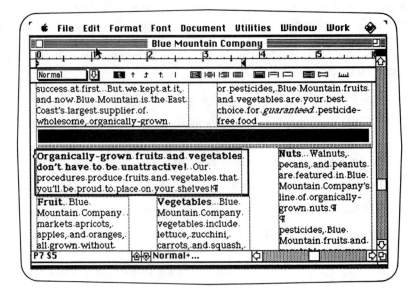

Fig. 14.5.

Positioning a banner over two columns in a three-column format.

Controlling Column Breaks

When you create snaking columns, Word breaks columns automatically, just as it breaks pages automatically in single-column documents. If you want, however, you can override Word's automatic column breaks by inserting a forced column break (like a forced page break, except that it forces Word to start a new column rather than starting a new page). To force a column break, you first create a section break and then format the new section using the New Column option in the Start dropdown box of the Section dialog box.

To control column breaks, follow these steps:

1. Position the cursor where you want the column break to occur.

2. Press ⌘-Enter.

   Word enters a double-dotted line to mark the location of the section break.

3. Place the insertion point below the new section break.

4. Choose Section from the Format menu.

5. Click the arrow on the Start dropdown box and choose the New Column option.

6. Type the number of columns you want in the Columns box.

7. Click OK.

Adding Newspaper Borders

If you're producing a newsletter, you may want to add vertical lines (called rules) to the sides of your columns (see fig. 14.6). To produce a single vertical rule between two columns, however, can be tricky.

The following steps outline a way around this problem. With this approach, you create columns with rules on both sides, but adjust the spacing so that the rules between the columns overlap. The result is a single rule between the two columns. Try these settings to add newspaper borders to two-column text:

1. Place the insertion point in the section containing the multiple-column text.

2. Choose Section from the Format menu.

3. Type *0.4 in* in the Spacing box and click OK.

4. Select all the paragraphs in the section.

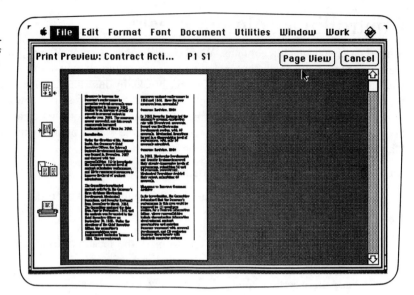

5. Choose Paragraph from the Format menu.

6. Click the Borders button.

7. When the Paragraph Borders dialog box appears, type *0.2 in* in the Spacing box.

   Be sure to do this step before you click the borders. If you do this step after you click the borders, the spacing you choose will not take effect.

8. Click the left and right borders of the page icon.

   To verify whether you have completed this step correctly, make sure that there is a space between the borders and the ''lines'' in the page icon.

9. Click OK.

To preview the borders, choose Print Preview from the File menu. Make sure that the center border is one line. If you see two lines down the center of two columns instead of one, experiment with the spacing options until the lines overlap in the center of the page.

Previewing Column Formatting

When you create multiple columns in Galley view, you see only one column on the screen, but Word operates at maximum speed. To view the multiple-column layout while you continue editing, choose Page View from the Document menu. (You will, however, have to sacrifice display and scrolling speed.) To view the overall layout of columns on the page, choose Print Preview from the File menu.

Creating Side-by-Side Paragraphs

Creating side-by-side paragraphs, multiple-column paragraphs that are linked so that they always print together (instead of ''snaking''), is very easy with Version 4 of Word. You simply create a table by using the Insert Table command, as discussed in Chapter 12, ''Creating Tables and Lists.'' When you choose the Insert Table command, you specify the number of columns you want, such as two or three. You also specify the number of rows of paragraphs you want. To create a table with ten pairs of paragraphs then, you would type *2* in the Columns text box and *10* in the Rows text box when you use the Insert Table dialog box. If you're not sure how many rows you need, you should underestimate the total: you can add rows more easily than you can delete unwanted ones.

To create a side-by-side paragraph format, use this procedure:

1. Position the insertion point where you want the side-by-side paragraphs to appear.

2. Choose Insert Table from the Document menu.

3. When the Insert Table dialog box appears, type the number of columns you want in the Columns box. Then type the number of rows of linked paragraphs you want in the Rows box.

   If you're not exactly sure how many rows or columns you need, don't worry; you can add or delete rows and columns later.

   After you type the number of rows and columns you want, Word calculates the column width automatically, assuming that each column is the same width. You can adjust column widths as you please later. To specify a column width (and override the automatic column width calculation), type a number in the Column Width box.

4. Click OK. Word creates the table and enters the grid pattern in your document.

Once you have created the format, typing the side-by-side paragraphs is a cinch. As you type, Word ''wraps'' the lines within each cell in the table, expanding the cell downward as necessary to accommodate the text you're entering (see fig. 14.7). Just press Tab to move to the next cell and keep typing.

Fig. 14.7.

*Side-by-side
paragraphs.*

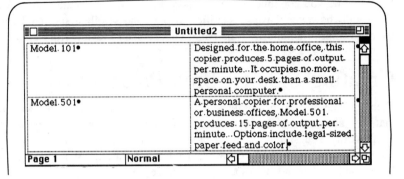

Integrating Text and Graphics

One of the joys of Macintosh computing is the ease with which you can blend text and graphics in a single document. Version 4 of Word includes many features that make integrating text and graphics very easy; the program even comes with a free copy of SuperPaint, an excellent graphics program that combines the painting tools of MacPaint with the drawing tools of MacDraw. By no means are you limited to SuperPaint files when you incorporate graphics into Word documents. In the Macintosh environment, you can create many different kinds of graphics files. Some formats are unique and cannot be imported or exported from one program to another. Most graphics files, however, conform to one of the following three standards:

❑ Bit-mapped graphics programs, such as MacPaint and SuperPaint (in its Paint mode), create graphics composed of pixels, discrete black or white dots on the screen. The advantage of bit-mapped graphics is that you can edit them, dot by dot, producing artistic effects. (Most paint programs include a ''blow-up'' mode that lets you manipulate individual dots at high magnification.) The drawback to bit-mapped graphics is that their resolution is limited to the 72-dots-per-inch resolution of the display screen; therefore, if you include a graphic in a document you print on a LaserWriter, the graphic (with 72-dots-per-inch resolution) will seem crude and rough in comparison to the text (with up to 300-dots-per-inch resolution). You can improve the appearance of bit-mapped graphics somewhat by scaling them down by 50 percent once you have pasted them into Word, but the appearance of bit-mapped graphics will usually seem crude and amateurish next to the fine-edged beauty of laser-printed text.

❑ QuickDraw object-oriented graphics are composed of graphics objects, such as circles and lines, that make up the image. Unlike bit-mapped graphics, which are nothing more than an assemblage of unconnected dots on the screen, the object-oriented graphics aren't just patterns of dots; they're entities generated by mathematical formulas. These entities (and their formulas) are encoded in your Macintosh's read-only memory (ROM), so a file made up of such graphics can contain just the information needed to ''point'' to these entities, making for more compact files. For printing, the advantage of object-oriented graphics is that they automatically print at your printer's highest level of resolution (up to 300 dots per inch for LaserWriters). Their disadvantage is that, unlike bit-mapped graphics, you cannot edit the image dot-by-dot on the screen. But programs such as MacDraw or SuperPaint (in its drawing mode) offer the tools you need to edit such drawings with ease.

❑ PostScript graphics use the PostScript printer language, which provides powerful tools for creating graphics on PostScript-compatible printers, such as the Apple LaserWriter. PostScript graphics are by far the sharpest and most detailed (a PostScript graphic can include dots as small as 1/2540 inch in width). Unlike bit-mapped or object-oriented graphics, PostScript graphics are programs, or lists of instructions, that generate the image on the printer. You can write such programs yourself, line by line, but you must learn the PostScript language. Happily, several graphics programs (such as Cricket Draw and Adobe Illustrator) generate PostScript graphics code from pictures you create on the screen; you can paste such pictures into Word and print them at the same time you print Word documents. The result is outstanding clarity and resolution.

Note: Because the Macintosh screen can display only 72 dots per inch, the screen version of a PostScript graphic created by a program such as Adobe Illustrator has less resolution than the image that appears on the printer. The PostScript code is hidden within the graphic image.

No matter what kind of picture you import, Word treats it as if it were a single character. For this reason, you can copy, cut, and paste graphics within a Word document just as you do any other character. What's more, you can size the ''frame'' in which a graphic is positioned by dragging the black boxes (called handles) on the frame enclosing the graphic. You can even adjust the scale of the graphic after pasting it into Word, enlarging the picture or reducing it to suit your needs.

After you insert a graphic into your document, Word pushes it down if you insert text above it. To control the position of a graphic on the page, therefore, you may want to "anchor" it by making it into a paragraph and using the Position command. For more information on the Position command, see the section titled "Anchoring Text and Graphics on the Page" later in this chapter.

Pasting a Graphic into a Word Document with the Clipboard

Designed for easy interchange of text and graphics among applications, the Macintosh's clipboard can store bit-mapped, object-oriented, or PostScript graphics temporarily while you switch from one program to another. If you have Multi-Finder and at least two megabytes of RAM, you can run Word and your graphics program simultaneously.

To create a graphic and paste it into a Word document via the clipboard, follow these instructions:

1. Create a graphic with your graphics program. Then copy the graphic to the clipboard.

2. Quit the graphics program, or if you have MultiFinder, click the program icon in the upper right corner or select Finder from the Apple menu to return to the Finder.

3. Start Word and open the document where you want to paste the graphic.

4. Position the insertion point where you want the graphic to appear.

5. Choose Paste from the Edit menu.

If you want to paste an entire graphics file into your document, you should know that Word can read SuperPaint files directly.

To import a SuperPaint file into a Word document, follow these steps:

1. Open a new Word document.

2. Choose Open from the File menu.

3. Choose the SuperPaint graphics file and click Open.

After you paste the graphic in your document, Word places the graphics in a graphics frame, a box made of dotted lines. On the frame's bottom and right borders you can see the sizing and scaling handles, small black rectangles. As you learn in the next section, you can use these handles to change the size of the graphics frame or to resize the graphic itself.

Sizing and Scaling a Graphic

Once you have pasted a graphic into a Word document, you can size it or scale it. To size a graphic is to enlarge or reduce the size of the frame in which the graphic is positioned; you don't actually change the size of the graphic image itself. For this reason, you can "crop" a graphic by sizing it, cutting off portions you don't want to print. To scale a graphic, in contrast, is to enlarge or reduce the actual graphic image.

To size or scale a graphic, you drag its handles, the little black boxes that appear on the left side, the bottom, and the lower right corner of the frame when you select the graphic. To view the frame (displayed with dotted lines), choose Show ¶ in the Edit menu. Note that the frame of the graphic doesn't print. If you want to add borders around the frame, select the graphic and use the Paragraph Borders command.

To size a graphic,

1. Select the graphic.

2. Drag one of the handles (the little black boxes) to size the graphic.

Choose the bottom handle to size the frame vertically; choose the right handle to size the frame horizontally. Choose the lower right corner's handle to size the frame vertically and horizontally at the same time.

When you choose the bottom or right handle, Word displays the vertical or horizontal size of the graphic in the status line. When you choose the lower right corner's handle, however, Word displays the scaling factor (100 percent for a full-size frame).

Note: When you change the size of a graphic's frame, the graphic itself stays the same size; only the frame that contains the graphic gets larger or smaller.

To scale a graphic, follow these steps:

1. Select the graphic.

2. Hold down the Shift key and drag one of the handles to scale the graphic.

Choose the bottom handle to scale the graphic vertically; choose the right handle to scale the graphic horizontally. Choose the handle in the lower right corner to scale the graphic vertically and horizontally at the same time.

When you choose the bottom or right handle, Word displays the vertical or horizontal size of the graphic in the status line. When you choose the handle in the lower right corner, Word displays the scaling factor (100 percent for a full-size frame).

Caution: When you scale a bit-mapped graphic, beware of choosing a scale that's out of proportion to the original. If you do, the scaling distortions may produce moire patterns, unwanted geometric lines. To avoid moire patterns, scale the graphic by dragging the lower right handle and choosing a scale of 50 percent or 75 percent.

Using QuickSwitch

With the clipboard, you copy a graphic from SuperPaint, store it temporarily, and paste it into Word. Once you have pasted the graphic into Word, however, you have severed the link between the Word picture and the SuperPaint graphic file from which you copied it. If you have MultiFinder and at least two megabytes of RAM, you can use QuickSwitch to create an active link between a SuperPaint graphics file and a Word picture. Once established, this link lets you update the graphic (paste in a new version, replacing the old one) or edit the graphic (switch to SuperPaint, revise the graphic, and repaste it into your Word document). When you use QuickSwitch, the effect is very much as if Word had been expanded to include sophisticated and flexible graphics capabilities, all of which are accessible with little more effort than it takes to pull down a menu or give a simple keyboard command.

To paste a SuperPaint graphic into Word and create an active link, follow these steps:

1. In SuperPaint, select the graphic (or the portion of the graphic) that you want to paste into your Word document.

2. Choose Copy from the Edit menu.

3. Start Word, or if you are using MultiFinder, switch to Word by clicking the program icon in the upper right corner or choosing Word from the Apple menu.

4. Position the insertion point where you want the graphic to appear.

5. Choose Paste Link from the Edit menu. When Word inserts the graphic, the program also inserts a line of hidden text that identifies the source of the graphic file. Don't erase this line; it will not print. It contains the information Word needs to maintain the active link between the Word picture and the SuperPaint file from which you copied it.

    Note: The SuperPaint document must be saved with a name other than Untitled for a link to be pasted into Word.

To update the Word picture, follow these steps:

1. Edit the graphic in SuperPaint.

2. Switch to Word by clicking the program icon in the upper right corner or choosing Word from the Apple menu.

3. Select the graphic you want to update.

4. Choose Update Link from the Edit menu.

To edit a graphic while using Word, follow these instructions:

1. In Word, select the graphic.

2. Hold down the Shift key and choose Edit Link from the Edit menu. **⌘-comma** Alternatively, press ⌘-comma, the QuickSwitch shortcut.

   Word copies the graphic to your graphics program, where you may revise it as you please.

3. To repaste the graphic into your Word document, display the graphic with your graphics program and press ⌘-comma.

Note: If you move the graphic while you are editing it in your graphics program, it may not paste properly into Word. QuickSwitch remembers a specific space in the graphic document to paste back into the Word document. If you move your graphic to another part of the window, the entire graphic may not paste back into Word.

Reserving a Blank Space with the Insert Graphics Command

Word's capability to import graphics is stunning, but you may very well prefer to create an illustrated document the old way: by leaving blank space for a graphic and pasting it in later. If you do, choose the Insert Graphics command to create a blank frame to hold the space blank.

To insert blank space for a graphic to be pasted in after printing, follow these steps:

1. Choose Insert Graphics from the Document menu.

2. After Word inserts the graphics frame, drag the bottom handle to expand the box vertically.

   Keep your eye on the lower left corner, which displays the current vertical dimension of the frame. When you reach the dimension you want, release the mouse button.

3. Now drag the left handle to expand the box horizontally.

   Keep your eye on the lower left corner, which now displays the current horizontal dimension of the frame. When you reach the dimension you want, release the mouse button.

Anchoring Text and Graphics on the Page

The Position command, new to Version 4, provides a tool of immense value for desktop publishing applications. With Position, you can fix the location of a paragraph (containing text or a graphic) on the page absolutely; no matter how much text you add or delete above it, the text or graphic you have formatted with Position stays put.

What makes Position especially flexible is the fact that you can anchor a paragraph anywhere on the page, regardless of the margins or column layout you have chosen. You can superimpose a graphic on an existing column layout, positioning it in the center of the page (see fig. 14.8), spanning multiple columns (see fig. 14.9), or even outside the text area within the margins (see fig. 14.10).

Fig. 14.8.

Graphic positioned in center of page.

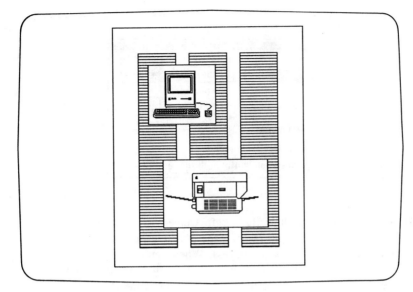

Fig. 14.9.

Graphic spanning multiple columns.

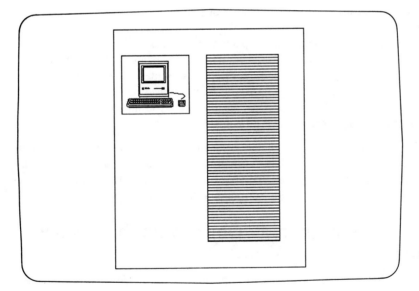

Fig. 14.10.

Graphic positioned outside the text area.

A paragraph of text positioned absolutely or a graphic is called an object. To position the object, you specify its horizontal and vertical position using the Position dialog box in the Format menu (see fig. 14.11):

Fig. 14.11.

The Position dialog box.

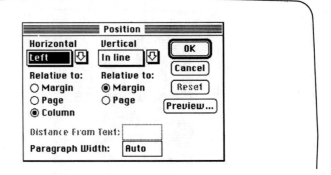

❏ Horizontal positions include flush Left, Center, Right, Inside (close to the binding when you print facing pages), or Outside (away from the binding when you print facing pages). When you choose one of these horizontal positions, you choose whether the object is positioned relative to the margin, the column, or the edge of the page. If you want, you may type a measurement in the Horizontal dropdown box.

❏ Vertical positions include In Line (not fixed), Top, Center, and Bottom. The In Line position is Word's default format for paragraph positioning; this option allows paragraphs to float up or down when you insert or delete text above the object. To anchor a paragraph, you choose the Top, Center, or Bottom options. With these options, you also choose whether the object is to be positioned relative to the margin or the edge of the page. If you want, you may type a measurement in the Vertical dropdown box.

As you can see, the Position dialog box allows a wide variety of positioning options. You can position an object virtually anywhere on the page, as long as the object is within the printing area that your printer allows (most laser printers cannot print within a 0.5-inch frame surrounding the perimeter of the page).

Tutorial: Anchoring an Object with the Position Command

The best way to understand what the Position command does is to experiment with it. The following tutorial walks you through all the basic Position techniques, including using the Position dialog box and repositioning an anchored graphic in the Print Preview mode.

1. Begin with an unwanted document that contains more than one page of text.

2. Choose Section from the Format menu and type *3* in the Number box to create a triple-column format.

3. Import a graphic via the clipboard and paste it at the beginning of your document.

4. Select the graphic and choose Position from the Format menu.

5. Choose Center, Relative to Margins, in the Horizontal dropdown box, and choose Center, Relative to Margins, in the Vertical dropdown box. Then click OK.

6. Choose Page View from the Document mode and view the location of the graphic.

7. Choose Print Preview to see the location of the graphic on the entire page.

8. Exit Print Preview by clicking the Cancel button.

9. Choose Position from the Format menu. This time, choose Top, Relative to Margins, in the Vertical dropdown box and click OK.

10. Preview the new location of the graphic in Page View.

11. Choose Print Preview.

12. Click the margins icon.

13. When you see the graphic surrounded by its boundary lines, move the mouse over the graphic until the pointer becomes a crosshair.

14. Drag the graphic down and right to position it in the lower right corner of the page.

15. Click anywhere outside the page.

16. Click Cancel to return to the document.

Editing or Canceling a Position Format

If you have positioned an object but you're not happy with the results, you can edit the formats you have chosen or cancel the Position formatting altogether. Just position the insertion point within the paragraph you have positioned, and choose the Position command again. To edit the format, make new choices in the Position dialog box. To cancel the Position formatting, click the Reset button.

Caution: Position formatting, like any other paragraph format, may be copied to the next paragraph if you press Return at the end of a paragraph formatted with the Position command. You may not realize that Word has copied the Position formatting, leading to unwanted results. If you choose Show ¶ in the Format menu, the paragraph properties mark provides a clue that you have chosen Position formats. (The paragraph properties mark is a little black box that Word places in the style bar next to any paragraph for which you have chosen formats not visible in Galley view.)

If you see the paragraph properties mark in a paragraph that follows a positioned paragraph, then you would be wise to investigate what's causing it. Position the insertion point in the paragraph, choose the Section command, and investigate the settings in the dialog box. To cancel unwanted Section formatting, click the Reset button.

Positioning Objects on a Specific Page

When you anchor a paragraph with the Position command, you have determined its position on the page, but you haven't determined which page it will print on. If you add additional text, Word may push the object to the next page. It will still print, however, in the position you have chosen relative to the page. If an object prints on the wrong page, just move it, using the Cut and Paste commands as you move any other paragraph, so that the object appears on the correct page.

Caution: After you use the Position command, the paragraphs you see on-screen in Galley view aren't necessarily in the order they will print. If the third paragraph has been formatted with the Position command so that it's anchored at the top of the page, for example, the third paragraph will come before the first two. To see the order of paragraphs as they will print, choose the Page View mode.

Using Positions in Styles

Because the choices you make in the Position dialog box are normal paragraph formats, you can include Position information in styles (see Chapter 7, ''Formatting with Style Sheets''). In figure 14.12, for instance, the document headings have been formatted 1 inch from the edge of the page, setting them off from the 2.5-inch left margins in a pleasing way. If you add the Position formats to the Heading style, all the headings you format with this style take the Position formatting automatically.

More Applications with the Position Command

Because you can use Position to fix text or graphics anywhere on the page, this command is ideal for a variety of desktop publishing applications, such as letterheads, ''drop-cap'' effects using a large capital letter to start a paragraph, and sidebars to highlight important passages of text. Here's a brief overview of the Position formats chosen for the text and graphics shown in the following figures:

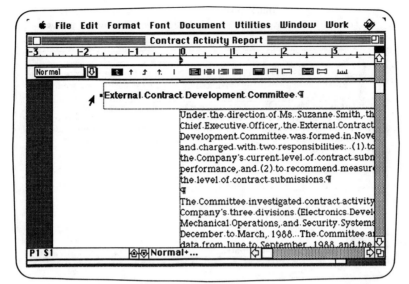

Fig. 14.12.

Heading style formatted with the Position command.

❏ Letterhead (see fig. 14.13). The text and thin rule spanning the page were imported as a graphic and positioned 0.5 inch from the top (Relative to Page) and centered (Relative to Page).

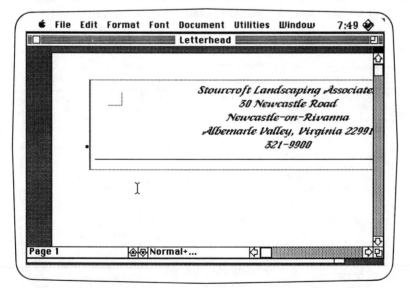

Fig. 14.13.

Letterhead using an imported graphic.

❏ Drop Cap (see fig. 14.14). The 72-point capital letter was created with SuperPaint and imported as a graphic. The graphic was positioned left (Relative to Margin) and top (Relative to Margin), with 0 distance from text.

Fig. 14.14.

Drop cap created in SuperPaint and imported as a graphic.

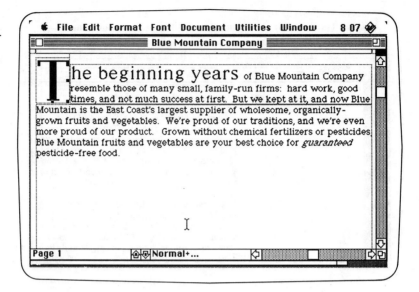

Note: The default distance from text is 0.125 inch, but it's necessary to change this setting to 0 to bring the drop cap closer to its text.

❏ Sidebar (see fig. 14.15). The sidebar text was positioned 6 inches from the top of the page and centered horizontally, with a 3.0-inch paragraph width. The sidebar has thick borders top and bottom.

Fig. 14.15.

A sidebar used in a Word 4 document.

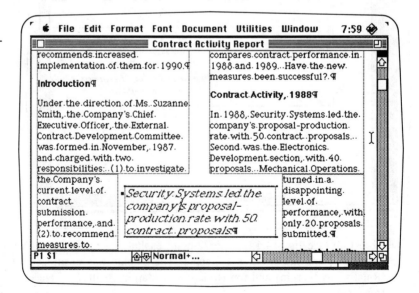

Note: When you position text, Word automatically sets the paragraph width to equal the width of the current column (the column in which the text you're positioning is located). You may need to adjust this width. If the sidebar is too wide, for instance, the text may not be able to "float" around it on either side; if so, narrow the paragraph width.

High-Productivity Techniques To Remember

❏ Multiple columns are section formats. Because you can create unlimited numbers of sections in your documents, you can change column formats as often as you want: you can start a document with a single-column section (in which you position the document's title or a headline), and follow with a two-column section. You can switch later to a three-column section or back to single-column formatting. To change section formats, enter a section break by pressing ⌘-Enter and choosing the Section command.

❏ If Word inserts an unwanted page break at a section break you have entered, place the insertion point after the section break and choose Section. Choose No Break in the Start dropdown box.

❏ To control column breaks, create a section break and place the insertion point below the break. Choose Section from the Format menu, and choose New Column in the Start dropdown box.

❏ To create a newsletter banner, type the banner in a single-column section. Then press ⌘-Enter to create a section break and insert a double- or triple-column format beneath the banner. Be sure to choose No Break in the Start dropdown box when you format the new section with the Section command.

❏ To prevent mismatched column lengths, do not format paragraphs with blank lines before or after, and click Widow Control off in the Document dialog box.

❏ To preview column formatting as you edit, choose Page View.

❏ To create side-by-side paragraphs, choose the Insert Table command and create a table with two or three columns.

❏ After importing a graphic, you can size it or scale it. To size, it, drag the handles. To scale it, press Shift before dragging the handles. When you scale graphics, be sure to choose a scaling ratio that does not introduce distortions into the graphic. Try 50 percent or 75 percent. To check the scaling ratio, watch the status line as you drag the lower right handle.

❏ If you have MultiFinder and at least two megabytes of RAM, use QuickSwitch to create a dynamic link between a SuperPaint graphic file and a picture in a Word document. When you paste a graphic using the Paste Link command, you can update it or edit it quickly; it's almost as if you had added a complete graphics package to Word's menus.

❏ Use the Position command whenever you want to position a paragraph of text or a graphic in an absolute position on the page, such as top left or centered. You specify the horizontal and vertical position relative to the edge of the page or the margins you have chosen.

15

Adding an Index and Table of Contents

Today's businesses must cope with a phenomenal amount of paperwork. The British firm of Marks and Spencer recently estimated that its employees crank out more than 30 million pages of paperwork per year. American firms generate enough paperwork each day to circle the globe many times over. In 1984 alone, more than 14 million filing cabinets were manufactured so that an estimated 200 billion pieces of paper could have some place to go! It's no wonder the paper business is so good these days.

Much of this paperwork involves the production of business reports and proposals. Just to cope with new regulations, the oil company Exxon had to submit a report to the Department of Energy that was just shy of 500,000 pages. To cope with the documentation for just one government contract, RCA's Missile and Surface Radar facility had to produce more than 100,000 pages of technical manuals a year. Obviously, anything an organization can do to cut down the labor involved in producing reports and proposals will pay off handsomely.

For many reasons, Word is handy for anyone faced with the job of creating a report or proposal. Some reasons already covered include Word's wonderful Outline mode, which greatly aids the tasks of planning, organizing, and restructuring complex documents. Covered in this chapter are two features sure to save you much time if your report or proposal must have an accurate index and table of contents.

Word can compile an index and table of contents, insert the correct page numbers, and print both tables for you automatically. What's more, if you make changes to your document, you can reprint these tables, and Word will make all the corrections without any intervention on your part. This feature alone is sure to save you much time as you struggle to meet deadlines.

This chapter will be useful for those whose reports and proposals will be reproduced directly from Word printouts, because the index references and table of

343

contents will refer to the pages Word creates. If you're preparing a document to be typeset, you must prepare the table of contents and index from the page proofs the printer gives you, so Word isn't of much help in such circumstances.

Creating an Index

To create an index with Word, you use the Insert Index Entry command (Document menu) to mark in your document the terms that you want to include in the index. This command inserts the special command .i., which tells Word that the characters that follow should be included in the index. This command also inserts a semicolon, which tells Word that the index entry ends at the semicolon. Both the command and the semicolon are formatted as hidden text, so they will not print (see fig. 15.1).

Fig. 15.1.

Index entry marked with the Insert Index Entry command.

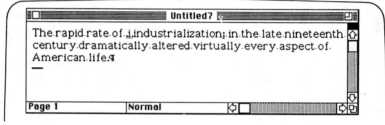

Once you have finished marking all the entries with Insert Index Entry, choose the Index command (Utilities menu) to compile your index. Word compiles the index automatically, adding page numbers, alphabetizing the entries, and creating the index at the end of your document in its own section.

You may wonder why Word's indexing features aren't completely automatic (you must mark the terms to be indexed manually). An automatically generated index that used every word in your document would run many times the length of the document itself. A good index begins with an idea of who the reader will be and what terms the reader is likely to use when searching for information. No computer program yet devised is capable of approaching this level of analytical ability.

Understanding Types of Index Entries

You can create several different kinds of index entries with Word:

❑ A *concordance entry* is a word in your document that you mark for indexing. Word prints the concordance entry and prints it again in the index. Use concordance entries to mark words for indexing that actually appear in your document. In figure 15.1, the word *industrialization* has been marked as a concordance entry.

❑ A *conceptual entry* is a word you embed in the text (formatted as hidden text so that it won't print) and mark for indexing. Word doesn't print the conceptual entry, but it appears in the index. Use conceptual entries when the words in your document aren't quite right for indexing. In figure 15.2, the word *industry* has been formatted as hidden text for indexing as a conceptual entry; the whole word is formatted as hidden text.

❑ A *subentry* is an index word that will be positioned beneath a main entry, as in figure 15.3.

❑ A *page range entry* indexes a subject that is discussed on two or more contiguous pages (see fig. 15.3).

❑ A *major entry* includes a boldface or italic page number, thus indicating to the reader that the topic receives its definitive or most important treatment on the page you have emphasized.

❑ A *text entry* includes text (such as *See industrialization*) instead of a page number.

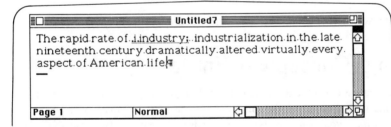

Fig. 15.2.

Hidden text for indexing a conceptual entry.

industrialization
    defined 7
    origins 9
    work roles 12
industry
    Third World 14-19

Fig. 15.3.

Subentries of a main entry.

These options are sufficiently flexible to generate a professional-looking index for virtually any publication project.

Before you begin experimenting with indexing, choose Preferences and click the Show Hidden Text option. You need to see hidden text on the screen so that you can tell whether you have coded the index entries correctly.

Marking Concordance Entries

If you used previous versions of Word, you know that coding each index entry by hand is a tedious job. Version 4 of Word, however, has a menu command called Insert Index Entry (Document menu). This command automatically formats a word or phrase as a concordance entry (an entry that prints in the document as well as appears in the index). The command inserts the index code and the semicolon, and formats both as hidden text.

If you're coding a concordance entry, the easiest technique is to type the word first, and then choose the Insert Index Entry command. If you're coding a conceptual entry, however, the easiest technique is to choose the Insert Index Entry command before you type the word.

To mark a concordance entry you have already typed, follow these steps:

1. Select the text you want entered as a concordance entry.

2. Choose Insert Index Entry from the Document menu.

Marking Conceptual Entries

When you create a conceptual entry, the word or phrase you're indexing does not appear in the text. You place the entry within the text, however, just before the material to which you want to draw the reader's attention. Because the whole entry is formatted as hidden text, the conceptual entry doesn't print in the text itself; it appears in the index only.

The easiest way to create a conceptual entry is to choose the Insert Index Entry command before typing the entry. That way, the entry you type automatically appears as hidden text.

To create a conceptual entry, follow these steps:

1. Position the insertion point where you want to type the entry.

2. Choose Insert Index Entry from the Document menu. Word enters the index code and the semicolon with the insertion point positioned between them.

3. Type the word or phrase you want to appear in the index as a conceptual entry.

Note that the word or phrase is formatted as hidden text. For this reason, it won't appear in your document.

Marking Subentries

Subentries are preferred when an entry would be followed by a long list of page numbers. In such cases, subentries, such as the following, help the reader locate the desired information:

Industrial ventures
    aluminum cookware 60
    graphite processing 32
    luxury goods 59
    matches 38
    textiles 23

Subentries are like conceptual entries in that the whole entry is formatted as hidden text—you don't want the subentry code to appear in your document.

To create subentries, use the following steps:

1. Place the insertion point before the discussion of the topic you want to index.

2. Choose Insert Index Entry from the Document menu.

3. Type the main entry, a colon, and the subentry, as shown in figure 15.4.

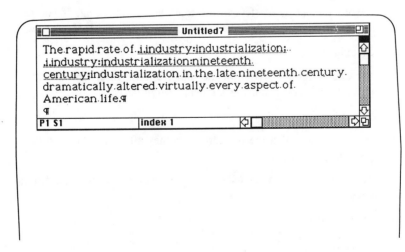

Fig. 15.4.

Subentry formatted as hidden text.

You can create additional levels of subentries, although you shouldn't use more than two levels. To create additional levels, add additional words or phrases after a semicolon.

.i.Main entry:Subentry1;

    Main entry
       Subentry1

.i.Main entry:Subentry1:Subentry2;

    Main entry
       Subentry1
          Subentry2

Marking a Range of Pages

Often, you may want to index a topic that's discussed on more than one page, such as

Industry 19-43

To create an entry that marks a range of pages, follow these steps:

1. At the beginning of the discussion of the topic, choose Insert Index Entry and type an entry using the following coding scheme:

   .i(.subject;

   The only difference between this entry and an ordinary conceptual entry is the beginning parenthesis. Note that the parenthesis comes after the *i*, but before the second period.

   The word *subject* here refers to the topic you're indexing. If you're indexing the topic *industry*, the beginning code would look like this:

   .i(.industry;

2. At the end of the discussion of the topic, choose Insert Index Entry again and type an entry using a closing parenthesis:

   .i).subject;

   Note, once again, that the parenthesis comes after the *i* but before the second period.

3. After Word compiles your index, the page range will be indicated as follows:

   Industry 19-43

Marking a Major Entry

Sometimes you want to guide the reader to the place where a topic receives its definitive or most important treatment. You can create concordance or conceptual entries for which the page number will appear in boldface or italic.

To mark a major entry, place an *i* or a **b** after the *i* in the index code (but before the second period) as shown in table 15.1.

Table 15.1
Formatting Codes for Major Entries

Code	Appearance in Index
.ii.subject;	Subject *7*
.ib.subject;	Subject **7**

Creating Text Entries

You can direct Word to print text after the index entry instead of a page number. You can use this feature to create cross-references (such as *See industrialization*).

To create a text entry:

1. When you come across a term that you want to cross reference, place the insertion point just before the term and choose Insert Index Entry from the Document menu.

2. Type the term using the following coding scheme:

   index entry#(See cross-reference entry)

   A properly coded text entry would look like the following:

   .i.industry#(See industrialization);

Understanding Indexing Techniques

The options for coding index entries are summarized in Table 15.2.

Table 15.2
Summary of Options for Coding Index Entries

Appearance in Index	Coding in Text
Capital investment 11	.i.capital investment;
Capital investment *11*	.ii.capital investment;
Capital investment **12**	.ib.capital investment;
Industry	.i.industry#();
capital goods 60	.i.industry:capital goods;
labor disputes 32	.i.industry:labor disputes;
luxury goods 59	.i.industry:luxury goods;
raw materials 19	.i.industry:raw materials;
Graphite 19-26	.i(.graphite; [text] .i).graphite;
mining 20	.i.graphite:mining;
capital 22	.i.graphite:mining:capital;
Manufacturing See industry	.i.manufacturing#(See industry);

Compiling the Index

When you are certain your document is in its final form and you have marked all the index entries, decide how you want your index to appear. You can choose from the following two formatting options:

❑ Nested subentries appear below the main entry and 0.25 inch to the right. Nested subentries can have distinct character styles.

❑ Run-in subentries continue on the same line and cannot have distinct character styles.

Figure 15.5 illustrates these two indexing styles.

Fig. 15.5.

The Nested and Run-in styles for automatically compiled indexes.

```
                      Untitled7
NESTED.INDEX.STYLE:

industry
    industrialization. 1
       nineteenth.century. 1

RUN-IN.INDEX.STYLE:¶

industry:.industrialization,. 1;.nineteenth.century,. 1

P2 S2              Normal
```

If you're indexing a long document with many index entries, Word may run out of memory before compiling the entire index. If this happens, you can compile the index in sections, beginning with A–L, for example, and continuing with M–Z. When you choose the Index command, click the From button and type the character range you want to index in the From and To boxes. After Word produces the index, choose Index again and repeat the procedure with the second range. If you still run out of memory, use smaller ranges.

To compile your index,

1. Choose Index from the Utilities menu.

2. When the Index dialog box appears, click the Nested or Run-in box (see fig. 15.6). If you are compiling an index for a long document with many entries, click the From button. Type *A* in the From box and *L* in the To box.

3. Click OK.

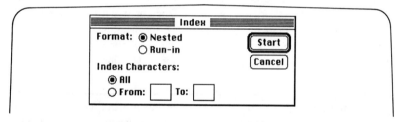

Fig. 15.6.

The Index dialog box.

When the index has been compiled, Word places it at the end of your document, beneath a section break.

If you find that terms are missing from your index or the index contains errors, insert or correct the codes in your document. Then use Index again to recompile the index. On your confirmation, Word deletes the existing index when it compiles the new one.

Don't index your document until you're sure that you have finished editing it. If you compile the index and then make changes, you may forget to update the index. Remember that the indexes Word creates aren't dynamic; they're a one-shot deal. Indexing should be the very last thing you do before printing.

If you do decide to make changes after compiling the index, however, you can always recompile the index. Word (on your confirmation) automatically deletes the previous index, so you cannot confuse the old one and new one. Just don't forget to use the Index command again if you make changes.

Understanding Index Styles

Once you have compiled the index, you will notice that Word has formatted each entry using the index styles in the default style sheet. These styles format the main entry with the normal character and paragraph style. Subentries are indented 0.25 of an inch. You can change these styles if you want. For instance, you can define the Index 1 style to print in boldface Helvetica 12 and have the subentries print in Helvetica 10 italic. To change the index styles, just redefine them as you would redefine any other automatic style. For information on redefining automatic styles, see Chapter 7, "Formatting with Style Sheets."

Creating a Table of Contents

To aid the reader and create a professional appearance, business and professional reports and proposals require a table of contents. Normally, it's a chore to compile such a table. But here's some good news: Word can do the job almost automatically, especially if you have organized your document with outlining, as recommended in Chapter 10, "Organizing Your Document with Outlining." If you haven't outlined your document, you can mark the headings in your document so that Word can compile a table of contents from them. But it's much easier to outline your document than it is to code every heading.

If you want to compile a table of contents, but you haven't outlined your document, it's probably easier to outline the document than to insert table-of-contents codes manually, as described later in this section. For information on outlining a document you have already created, see the "Outlining an Existing Document" section in Chapter 10.

Creating a Table of Contents by Using an Outline

One of the advantages of outlining your documents is that you can compile a table of contents from an outline almost automatically. This procedure is so simple that you can make extensive use of this feature.

To create a table of contents from an outlined document, follow these steps:

1. Choose Outline from the Document menu to switch to the Outline view.

2. Click one of the heading-level numbers on the outline bar to show just the headings you want to print.

3. Choose Table of Contents from the Utilities menu.

4. When the Table of Contents dialog box appears, click the Outline button (see fig. 15.7).

5. Click the Start button.

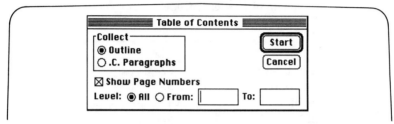

Fig. 15.7.

The Table of Contents dialog box.

Word compiles the table of contents and places it at the beginning of your document in its own, unpaginated section. You can format the table of contents as you please. Add character emphases, indentations, blank lines, and other formats to suit your tastes and style guidelines.

Creating a Table of Contents by Coding Entries

If you haven't outlined your document, you can create a table of contents by marking the headings you want Word to place in the table. But it's much easier to create an outline for your document than to place the codes on each heading manually. For information on outlining a document you have already created, see Chapter 10, "Organizing Your Document with Outlining."

If you're determined to create your table of contents by coding headings manually, however, you will find the instructions in this section.

Marking headings for inclusion in a table of contents is much like creating concordance entries for an index. You must distinguish between three parts of each marked heading, as follows:

❑ *Table of contents code (.c.)*. This code, a lowercase *c* surrounded by periods, must be formatted as hidden text. The code tells Word that the text to follow should be treated as a table of contents entry. The number after the *c* code (see table 15.3) tells Word the level of the heading (you can distinguish up to nine levels). If there is no number, Word assumes that the heading is a first-level heading.

❏ *The heading*. So that the heading will print in your document, the heading should not be formatted as hidden text. If the heading contains a colon, semicolon, or quotation marks, enclose the whole heading with quotation marks formatted as hidden text.

❏ *End mark (;)*. This code, a semicolon formatted as hidden text, tells Word where the table of contents entry stops.

Table 15.3
Table of Contents Codes

Level	Code
First level	.c. or .c1.
Second level	.c2.
Third level	.c3.
Fourth level	.c4.
Fifth level	.c5.
Sixth level	.c6.
Seventh level	.c7.
Eighth level	.c8.
Ninth level	.c9.

To create a table of contents using the manual marking technique, follow these steps:

1. Select the heading you want to appear in the table of contents.

2. Choose Insert Toc Entry from the Utilities menu.

3. After the letter *c* in the table of contents code, type the number of the heading's level. For a second-level heading, for instance, type *.c2*. Table 15.3 lists the heading-level codes.

4. Continue coding the headings as explained in step 3.

5. When you finish coding all the headings, choose Table of Contents from the Utilities menu.

6. When the Table of Contents dialog box appears, click the .C. paragraphs options under Collect.

7. Click Start.

Word compiles the table of contents and places it at the beginning of your document in its own unpaginated section. You can format the table of contents as you please. Add character emphases, indentations, blank lines, and other formats to suit your tastes and style guidelines.

Understanding TOC Styles

Like entries in the indexes Word automatically creates, table of contents entries are formatted by automatic styles in Word's default style sheet, but you can modify these styles. By default, Word formats so that the headings are formatted with the normal character format and a flush-right tab stop (with dot leaders) at 6 inches. Subordinate headings are formatted with additional half-inch indentations. You can reposition the tab stops, redefine the character style, or change the pattern of indentations. For information on redefining automatic styles, see Chapter 7, "Formatting with Style Sheets."

High-Productivity Techniques To Remember

❑ If you're producing reports and proposals that will be reproduced directly from Word printouts, you can save time and money by generating indexes and tables of contents automatically. To generate an index, you must code each term you want the index to contain. If you have outlined your document, Word can compile a table of contents with very little effort on your part.

❑ To create a good index for your document, try to anticipate what your readers will want to look up. Distinguish between concordance entries (words that appear in the text as well as in the index) and conceptual entries (words that don't appear in the text, but do appear in the index). A good index has both concordance and conceptual entries.

❑ Resist the temptation to use too many levels of subentries; use two levels at the most.

❑ To create concordance entries, type the word you want to index, select it, and choose the Insert Index Entry command from the Document menu. To create conceptual entries, choose the Insert Index Entry command first. Then type the term.

❑ If you want, add page range, major entry, and text entries to your index. Use text entries to cross-reference other topics in your index.

❑ If you want to create a table of contents, but you haven't outlined your document, it's easier to add an outline than it is to code the headings manually. See Chapter 10, "Organizing Your Document with Outlining," for information on outlining an existing document.

CHAPTER 16

Creating Form Letters and Mailing Labels

Form letters can be a help or a nusance. Surely at some time, you have received a letter like this one:

Dear Mr. or Ms. **So-and-So**, here's great news for you and the **So-and-So** family. You have definitely won at least one of the following fantastic prizes: a Lincoln Continental Town Car, a six-month trip to the South Seas, $30,000 in cash, or a cheap digital wrist watch. To claim your prize, all you have to do is visit our fine new recreational center, the Happy Acres Landfill and Hazardous Waste Repository, and listen to six hours of grueling cross-examination by our sadistic sales staff!

More than likely, your name is printed slightly out of register, betraying the fact that everyone in your neighborhood is getting the same letter. You have received a personalized form letter—a letter sent to many people, but personalized by a computer so that it appears as if it were sent to only you.

Letters of this sort are irritating, but personalized form letters have many legitimate uses in business. Whenever you find yourself wanting to send the same message to many people but with a personal touch, think of sending a personalized form letter. When you do, bear in mind that Word offers one of the most powerful form-letter features that you will find in any word processing package.

Unfortunately, these features also are among the most challenging Word features to use. It isn't easy to get a form letter application working correctly with Word. To be fair to Microsoft, similar features in other programs aren't noted for their ease of use either; the difficulties come with the territory. But even a novice Word user, given enough guidance, can develop and use a simple form letter application, and that guidance is the aim of this chapter.

This chapter doesn't cover every aspect of Word's powerful form letter capabilities, but it does show you, by means of an extended tutorial, how to create a form letter application successfully. You later can build on this knowledge to take full advantage of all the features. You also learn how you can print mailing labels automatically, using the techniques presented in this chapter.

About Form Letter Applications

A form letter application uses information from a mailing list and, one by one, creates copies of a letter personalized with each person's name, address, city, state, ZIP code, and other information. Such an application requires two Word documents: the data document and the main document.

The *data document* contains the personalized information you want Word to insert automatically into each copy of the letter. Each line contains a *data record*, a unit of information, which contains *data fields*. Each field is a place for a particular kind of information, such as street address, city, state, or last name.

The *main document* contains the text you want to send to everyone—the text of the letter. You write this document just as you would an ordinary Word document, except that you don't fill in the particulars about the person who will receive the letter. Instead, you type the names of the data fields you used in the data document, using special symbols (chevrons), which tell Word that the field name isn't ordinary text.

After you create the data document and the main document, you use the Print Merge command (File menu) to print the main document. Word makes one copy of the main document for each record in the data document. For each copy, when Word encounters a field name, it goes to the data document and retrieves the text you have placed in the data record.

In figure 16.1, for instance, the data document contains three records (for Ed, Mary, and Sue), and each record contains two fields (Name and State). In the main document, there are two field names, Name and State. When you print the main document using Print Merge, you get three letters, one each to Ed, Mary, and Sue.

The basic concept is simple enough, but it's a challenge to get the application to work correctly. So remember, you're not a failure at personal computing if your form letter application doesn't work the first time—or the second or third. Just follow the tutorial carefully and you will be in good shape.

You will use many chevrons in this chapter. You can type them from the keyboard by pressing Option-\ for the left chevron and Shift-Option-\ for the right chevron, but that process can get tedious. Happily, Word's standard glossary contains an entry called Print Merge, which enters the chevrons automatically, and, what's more, it positions the insertion point conveniently between the chevrons so that you can type the field name.

If you're going to work through the material in this chapter, you will want to use this glossary often, so put it in the Work menu. To add the glossary item to the Work menu, press ⌘-Option-Plus (on the keyboard, not the keypad), choose Glossary from the Edit menu, and choose the Print Merge glossary.

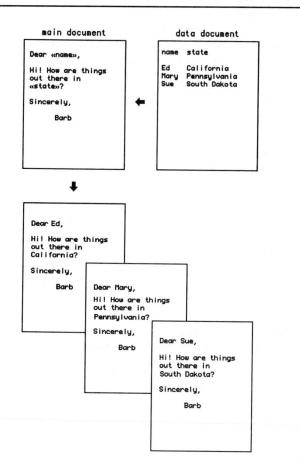

Fig. 16.1.

Examples of simple form letters.

Creating the Data Document

First, you create the data document, which is the Word file that contains the information you want Word to insert into your form letter automatically.

Most experienced Word users would probably agree that the data document is the weakest part of Word's form-letter capabilities. When you use the standard comma-delimited format, it's difficult to enter data in a way that's easy to update or correct.

In the tutorial that follows, however, you will learn how put Word 4's new Table features to work to create an attractive and useful format for data documents. This approach makes it much easier to fix the problems that inevitably arise the first time you run a form letter application. Because you cannot create a table with more than 22 columns, however, you're limited to 22 data fields in your form letter application. However, you will rarely need to use more than 10 or 12 fields.

If you use a table to store the data in your data document, the table must be the first character in the data document—you cannot place anything above it.

1. Choose New from the File menu to open a new file.

2. Choose Page Setup from the File menu.

3. When the Page Setup dialog box appears, click the horizontal orientation icon (the right-hand printer icon under Orientation).

4. Choose Document from the Format menu and type *0.5* in the Left and Right margin boxes.

   Now your document can accommodate a 10-inch line length. You can exceed this length if you want, but if you stay within it, you can print your data document.

5. Choose Insert Table from the Document menu.

6. When the Insert Table dialog box appears, enter *7* in the Number of Columns box and *10* in the Number of Rows box.

   You can always add more columns or rows, so don't worry if you cannot predict exactly how many rows or columns you will need.

7. Click the Format button.

8. Click the Borders button.

9. Click Every Cell in Selection. Then click the thick line option, and click borders on all four sides of the cell boundary diagram.

10. Click OK in the Cell Borders box and click OK in the Cell dialog box.

The data document begins with a *header record*, a special record that lists the field names you plan to use. Without the header record, Word would not know what field names you have chosen for the data you will enter.

11. Create the header record by typing, in the first row of the table, the following headings in each cell:

    Firstname
    Lastname
    Salutation
    Address
    City
    State
    Zip

    Field names can include up to 65 characters, although in practice you will want to keep them shorter. If you use no more than 6 or 8 characters, you can fit more columns on the screen.

    You can define up to 127 fields for each form letter application. If you're using a table to hold your data, however, you cannot exceed the maximum number of columns (22). Don't name a field using any of the words reserved for Print Merge applications, such as IF, NEXT, ELSE, INCLUDE, or DATA.

12. Position the insertion point in the first cell in the first column and hold down the Option key. When you see the down arrow, click to select the column.

13. Click the scale icon on the Ruler until the column boundary markers, which look like uppercase T's, appear. Drag the first column's marker to widen the first column.

14. Adjust the size of other columns to make room for the text you will enter (but don't exceed the 10-inch line length).

    The text you enter in each cell will wrap to the next line if there isn't room, so don't worry about making the cells wide enough for the longest entry. Your table should look like the one shown in figure 16.2.

15. Place the insertion point in the first cell of the second row and begin entering data. Don't leave a blank line below the header record. To move to the next cell after entering the last name, press Tab. (Don't press Return at the end of the line; press Tab to go to the first cell of the next row.) To move back to correct mistakes, press Shift-Tab.

Enter data to fill all the rows you have added (make up the names and addresses). Be sure to fill in every cell.

16. Drag down to select all the last names in the first column, but don't select the first cell in the first row (see fig. 16.3).

17. Choose Sort from the Utilities menu.

Word sorts the data document in alphabetical order by last name. You also can sort the data document by ZIP code by selecting the ZIP code column. (Be careful not to select the cell in the first row, or Word will include it in the sort.)

18. Save your data document.

Fig. 16.2.

Creating the table for the main document.

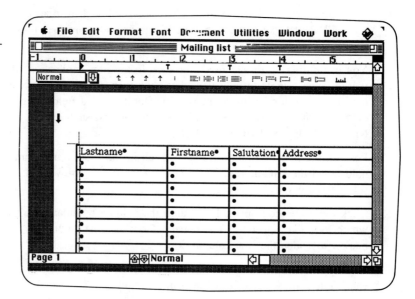

Creating the Main Document

Now you're going to create the main document. This document is like any other letter you write with Word, except that you leave out the specifics (name, address, city, and so on). Instead, you enter field names surrounded by chevrons. To create the main document, follow these steps:

1. Choose New from the File menu to create a new Word document.

2. On the first line, enter a left chevron by pressing Option-\.

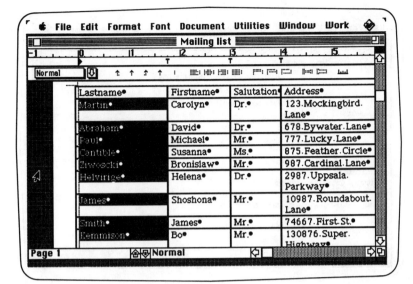

Fig. 16.3.

*Selecting a column
for sorting.*

3. Type *DATA*, press the space bar, and type the name of the data document.

4. Enter a right chevron by pressing Shift-Option-\.

5. Type your return address.

6. Type the correspondent's address using field names as follows:

   «firstname» «lastname»
   «address»
   «city», «state» «zip»

Double-check your spelling. The spelling of the field names you type in the main document must match exactly the spelling of the field names in the header record of the data document.

You don't need to use all the fields you created in your data document, and you can use the same field name twice.

7. Instead of the usual salutation, type

   Dear «salutation» «lastname»:

   Your document should resemble figure 16.4.

8. Type the rest of the text of the letter as shown in figure 16.5

9. Save the main document.

Fig. 16.4.

Creating the main document.

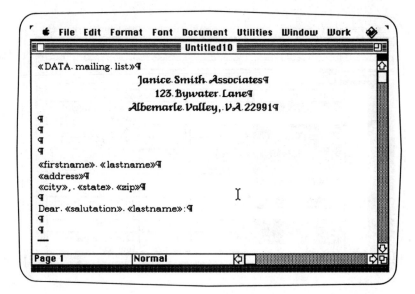

Fig. 16.5.

Finishing the main document.

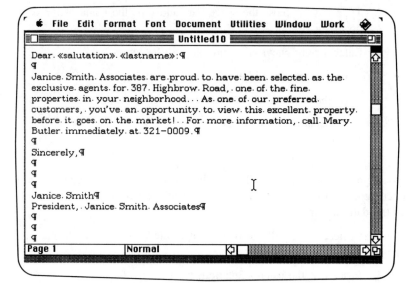

Printing the Form Letters

Next, you are going to print. If something goes wrong the first time, don't worry. In the section that follows, you will find a troubleshooting guide. To print your form letter, follow these steps:

1. Open the main document.

2. Choose Print Merge from the File menu.

3. When the Print Merge dialog box appears (see fig. 16.6), click the Print button to print the letters.

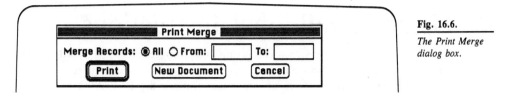

Fig. 16.6.

The Print Merge dialog box.

You can print a selected range of the records in the data document by clicking the From button and typing the row numbers in the From and To boxes. The first data record under the header record is Record 1, and the rest of the records are numbered sequentially.

If you want to see the filled-in letters before printing them, click New Document. Word prints the letters to a new document file, with each letter separated by a page break. You can review the letters and add additional text before printing them.

To cancel printing, press ⌘-period.

Troubleshooting Print Merge Problems

If you create your form letter application with Word's new Table commands, you minimize the number of possible problems. In previous versions, you had to separate the data fields using commas or tabs and, in practice, it was hard to tell whether you had entered all the data. Print Merge won't work correctly unless each data record has exactly the same number of data fields.

Here's an overview of the alert boxes you're likely to see if something goes wrong with your merge application:

❏ Unknown Field Name alert box. A field name in your main document doesn't match the names you have used in your data document. Check both documents to make sure that you have used exactly the same field names.

❏ Letter Printed Without Data. One of the rows in your data document is blank. Select it and choose Table in the Edit menu to delete it.

❑ Data Record Too Long alert box. You're not likely to see this alert box if you create your data document with Word's Table commands. If you delimit your data fields with commas or tabs, however, you're very likely to see it. As it displays the alert box, Word opens the data document and highlights the error.

Using Conditional Instructions

With Word's IF instructions, you can set up your form letter so that Word checks the data record to see whether it meets a criterion you specify. If the record does meet the criterion, Word prints the text that follows the IF instruction. If the record doesn't meet the criterion, Word skips the text. Using this instruction, which is called a conditional instruction, you can tailor your form letters to the special situation of each recipient.

To illustrate how conditional instructions are used, the data document developed in this chapter's tutorial has been expanded with an additional column (see fig. 16.7). This column, with the heading Contacted, contains either a Yes (meaning that the customer has been contacted by sales staff) or a No (meaning that the customer hasn't yet been contacted).

Fig. 16.7.

Additions to the data document.

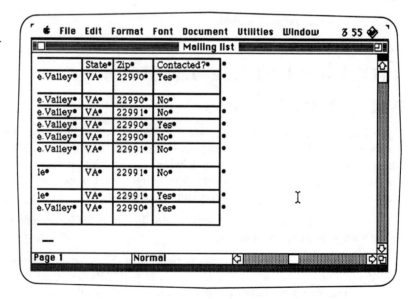

In figure 16.8, note the additions to the main document, which contains the two following IF instructions:

❏ «IF contacted = "Yes"» We would like to thank you for giving us a moment the other day to explain our newsletter about real estate investment opportunities in Albemarle Valley. Please let us know if we can assist you in any way.«ENDIF»

❏ «IF contacted = "No"» In a few days, Charles Smith, your Investment Properties Representative, will contact you with an exciting free offer—a free subscription to our one-of-a-kind newsletter about real estate investment opportunities in Albemarle Valley.«ENDIF»

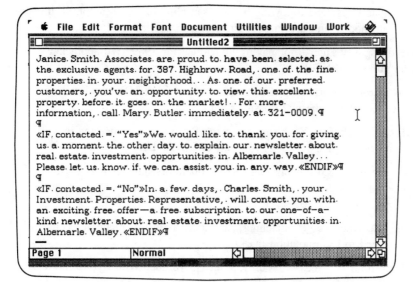

Fig. 16.8.

Additions to the main document.

The text following the first IF instruction prints only if the data record contains Yes in the Contacted column. If the data record contains No in that cell, Word prints the text following the second data record. If the cell is blank, Word doesn't print either of the units of text that follow the IF instructions.

When you use IF instructions, bear in mind the following rules:

❏ Each IF instruction must be followed by an ENDIF. If you forget the ENDIF, you will see an alert box when you choose Print Merge.

❏ The text you want Word to match must be enclosed in quotation marks.

As you develop your Print Merge application, think about what kinds of information you could collect and place in your data document, that would help you take advantage of Word's conditional instruction capabilities. Add new field names and columns to accommodate this information. If you're maintaining a membership mailing list, for example, you want to record whether the members have paid their dues for the current year. If the Duespaid field contains No, you can add an instruction that prints a request for payment in the next mailing.

As you explore conditional instructions, you may want to take advantage of more advanced capabilities. The following list is a sampling of some sample IF instructions you can modify and use in your Print Merge applications:

❏ «IF duespaid» Thanks for paying your dues for 1989. We appreciate your support.«ENDIF»

This instruction prints its text if something is in the Duespaid cell. If the cell is blank, the text doesn't print.

❏ «IF dues > 20.00» Your support at the Patron level is helping us expand our services. Thanks from all of us.«ENDIF»

You can use the following comparison operators: greater than (>), greater than or equal to (=>), less than or equal to (<=), less than (<), and not equal to (<>).

Note that when you're matching a number, as in this example, you don't need to use quotation marks.

❏ «IF overdue = ''Yes''» Your account is overdue. Won't you send a check today?«ELSE»We really appreciate the fine way you have handled your account.«ENDIF»

In this example, Word prints ''Your account is overdue...'' if the Overdue cell contains ''Yes.'' Otherwise, it prints ''We really appreciate....''

You can use the ASK instruction to prompt the user to supply information from the keyboard when a form letter is being printed. For more information on ASK, see Chapter 13, ''Creating Business Forms.''

Printing Mailing Labels

If you have created a mailing list data document like the one discussed in this chapter, you can print mailing labels automatically. All you need is a main document that sets up correctly the label-printing operation.

Most mailing labels for Apple Macintosh printers fall into the following categories:

❑ Continuous labels. These labels, designed for use on ImageWriter printers, come in one-column or three-column formats. The tops of the labels are exactly one inch apart.

❑ Sheet labels. Designed for laser printers, each sheet contains 27 one-inch labels, in 3 columns of 9 labels each.

Printing One-Column Continuous Labels with an ImageWriter

The easiest way to print mailing labels is to choose one-column, continuous feed labels. If you choose three-column labels, you must set up a three-column format, which is a longer (and trickier) process.

To print labels in one column, use the following steps:

1. Open a new Word document. On the first line, type a «DATA» instruction that names the data document you're using.

   If your data document is called Mailing List, for example, you would type

   «DATA Mailing List»

   For instructions on creating a data document, see the ''Creating the Data Document,'' section in this chapter.

   To enter the chevrons, press Option-\ to enter the left chevron and Shift-Option-\ to enter the right chevron. Alternatively, choose the Print Merge entry in the Glossary.

2. On the same line as the DATA instruction, type

   «firstname» «lastname»

   and press Return.

   If you have used different names for the fields, type the field names you have used.

3. Type *«address»* and press Return.

4. Type *«city», «state» «zip»*. Your main document should look like the one in figure 16.9.

«DATA·Mailing·List»«firstname»·«lastname»¶
«address»¶
«city»,·«state»·«zip»¶

5. Choose Preferences from the Edit menu and, when the Preferences dialog box appears, enter the width of your label paper in the Custom Paper Size Width box.

6. Type *1* (the label height in inches) in the Custom Paper Size Height box.

7. Click OK and choose Page Setup from the File menu.

8. Click the Custom Paper Size and No Gaps Between Pages buttons.

9. Click OK and choose Document from the Format menu.

10. Enter *0* in the Top, Bottom, and Right boxes, and enter *0.2* in the Left box.

11. Click OK.

12. Load the continuous label paper so that the top of the first label is even with the print head. (Remember, there's no top margin.)

13. Choose Print Merge from the File menu.

14. Click the From button. Enter *1* in the From box and *1* in the To box.

15. Click Print and inspect the alignment of the first label. If the printing is satisfactory, choose Print Merge again and click the All button. If not, adjust the label paper. Then choose Print Merge and click the From button, and try another test.

Printing Three-Column Continuous Labels with an ImageWriter

Printing three-column labels requires you to create a multiple-column main document. You type in three sets of address fields, one for each column. To print labels in three columns, follow these steps:

1. Open a new Word document. On the first line, type a «DATA» instruction that names the data document you're using. If your data document is called ''Mailing List,'' for instance, you would type

    «DATA Mailing List»

    For instructions on creating a data document, see the ''Creating the Data Document,'' section earlier in this chapter.

    To enter the chevrons, press Option-\ for the left chevron and Shift-Option-\ for the right chevron. Alternatively, choose the Print Merge entry in the Glossary.

2. On the same line as the DATA instruction, type

    «firstname» «lastname»

    and press Return. If you have used different field names for the name fields, type the field names you have used.

3. Type *«address»* and press Return. Type

    «city», «state» «zip»

    and press Return.

4. Press ⌘-Enter to enter a section mark.

5. Below the section mark, type

    «NEXT»«firstname» «lastname»

    all on the same line. Press Return and repeat steps 3 and 4. The NEXT instruction tells Word to print the next data record without starting a new page, which in this case would mean moving down to the next row of labels.

6. Press ⌘-Enter to enter a second section mark, and type another «NEXT» instruction and a third set of field names. Your main document should look like the one in figure 16.10.

7. Select the whole document and choose Section from the Format menu.

8. Enter *3* in the Number box and *0* in the Column Spacing box.

9. Choose New Column in the Start box and click OK.

10. With the whole document still selected, drag the left indent marker right to 1/4 inch. If the ruler isn't displayed, choose Show Ruler from the Format menu or press ⌘-R.

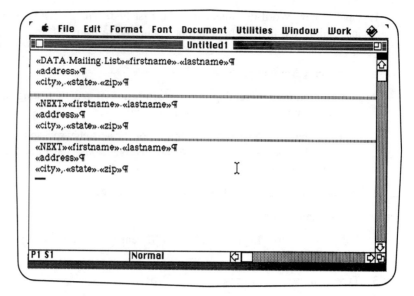

11. Choose Preferences from the Edit menu and, when the Preferences dialog box appears, type the width of your label paper in the Custom Paper Size Width box.

12. Enter *1* (the label height) in the Custom Paper Size Height box.

13. Click OK and choose Page Setup from the File menu.

14. Click the Custom paper size and No gaps between pages buttons.

15. Click OK and choose Document from the Format menu.

16. Enter *0* in the Top, Bottom, and Right boxes, and enter *0.2* in the Left box.

17. Click OK and load the continuous label paper so that the top of the first label is even with the print head (remember, there's no top margin.)

18. Choose Print Merge from the File menu.

19. Click the From button, and enter *1* in the From box and *1* in the To box.

20. Click Print and inspect the alignment of the first label. If the printing is satisfactory, choose Print Merge again and click the All button. If not, adjust the label paper. Then choose Print Merge and click the From button, and try another test.

Printing Laser Labels with the LaserWriter

To print laser label sheets, you must create a main document with the same number of address field sets as there are *printable* labels on the sheet (27), and you must use a multiple-column format so that they will print correctly. Most laser label sheets contain 33 labels (three rows of 11 labels), but the LaserWriter, like other laser printers, cannot print on the first and last half inch of the page. So you can use only 27 of the labels, leaving the top and bottom rows blank.

If you try printing mailing labels using the following instructions, make sure that your data and main documents are formatted with 12-point characters. In this application, line height is critical because you use Return keystrokes to determine the spacing between the labels. With a 12-point font, there are exactly six lines to the inch.

To print laser label sheets with a LaserWriter, follow these steps:

1. On the first line, type the DATA instruction as shown in figure 16.11.

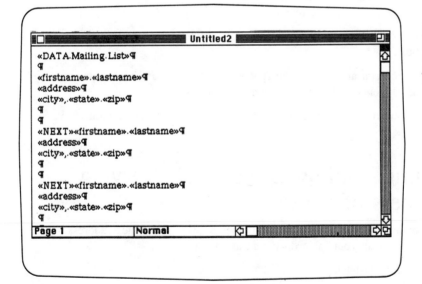

Fig. 16.11.

Starting a main document for printing laser label sheets.

2. Press Return to enter one blank line beneath the DATA instruction.

3. Type the first set of address fields as shown in figure 16.11 and press Return twice.

4. Type *«NEXT»*. The NEXT instruction tells Word to print the next data record without ejecting the page and starting a new one.

5. Type the second set of address fields as shown in figure 16.11 and press Return twice.

6. Repeat steps 4 and 5 until you have typed a total of 27 address fields. Use the Copy and Paste commands to speed the process.

7. Choose Section from the Format menu. Enter *3* in the Number of Columns box and *0* in the Column Spacing box.

8. Click OK and select the entire document by moving the pointer to the selection bar, holding down the ⌘ key, and clicking.

9. Choose Paragraph from the Format menu and enter *12* in the Line box.

10. Click OK and choose Document from the Format menu.

11. Enter *1* in the Top box, *1* in the Bottom box, *0.2* in the Left box, and *0.2* in the Right box.

12. After loading the laser label sheets in your printer, choose Print Merge from the File menu.

13. Click the From button and enter *1* in the From box and *27* in the To box.

14. Click Print and inspect the spacing on the sheet and make spacing adjustments in the main document, if necessary.

15. Choose Print Merge from the File menu, click the All button, and click Print.

Printing Mailing Labels with Varying Numbers of Lines

If your mailing list includes home addresses as well as business addresses, you will have to set up your main document as follows:

«firstname» «lastname»
«company»
«address»
«city», «state» «zip»

The problem is that the home-address labels have only three lines. Because the Company field is blank, the labels print with a blank line between the name and address, like the following:

Sue Smith

123 Mockingbird Lane
Happy Valley, CA 90570

To prevent this problem, you can use an IF instruction in your main document. To use this instruction, your data document must contain two additional fields, Home and Company. In the Home field, type any character (such as X or Yes) to indicate that the address is a home address. In the Company field, type the name of the company or organization.

«firstname» «lastname»«IF company»¶
«company»«ENDIF»
«street»
«city», «state» «zip»
«IF home»
«ENDIF»¶

These instructions print a four-line address if something is entered in the Company field. If nothing is entered in the Company field but there is text in the Home field, Word prints a three-line address with a blank line following.

The insertion of the blank line is very important if you're printing laser label sheets. When printing such sheets, you must use blank lines to separate one set of fields from the next. So it is vital that every address takes up exactly four lines. You use two blank lines to separate one set of address labels from the next set.

High-Productivity Techniques To Remember

❏ If you need to send the same message to many people, but you want to personalize it, use Word's form letter capabilities. To create a form letter application, you need a data document (which contains the mailing list) and a main document (which contains the text you are sending to all the recipients).

❏ If you decide to create a Print Merge application, add the Print Merge glossary to the Work menu.

❏ Unless your data document contains more than 22 fields, which is unlikely, use Word 4's new Table features to store your data. Unlike the former required storage format (comma or tab delimited), tables make it easy to tell whether all records have the same number of fields. When you create your data document with the Table commands, it is easier to update and edit.

❑ When you create your data document, choose the Page Setup options that print horizontally, producing a 10-inch line length (with 1-inch margins). That way you easily can produce a hard copy backup of your mailing list.

❑ Add borders to your table so that you can see each data record and field clearly. Size the columns so that you can keep all the data within the 10-inch line length of the horizontally printed page, if possible. If the data you type will not fit on one line, Word expands the cell.

❑ Keep your field names short so that you can keep your columns narrow. Sort the table to arrange your records in alphabetical or numerical order. To sort by last name, select the last name column and choose Sort from the Utilities menu. To sort by ZIP code, select the ZIP code column and choose Sort.

❑ The main document must begin with a DATA instruction that names the data document. The main document also must contain field names, which tell Word where to print the information found. Be sure that the spelling of the field names you enter matches the spelling you used in your data document.

❑ You can print form letters to a document by clicking the New Document option in the Print Merge application. Choose this option to personalize the form letters or to check the application's performance.

❑ If you run into problems, make sure that you have spelled the field names exactly the same in the data and main documents. Eliminate blank records from the data document. Check to make sure that every data field in the main document is enclosed by opening and closing chevrons. Don't use less-than or greater-than signs in place of chevrons.

❑ Use conditional instructions to personalize your form letter application. You can write conditional instructions that include a passage of text only if the record meets criteria you specify.

❑ Once you have created a data document containing a mailing list, you easily can print mailing labels, especially if you're printing one-column labels on an ImageWriter. If you're printing three-column labels on an ImageWriter or a LaserWriter, you must create a multiple-column main document, and you will probably have to experiment with column and line spacing until you get everything right.

Installing Word 4 and Configuring Your System

Installing Word is an easy process, especially if your system is equipped with a hard disk.

What You Need To Run Word

As Word has increased in size and complexity over the years, it has grown too large to run on the original 128K Macintosh or the 512K "Fat Mac." To run Word 4, you must have an enhanced 512K Macintosh, a Macintosh Plus, a Macintosh SE, or a Macintosh II. You will need a minimum of two 800K drives.

Unlike many Macintosh programs, Word's program disk doesn't include the System file and Finder. To run the program on your Macintosh, you must make sure that your system is equipped with the versions of the System and Finder that Word 4 requires:

❏ *Macintosh 512K (enhanced) and Macintosh Plus*. Word 4 requires System Version 3.2 or later versions, and it also requires Finder 5.3 or later versions.

❏ *Macintosh SE and Macintosh II*. For these models, Word 4 requires System Version 4.1 or later versions, and it also requires Finder 6.0 or later versions.

If you don't have the System and Finder you need, contact your Apple dealer to obtain an update.

The Optimum System for Word

Although you can use Word conveniently on a system with two 800K disk drives and one megabyte of RAM, the program's performance improves significantly when your system includes a hard disk and at least two megabytes of memory. Using a hard disk greatly speeds file retrieval and saving operations. And if you have two megabytes of RAM, you can use Word with MultiFinder, which enables you to move text and graphics among programs much more quickly.

The Knowledge You Need

This book (including this Appendix) assumes that you have a basic familiarity with the Macintosh. Before you begin, you should understand basic Macintosh concepts and fundamental skills. These concepts and skills apply to all or most of the programs you use on your Macintosh, and include the following:

❏ Using the mouse for pointing, clicking, dragging, double-clicking, and Shift-clicking

❏ Initializing new disks

❏ Copying files from one disk to another disk

❏ Starting applications using the Finder

❏ Pulling down menus and choosing commands

❏ Using the Clipboard to copy and move text or graphics

❏ Using dialog boxes, list boxes, check boxes, and buttons

❏ Scrolling, moving, and sizing windows

For more information on these concepts and skills, see the manual that came with your Macintosh.

Installing and Starting Word on a System with Two 800K Drives

When Word was a smaller program, you could create a Word startup disk: a disk that contained the System files as well as the Word program files. Now that Word has grown, however, the best method is to start your system with a startup disk that doesn't contain Word. Use this disk in the internal drive to contain your documents. The Word disk has enough room for the Word program and the Spell dictionary. Place the Word disk in the external drive.

Installing Word on a Two-Drive System

To install Word on a system with two 800K drives, follow these steps:

1. Make backup copies of the three Word disks. Name the backups Word Program Backup, Word Utilities 1 Backup, and Word Utilities 2 Backup.

2. Starting with a blank, initialized disk, create a Working System Disk with the following system documents:

   - ❏ System
   - ❏ Finder
   - ❏ General
   - ❏ Keyboard
   - ❏ Mouse
   - ❏ Startup Device
   - ❏ Clipboard
   - ❏ ImageWriter or LaserWriter printer driver

   You will find these files on your Macintosh system disk.

3. On a blank, initialized disk, copy the Microsoft Word file from the Word Program Backup disk. Label this disk appropriately, for example, the Word Working Disk.

4. Now copy the following files from the Word Utilities 1 Backup disk to the Word Working Disk:

   - ❏ Standard Glossary
   - ❏ MS Dictionary
   - ❏ Word Help
   - ❏ Word Hyphenation

Starting Word on a Two-Drive System

To start Word on a two-drive system, place the Working System Disk in the internal drive, and place the Working Word Disk in the external drive. Then turn on your Macintosh. When the Finder desktop appears, double-click on the Word icon to start Word. Save your documents to the Working System Disk.

Because you must save your work to the Working System Disk, you will find it helpful to conserve disk space on this disk. Erase unwanted files and copy files you are not using to backup disks.

Installing and Starting Word on a Hard Disk System

If you have a hard disk system, you can copy all the Word files so that they are available when you need them. The optimum configuration involves the use of two folders:

❑ *System Folder*. This folder was created when you (or the dealer from whom you bought your Macintosh) set up your hard disk. Place the printer driver you need in this folder.

❑ *Word Folder*. Use this folder for all the Word files you copy from the Word Program disk and Word Utilities 1 disk. When you set up your hard disk this way, you speed Word's operation. The program looks for the files it needs by checking the other files in its folder before searching other files. Therefore, if you create a folder for Word and place all the Word files in it (such as the Hyphenation and MS Dictionary files), Word finds them right away.

To start Word on a hard disk system, open the Word folder and double-click the Word icon. Alternatively, double-click on a Word document.

Installing the WordFinder Thesaurus

Word 4 comes with a free version of an outstanding electronic thesaurus, Word-Finder, which employs a synonym dictionary containing 220,000 synonyms. To use WordFinder, you need two files: the WordFinder desk accessory and the WordFinder Thesaurus. Using Font/DA Mover, an Apple utilities program, you place the WordFinder desk accessory in the System Folder of your startup disk. If you have a hard disk, you can copy the Thesaurus file to your Word folder. If you have a two-drive system, you can insert the Thesaurus disk when it's needed.

To install WordFinder, follow these steps:

1. Make a backup copy of the Word Utilities 2 disk. Put the original away and work only with the backup.

2. If you have a two-drive system, start your Macintosh with the Working System Disk you created when you installed Word 4. If you have a hard disk, start your system as you do normally.

3. Place the Word Utilities 2 Backup disk in the external drive. Double-click on the disk icon to open the disk on the desktop.

4. Double-click the WordFinder DA icon.

   Your Macintosh starts the Font/DA Mover program automatically.

5. When the Font/DA Mover window appears, click the Open button and the Drive button. Choose the System Folder on your Working System Disk.

6. Click the Copy button to copy the WordFinder desk accessory to the System Folder.

7. Choose Quit.

   The WordFinder desk accessory should now be listed in the Apple menu.

8. If you have a hard disk, copy the Thesaurus file to the System Folder.

   If you don't have a hard disk, you will have to swap disks to use the Thesaurus.

Installing the AutoMac III Macro Recorder

AutoMac III, supplied free with Word 4, is an excellent macro-recording program. You can use this program to record a series of commands, as explained in Chapter 9. To install AutoMac III, perform the following steps:

1. Place the Word Utilities 2 disk in the external disk drive. If you have a two-floppy system, place the Working System Disk you created in the internal drive.

2. Copy the AutoMac application to the System Folder.

3. Choose Restart from the Special menu to restart your computer.

The AutoMac RAS icon now appears in the upper-left corner of the menu bar next to the Apple menu. To use AutoMac, you pull down this menu and choose commands.

Word and Your Printer

In previous versions of Word, a special installation process was needed to install Word for your printer. This process is no longer necessary. You install your printer by using the Chooser desk accessory, as explained in your Macintosh manual. Word automatically detects the correct printer information.

If you want to change printers while you're using Word, just choose the Chooser desk accessory and select a different printer driver.

B

Using Word's Mathematical Typesetting Commands

With its capability to integrate text and graphics, Microsoft Word is increasingly favored in engineering and scientific settings. In such settings, however, the Macintosh's built-in facilities for scientific and mathematical symbols come up short. To be sure, you can type simple formulas, such as

$a = b^2 + c^2$

using the normal characters, symbols, and character position commands. To create a more complex formula using square root, summation symbols, and brackets, you can take advantage of Word's mathematical typesetting commands.

These commands depart somewhat from Word's "what you see is what you get" screen philosophy; you create the formula by typing the commands within your text. But you need not wait until your document is printed before you see the results of your work. For instance, you create the following formula:

$a = \sqrt{b^2 + c^2}$

by typing

$a = .\backslash R(b^2 + c^2)$

When you choose Show ¶ from the Edit menu, you see the radical on the screen. To make the entry of such formulas even easier, you can use the Formula Glossary provided on Word Utilities Disk 1. This glossary contains "generic" versions of integrals, radicals, and other commonly used mathematical symbols. You can construct complex formulas quickly just by choosing a glossary entry and modifying it.

Thanks to the interactive, on-screen display of Word's mathematical typesetting commands, they aren't difficult to use. So if your document production tasks involve the inclusion of mathematical formulas in your written work, don't just leave a blank space and draw the symbols by hand; put Word's mathematical typesetting commands to work.

Preparing To Use Word's Mathematical Typesetting Commands

To use Word's mathematical typesetting capabilities, you need to add the Symbols font to your System Folder. Opening the Symbols Glossary, which contains many symbols, including a full set of Greek characters, is also helpful. To facilitate the use of these features, you can use the Symbols configuration file, which places the formula commands you need in the Work menu. The following three sections give step-by-step instructions for these preparatory steps.

Adding the Symbols Font to the System Folder

To add the Symbols font to your System Folder, you use the Font/DA Mover desk accessory. Before you start, copy the Font/DA Mover software to your startup disk.

1. Place in the external drive the Macintosh Utilities Disk that contains the Fonts folder.

   This disk was supplied with your Macintosh. If you don't have a hard disk, place your System Disk in the internal drive.

2. Start the Font/DA Mover desk accessory.

3. Click the Open button to open the Macintosh Utilities disk. When the disk directory appears, click the Fonts document.

4. When the list of fonts appears, highlight the Symbols font.

5. Click Copy.

6. When Font/DA Mover finishes copying the fonts, click Quit.

Note: If you're running Font/DA Mover under MultiFinder, you must restart your Macintosh before the Symbols fonts will appear in Word menus.

Opening the Formula Glossary

Once you have added the Symbols font to your System Folder, you can use the many Greek, mathematical, and technical characters contained in these font files; and you can construct mathematical expressions using the mathematical symbol commands. But using the Formula Glossary, located on Utilities Disk 1, is much easier. In this glossary are ready-made, "generic" versions of several frequently used symbols, such as integrals, arrays, and radicals (see table B.1); Greek symbols (see table B.2); and additional symbols found in the Symbols fonts (see table B.3).

To use the Formula Glossary, follow these steps:

1. Insert Word Utilities Disk 1 into the external drive.

2. Choose Glossary from the Edit menu.

3. While the Glossary dialog box is still on the screen, choose Open from the File menu.

4. Open the Formula Glossary folder and open the Formula Glossary file.

5. Click Cancel to close the Glossary dialog box.

After you open the Formula Glossary, you can choose any of these entries to help you create a mathematical formula. When the glossary entry appears, you will see words in caps such as REPLACE or TOP, indicating where you substitute the constants or variables you are using. Erase the all-caps words and type the constants or variables to create your formula.

If you plan to work with the Formula Glossary frequently, add the formula glossary entries you use most frequently to the Work menu. To add the entries, press ⌘-Option-Plus (on the keyboard, not the keypad), and choose a glossary entry. Repeat this step until you have added the entries you want. To add all the Formula Glossary entries to the Work menu in one command, see the next section.

Power
User
Tip

Table B.1.
Formula Glossary Entries for Mathematical Symbols

Glossary Entry	*Appearance in Document (Hide ¶ Options Selected)*
Abs	|REPLACE|
Array	LIST ARRAY HERE
Backward (moves character back by the number of points you specify)	REPLACE
Box	REPLACE
Brackets — br[br{, br<, br(, paren	[REPLACE]
Forward (Moves character forward by the number of points you specify)	REPLACE
Fraction	TOP BOTTOM
Integral	TOP ∫RIGHT BOTTOM
Lbrace	{REPLACE
Lbracket	[REPLACE
Limit	lim nÆ◆
List	REPLACE,THESE,LIST,ITEMS
Not	REPL̸ACE
Product	TOP ∏RIGHT BOTTOM
Rbrace	REPLACE}
Rbracket	REPLACE]

Sqrt	$\text{OUTSIDE} \sqrt{\text{INSIDE}}$
Stack	TOP BOTTOM
Subscript	REPLACE
Sum	TOP ΣRIGHT BOTTOM
Superscript	REPLACE

Table B.2.
Greek Symbols in the Formula Glossary

Choose This Formula Glossary Entry	To Enter This Greek Symbol
alpha	α
beta	β
chi	χ
delta	δ
!delta	Δ
eta	η
gamma	γ
!gamma	Γ
iota	ι
kappa	κ
lambda	λ
!lambda	Λ
mu	μ
nabla	∇

nu	ν
o	o
omega	ω
!omega	Ω
phi	ϕ
!phi	Φ
pi	π
!pi	Π
psi	ψ
!psi	Ψ
rho	ρ
sigma	σ
!sigma	Σ
tau	τ
theta	θ
!theta	Θ
upsilon	υ
!upsilon	Υ
epsilon	ϵ
varpi	ϖ
varsigma	ς
vartheta	ϑ
xi	ξ
!xi	Ξ
zeta	ζ

Table B.3.
Additional Symbols in the Formula Glossary

Choose This Formula Glossary Entry	To Enter This Symbol
!dagger	‡
!darrow	⇓
!langle	⟪
!larrow	⇐
!lrarrow	⇔
!plus	⊕
!rangle	⟫
!rarrow	⇒
!times	⊗
!uarrow	⇑
!udarrow	⇕
aleph	ℵ
angle	∠
approx	≈
bullet	•
cap	∩
cdot	·
circle	∘
clubsuit	♣
cong	≅
cup	∪
dagger	†
darrow	↓
diamond	◇

diamondsuit	◆
div	÷
emptyset	∅
equiv	≡
exists	∃
f1	f_1
f2	f_2
forall	∀
geq	≥
gg	»
heartsuit	♥
idots	⋯
imag	ℑ
in	∈
infinity	∞
langle	⟨
larrow	←
lb, pound	£
leq	≤
ll	«
lrarrow	↔
mid	∣
neg	¬
ni	∋
noteq	≠
notin	∉

para	¶
parallel	∥
partial	∂
perp	⊥
pm	±
prime	′
propto	∝
rangle	⟩
rarrow	→
real	ℜ
s6	§
sim	∼
simeq	≃
spadesuit	♠
supset	⊃
supseteq	⊇
surd	√
times	×
tm	™
triangle	Δ
uarrow	↑
udarrow	↕
vee	∨
wedge	∧

When you quit Word after opening the Formula Glossary, an alert box appears asking you whether you want to save the glossary. If you don't want to use the Formula Glossary's entries again, click No. If you click the Yes button, you see a Save As box that lets you specify where you want to save the new entries you have added. If you plan to use these symbols frequently, you may want to add them to the Standard Glossary. Use the file selection box to choose the Standard Glossary and click the Save button.

Opening the Formula Settings File

As explained in Chapter 9, "Customizing Word 4's Menus and Keyboard," you can create and save for Word configuration files that include menu and keyboard choices you have made. Several such configuration files are provided on Word Utilities Disk 1, including the Formula Settings file. This file places all the Formula Glossary entries on the Work menu so that you can choose them easily. Otherwise, this configuration file is identical to the default Full Menus configuration.

To use the Formula Settings File, follow these steps:

1. Insert Word Utilities Disk 1 into the external drive.

2. Choose Commands from the Edit menu.

3. Click the Open button in the Command dialog box.

4. Open the Formula Settings file in the Formula Glossary folder.

5. Click Cancel to close the Command dialog box.

The Work menu now contains the Formula Glossary entries, divided into sections. The first section contains "generic" versions of common mathematical symbols, such as integrals and radicals. These symbols are listed in table B.1. The second section contains the Greek characters listed in table B.2. The third section contains the additional characters and symbols listed in table B.3.

Creating Formulas Manually

The easiest way to create mathematical formulas with Word is to build them from the Formula Glossary entries. If you want, however, you can type the commands yourself instead of choosing glossary entries. Table B.4 provides a reference guide to these commands. As you experiment with them, note the following points:

❏ To enter the special formula typesetting command (.\), press ⌘-Option-\.

❏ So that you can see what you're doing, choose Show ¶ from the Edit menu.

❏ When you finish typing the expression, choose Hide ¶ to see how it looks. If you still see the formula typesetting commands (instead of the printed appearance of the formula), you have made a mistake. Double-check your work; you have probably forgotten to include a closing parenthesis.

❏ You can type the formula typesetting commands in uppercase or lowercase.

❏ You can add more than one command option. For example,

.\X.\LE.\RI(Hi!)

prints the following:

|Hi!|

❏ Don't try to edit a formula in the Hide ¶ mode; you can't see what you're doing well enough. To copy, move, or edit a formula, choose Show ¶.

❏ You can nest elements within another, up to a maximum of 40 nested elements. The following expression, for instance,

.\R(.\X.\LE.\RI(Hi!))

produces the following result:

$$\sqrt{|Hi!|}$$

The following example illustrates how these commands can be combined to create a complex formula. The following typesetting commands appear this way in the Hide ¶ mode:

x = \F(.\I.\SU(i=1,n.\S(2),.\R(a)),.\R(b² − c²))

In the Show ¶ mode, they appear as the following formula:

$$x = \frac{\sum\limits_{i=1}^{n^2} \sqrt{a}}{\sqrt{b^2 - c^2}}$$

Table B.4.
Reference Guide to Mathematical Symbol Commands

Command	Explanation
.\A.\AL(list)	Array, align list left
.\A.\AR(list)	Array, align list right
.\A.\AC(list)	Array, align list center
.\A.\COn(list)	Array with list formatted in columns
.\A.\VSn(list)	Array with list formatted with n points spacing between lines
.\A.\HSn(list)	Array with list formatted with n points horizontal spacing between columns
.\B.\LC.\c(argument)	Draws a bracket with the bracketing character c on the left side of the argument
.\B.\RC.\c(argument)	Draws a bracket with the bracketing character c on the right side of the argument
.\B.\BC.\c(argument)	Draws a bracket with the bracketing character c on both sides of the bracket
.\D.\FOn(character)	Displaces character forward n points
.\D.\BAn(character)	Displaces character backward n points
.\D.\LI(character)	Draws a line from the end of the preceding character to the beginning of the next character
.\F(*numerator*, *denominator*)	Fraction
.\I(lowerlimit, upperlimit, integrand)	Integral
.\I.\SU(lowerlimit, upperlimit, integrand)	Capital sigma

Command	Explanation
.\I.\PR(lowerlimit, upperlimit, integrand)	Capital *pi*
.\I.\IN(lowerlimit, upperlimit, integrand)	In-line format with limits displayed to the right of the symbol
.\I.\FC.\c(lowerlimit, upperlimit, integrand)	Uses fixed-height character *c* as the operator
.\I.\VC.\c(lowerlimit, upperlimit, integrand)	Uses fixed-height character *c* as the operator but automatically matches the height of the integrand
.\L(a,b,c)	Lists values within parentheses
.\O(a,b)	Prints character *a* on top of character *b*
.\R(outside, inside)	Creates a radical. If you specify only one argument, Word creates a square root.
.\S	Superscript
.\S.\UP*n* (argument)	Superscripts the argument *n* point above the baseline
.\S.\DO*n*(argument)	Subscripts the argument *n* points below the baseline
.\X(argument)	Draws a box around the argument
.\X.\BO(argument)	Draws a border beneath the argument
.\X.\LE(argument)	Draws a border left of the argument
.\X.\RI(argument)	Draws a border right of the argument
.\X.\TO(argument)	Draws a border above the argument

C

Word 4's Keyboard Shortcuts

T his appendix lists Word 4's default keyboard configuration in two ways: The first list is alphabetized by the command name (such as Bold), while the second is alphabetized by the key you press to use the command (such as ⌘-Shift-B).

Bear in mind that Word's keyboard is fully customizable. You can use the Commands command to reconfigure the keyboard just the way you want. (For more information on customizing the keyboard, see Chapter 9, "Customizing Word 4's Menus and Keyboard.") This appendix lists the key assignments for Word in its default version. If you change the key assignments, Word will create a new keyboard shortcut list for you. Just choose the Commands command from the Edit menu and click the List button. You can print the list after Word compiles it.

Note: If you have an extended keyboard with function keys, you can use the function-key assignments listed in both tables. You can redefine the function-key assignments just as you would redefine any other key.

For some commands, you must press a key on the numeric keypad; you cannot use the corresponding key on the regular keyboard. These letters are preceded by a K. For example, K+ means the + key on the numeric keypad.

Guide to Keyboard Commands (Sorted by Command)

Command	Key
Activate Keyboard Menus	⌘-Tab
Activate Keyboard Menus	K. (keypad period)
Add to Menu	⌘-Option-=
Add to Menu	⌘-Shift-Option-=
Again	⌘-A
All Caps	⌘-Shift-K
All Caps	Shift-F10
Assign to Key	⌘-Option-K+
Assign to Key	⌘-Shift-Option-←
Backspace	Delete
Bold	⌘-Shift-B
Bold	F10
Calculate	⌘-=
Cancel	⌘-. (period)
Centered	⌘-Shift-C
Change Font	⌘-Shift-E
Change Style	⌘-Shift-S
Change	⌘-H
Character...	⌘-D
Character...	F14
Close	⌘-W
Context Sensitive Help	⌘-/
Copy	⌘-C
Copy	F3
Copy as Picture	⌘-Option-D

Command	Key
Copy Formats	⌘-Option-V
Copy Formats	Shift-F4
Copy Text	⌘-Option-C
Copy Text	Shift-F3
Cut	⌘-X
Cut	F2
Define Styles...	⌘-T
Delete Forward	⌘-Option-F
Delete Forward	Del
Delete Next Word	⌘-Option-G
Delete Previous Word	⌘-Option-Delete
Document...	⌘-F14
Dotted Underline	⌘-Shift-\
Dotted Underline	Option-F12
Double Space	⌘-Shift-Y
Double Underline	⌘-Shift-[
Double Underline	Shift-F12
Edit Link (QuickSwitch)	⌘-,
Edit Link (QuickSwitch)	Option-F2
Extend to Character	⌘-Option-H
Extend to Character	K −
Find Again	⌘-Option-A
Find Again	K =
Find Formats	⌘-Option-R
Find...	⌘-F
First Line Indent	⌘-Shift-F

Command	Key
Flush Left	⌘-Shift-L
Flush Right	⌘-Shift-R
Footnote…	⌘-E
Glossary…	⌘-K
Go Back	⌘-Option-Z
Go Back	K0
Go To…	⌘-G
Hanging Indent	⌘-Shift-T
Hidden Text	⌘-Shift-V
Hidden Text	⌘-Shift-X
Hidden Text	Option-F9
Hyphenate…	Shift-F15
Insert Formula	⌘-Option-\
Insert Glossary Text	⌘-Delete
Insert Line Break	Shift-Return
Insert New Paragraph	Return
Insert New Paragraph	Enter
Insert New Section	⌘-Enter
Insert Nonbreaking Hyphen	⌘-'
Insert Nonbreaking Space	Option-space bar
Insert Nonbreaking Space	⌘-space bar
Insert Optional Hyphen	⌘-- (hyphen)
Insert Page Break	Shift-Enter
Insert Tab	Tab
Insert Tab	Option-Tab
Insert ¶ Above Row	⌘-Option-space bar
Italic	⌘-Shift-I
Italic	F11

Command	Key
Justified	⌘-Shift-J
L Thick Paragraph Border	⌘-Option-2
Larger Font Size	⌘-Shift-. (period)
Larger Font Size	⌘-Shift->
Move Keyboard Prefix	⌘-Option-'
Move Text	⌘-Option-X
Move Text	Shift-F2
Move to Bottom of Window	End
Move to End of Document	⌘-K3
Move to End of Document	⌘-End
Move to End of Line	K1
Move to Next Character	→
Move to Next Character	⌘-Option-L
Move to Next Character	K6
Move to Next Line	↓
Move to Next Line	⌘-Option-,
Move to Next Line	K2
Move to Next Page	⌘-page down
Move to Next Paragraph	⌘-↓
Move to Next Paragraph	⌘-Option-B
Move to Next Paragraph	⌘-K2
Move to Next Sentence	⌘-K1
Move to Next Window	⌘-Option-W
Move to Next Word	⌘-→
Move to Next Word	⌘-Option-;
Move to Next Word	⌘-K6
Move to Previous Cell	Shift-Tab

Command	Key
Move to Previous Character	←
Move to Previous Character	⌘-Option-K
Move to Previous Character	K4
Move to Previous Line	↑
Move to Previous Line	⌘-Option-0
Move to Previous Line	K8
Move to Previous Page	⌘-page up
Move to Previous Paragraph	⌘-↑
Move to Previous Paragraph	⌘-Option-Y
Move to Previous Paragraph	⌘-K8
Move to Previous Sentence	⌘-K7
Move to Previous Text Area	⌘-Option-K9
Move to Previous Word	⌘-←
Move to Previous Word	⌘-Option-J
Move to Previous Word	⌘-K4
Move to Start of Document	⌘-K9
Move to Start of Document	⌘-Home
Move to Start of Line	K7
Move to Top of Window	⌘-K5
Move to Top of Window	Home
Nest Paragraph	⌘-Shift-N
New	⌘-N
New	F5
New Window	Shift-F5
New ¶ After Ins. Point	⌘-Option-Return
New ¶ with Same Style	⌘-Return
No Paragraph Border	⌘-Option-1
Normal Paragraph	⌘-Shift-P

Command	Key
Numeric Lock	(Keypad)-Clear
Open Any File...	Shift-F6
Open Footnote Window	⌘-Shift-Option-S
Open Spacing	⌘-Shift-O
Open...	⌘-O
Open...	F6
Outline	⌘-Shift-D
Outline	Shift-F11
Outline Command Prefix	⌘-Option-T
Outlining	⌘-U
Outlining	Shift-F13
Page Setup...	Shift-F8
Page View	⌘-B
Page View	F13
Paragraph...	⌘-M
Paragraph...	Shift-F14
Paste	⌘-V
Paste	F4
Paste Link	Option-F4
Paste Special Character	⌘-Option-Q
Plain For Style	⌘-Shift-space bar
Plain For Style	F9
Plain Text	⌘-Shift-Z
Plain Text	Shift-F9
Print Preview...	⌘-I
Print Preview...	Option-F13
Print...	⌘-P
Print...	F8

Command	Key
Quit	⌘-Q
Remove From Menu	⌘-Option-- (hyphen)
Renumber...	⌘-F15
Repaginate Now	⌘-J
Save	⌘-S
Save	F7
Save As...	Shift-F7
Scroll Line Down	⌘-Option-/
Scroll Line Down	K +
Scroll Line Up	⌘-Option-[
Scroll Line Up	K*
Scroll Screen Down	⌘-Option-. (period)
Scroll Screen Down	K3
Scroll Screen Down	page down
Scroll Screen Up	⌘-Option-P
Scroll Screen Up	K9
Scroll Screen Up	page up
Section...	Option-F14
Select Whole Document	⌘-Option-M
Shadow	⌘-Shift-W
Shadow	Option-F11
Show/Hide Ruler	⌘-R
Show/Hide ¶	⌘-Y
Small Caps	⌘-Shift-H
Small Caps	Option-F10
Smaller Font Size	⌘-Shift-<
Smaller Font Size	⌘-Shift-,
Spelling...	⌘-L

Command	Key
Spelling...	F15
Split Window	⌘-Option-S
Strikethru	⌘-Shift-/
Subscript 2 pt	⌘-Shift-- (hyphen)
Superscript 3 pt	⌘-Shift-=
Symbol Font	⌘-Shift-Q
Underline	⌘-Shift-U
Underline	F12
Undo	⌘-Z
Undo	F1
Unnest Paragraph	⌘-Shift-M
Update Link	Option-F3
Word Count...	Option-F15
Word Underline	⌘-Shift-]
Word Underline	⌘-F12
Zoom Window	⌘-Option-]

Guide to Keyboard Commands (Sorted Alphabetically by Key)

Key	Command
Clear	Cancel
⌘-,	Edit Link (QuickSwitch)
⌘--	Insert Optional Hyphen
⌘-.	Cancel
⌘-/	Context Sensitive Help
⌘-=	Calculate
⌘-'	Insert Nonbreaking Hyphen
⌘-A	Again
⌘-B	Page View
⌘-C	Copy
⌘-D	Character...
⌘-Delete	Insert Glossary Text
⌘-↓	Move to Next Paragraph
⌘-E	Footnote...
⌘-End	Move to End of Document
⌘-Enter	Insert New Section
⌘-F	Find...
⌘-F12	Word Underline
⌘-F14	Document...
⌘-F15	Renumber...
⌘-G	Go To...
⌘-H	Change...
⌘-Home	Move to Start of Document
⌘-I	Print Preview...
⌘-J	Repaginate Now

Key	Command
⌘-K	Glossary…
⌘-L	Spelling…
⌘-←	Move to Previous Word
⌘-M	Paragraph…
⌘-N	New
⌘-O	Open…
⌘-P	Print…
⌘-page down	Move to Next Page
⌘-page up	Move to Previous Page
⌘-Q	Quit
⌘-R	Show/Hide Ruler
⌘-Return	New ¶ with Same Style
⌘-→	Move to Next Word
⌘-S	Save
⌘-space bar	Insert Nonbreaking Space
⌘-T	Define Styles…
⌘-Tab	Activate Keyboard Menus
⌘-U	Outlining
⌘-↑	Move to Previous Paragraph
⌘-V	Paste
⌘-W	Close
⌘-X	Cut
⌘-Y	Show/Hide ¶
⌘-Z	Undo
⌘-K1	Move to Next Sentence
⌘-K2	Move to Next Paragraph
⌘-K3	Move to End of Document
⌘-K4	Move to Previous Word

Key	Command
⌘-K5	Move to Top of Window
⌘-K6	Move to Next Word
⌘-K7	Move to Previous Sentence
⌘-K8	Move to Previous Paragraph
⌘-K9	Move to Start of Document
⌘-Option-'	Move Keyboard Prefix
⌘-Option-,	Move to Next Line
⌘-Option--	Remove From Menu
⌘-Option-.	Scroll Screen Down
⌘-Option-/	Scroll Line Down
⌘-Option-1	No Paragraph Border
⌘-Option-2	L Thick Paragraph Border
⌘-Option-;	Move to Next Word
⌘-Option-=	Add to Menu
⌘-Option-[	Scroll Line Up
⌘-Option-\	Insert Formula
⌘-Option-]	Zoom Window
⌘-Option-A	Find Again
⌘-Option-B	Move to Next Paragraph
⌘-Option-C	Copy Text
⌘-Option-D	Copy as Picture
⌘-Option-Delete	Delete Previous Word
⌘-Option-F	Delete Forward
⌘-Option-G	Delete Next Word
⌘-Option-H	Extend to Character
⌘-Option-J	Move to Previous Word
⌘-Option-K	Move to Previous Character
⌘-Option-L	Move to Next Character

Key	Command
⌘-Option-M	Select Whole Document
⌘-Option-O	Move to Previous Line
⌘-Option-P	Scroll Screen Up
⌘-Option-Q	Paste Special Character
⌘-Option-R	Find Formats
⌘-Option-Return	New ¶ After Ins. Point
⌘-Option-S	Split Window
⌘-Option-space bar	Insert ¶ Above Row
⌘-Option-T	Outline Command Prefix
⌘-Option-V	Copy Formats
⌘-Option-W	Move to Next Window
⌘-Option-X	Move Text
⌘-Option-Y	Move to Previous Paragraph
⌘-Option-Z	Go Back
⌘-Option-K +	Assign to Key
⌘-Shift-,	Smaller Font Size
⌘-Shift- −	Subscript 2 pt
⌘-Shift-.	Larger Font Size
⌘-Shift-/	Strikethru
⌘-Shift-<	Smaller Font Size
⌘-Shift- =	Superscript 3 pt
⌘-Shift->	Larger Font Size
⌘-Shift-[	Double Underline
⌘-Shift-\	Dotted Underline
⌘-Shift-]	Word Underline
⌘-Shift-B	Bold
⌘-Shift-C	Centered
⌘-Shift-D	Outline

Key	*Command*
⌘-Shift-E	Change Font
⌘-Shift-F	First Line Indent
⌘-Shift-H	Small Caps
⌘-Shift-I	Italic
⌘-Shift-J	Justified
⌘-Shift-K	All Caps
⌘-Shift-L	Flush Left
⌘-Shift-M	Unnest Paragraph
⌘-Shift-N	Nest Paragraph
⌘-Shift-O	Open Spacing
⌘-Shift-P	Normal Paragraph
⌘-Shift-Q	Symbol Font
⌘-Shift-R	Flush Right
⌘-Shift-S	Change Style
⌘-Shift-space bar	Plain For Style
⌘-Shift-T	Hanging Indent
⌘-Shift-U	Underline
⌘-Shift-V	Hidden Text
⌘-Shift-W	Shadow
⌘-Shift-X	Hidden Text
⌘-Shift-Y	Double Space
⌘-Shift-Z	Plain Text
⌘-Shift-Option- =	Add to Menu
⌘-Shift-Option-←	Assign to Key
⌘-Shift-Option-S	Open Footnote Window
Del	Delete Forward
Delete	Backspace
↓	Move to Next Line

Key	Command
End	Move to Bottom of Window
Enter	Insert New Paragraph
F1	Undo
F2	Cut
F3	Copy
F4	Paste
F5	New
F6	Open…
F7	Save
F8	Print…
F9	Plain For Style
F10	Bold
F11	Italic
F12	Underline
F13	Page View
F14	Character…
F15	Spelling…
Home	Move to Top of Window
K*	Scroll Line Up
K+	Scroll Line Down
K−	Extend to Character
K.	Activate Keyboard Menus
K0	Go Back
K1	Move to End of Line
K2	Move to Next Line
K3	Scroll Screen Down
K4	Move to Previous Character
K6	Move to Next Character

Key	Command
K7	Move to Start of Line
K8	Move to Previous Line
K9	Scroll Screen Up
K=	Find Again
Clear (Keypad)	Numeric Lock
←	Move to Previous Character
Option-F2	Edit Link (QuickSwitch)
Option-F3	Update Link
Option-F4	Paste Link
Option-F9	Hidden Text
Option-F10	Small Caps
Option-F11	Shadow
Option-F12	Dotted Underline
Option-F13	Print Preview...
Option-F14	Section...
Option-F15	Word Count...
Option-space bar	Insert Nonbreaking Space
Option-Tab	Insert Tab
page down	Scroll Screen Down
page up	Scroll Screen Up
Return	Insert New Paragraph
→	Move to Next Character
Shift-Enter	Insert Page Break
Shift-F2	Move Text
Shift-F3	Copy Text
Shift-F4	Copy Formats
Shift-F5	New Window
Shift-F6	Open Any File...

Key	Command
Shift-F7	Save As…
Shift-F8	Page Setup…
Shift-F9	Plain Text
Shift-F10	All Caps
Shift-F11	Outline
Shift-F12	Double Underline
Shift-F13	Outlining
Shift-F14	Paragraph…
Shift-F15	Hyphenate…
Shift-Return	Insert Line Break
Shift-Tab	Move to Previous Cell
Tab	Insert Tab
Up	Move to Previous Line

Index

G

H

M

Q–R

More Computer Knowledge from Que

SELECT QUE BOOKS TO INCREASE
YOUR PERSONAL COMPUTER PRODUCTIVITY

Using PageMaker: Macintosh Version

by C. J. Weigand

Help your customers use their Macintoshes to become professional publishers with the valuable information presented in Que's *Using PageMaker: Macintosh Version*. Covering both program fundamentals and basic design principles, this informative text presents all the details needed to produce professional-quality douments. Numerous applications and examples are included.

Using Excel

by Mary Campbell

Functioning as both a step-by-step tutorial and a comprehensive reference, *Using Excel* offers a thorough examination of Microsoft's powerful spreadsheet for the Macintosh. This book presents the features of Excel in a logical manner with clear, easy-to-understand examples. You will learn how to navigate through the Excel worksheet, use windows, set up a database, create graphs, and develop timesaving macros. Use Que's *Using Excel* to progress from simple program installation to advanced application design—and become a Macintosh spreadsheet master!

Using HyperCard: From Home to HyperTalk

by W. Tay Vaughan III

Move beyond the Home card to advanced HyperTalk programming with Que's new *Using HyperCard: From Home to HyperTalk*. This comprehensive guide serves as a complete tutorial and lasting reference to all aspects of HyperCard. Using HyperCard introduces you to HyperCard basics, shows you how to create new stacks, teaches you the fundamentals of the HyperTalk programming language, and presents techniques for improving the performance of HyperCard applications. Learn all there is to know about HyperCard with Que's *Using HyperCard*!

Networking Personal Computers, 3rd Edition

by Michael Durr

An excellent overview of local area networks. This well-written book discusses LAN standards, evaluates LAN hardware, covers LAN installation, and gives practical solutions to common LAN problems. This new edition also includes information on networking IBM-compatible PCs with Macintosh machines. Whether your customers are small-business owners, MIS directors, or network managers, this is the book to stock!

ORDER FROM QUE TODAY

Item	Title	Price	Quantity	Extension
949	Using PageMaker: Macintosh Version	$24.95		
198	Using Excel	21.95		
840	Using HyperCard: From Home to HyperTalk	24.95		
955	Networking Personal Computers, 3rd Edition	22.95		

Book Subtotal	
Shipping & Handling ($2.50 per item)	
Indiana Residents Add 5% Sales Tax	
GRAND TOTAL	

Method of Payment

☐ Check   ☐ VISA   ☐ MasterCard   ☐ American Express

Card Number _____ Exp. Date _____

Cardholder's Name _____

Ship to _____

Address _____

City _____ State _____ ZIP _____

If you can't wait, call **1-800-428-5331** and order TODAY.
All prices subject to change without notice.

FOLD HERE

Que Corporation
P.O. Box 90
Carmel, IN 46032

Using Microsoft Works: Macintosh Version, 2nd Edition

by Ronald Mansfield

Updated for Version 2! This practical text covers both basic and advanced features of all four Works' applications: word processing, database, spreadsheet, and communications. Also includes expanded coverage of desktop publishing and a new section on recording and using macros.

Order #1009
$21.95 USA
0-88022-461-4, 500 pp.

Using Dollars and Sense

by John Hannah

Written especially for those of you who use Macintosh and Apple II computers! *Using Dollars and Sense* shows you how to track accounts, determine net worth, and estimate your tax liability. Packed with business application examples, this information-packed resource helps improve your financial management skills.

Order #182
$19.95 USA
0-88022-164-X, 174 pp.

Using FullWrite Professional

by Rebecca Kenyon

Clear, concise guide to the basics of FullWrite Professional's word processing and desktop publishing capabilities. Includes QuickStart tutorials, numerous sample documents, helpful design tips, and a complete command chart for easy reference.

Order #885
$21.95 USA
0-88022-398-7, 566 pp.

Using WordPerfect: Macintosh Version

by Ralph Blodgett

Advance step-by-step from word processing basics to advanced WordPerfect operations with this useful text from Que. This easy-to-use handbook covers customized style sheets and timesaving macros. Also includes Quick Start tutorials for fast, easy start-ups.

Order #833
$19.95 USA
0-88022-342-1, 559 pp.

Excel Tips, Tricks, and Traps

by Ron Person

The power user's guide to Excel! Contains hundreds of time-saving techniques and troubleshooting tips for both the IBM and Macintosh versions of Excel. Teaches you how to manipulate charts, customize fonts, and program high-level macros.

Order #959
$22.95 USA
0-88022-421-5, 500 pp.

Excel QuickStart

Developed by Que Corporation

Teach yourself Excel! Illustrations are the focus of this unique guide to Excel spreadsheets, graphs, and databases. Contains more than 200 pages of graphics to get you up and running fast. Covers both IBM and Macintosh versions of Excel.

Order #957
$19.95 USA
0-88022-423-1, 400 pp.

Using dBASE Mac

by Paul Springer and Ralph DeFranco

An expert look at fundamental dBASE concepts for Macintosh computers! The authors—both involved with Ashton-Tate's development of dBASE Mac—provide detailed insight to the program's operations. The text contains Quick Start lessons and explores several undocumented features of the program.

Order #810
$19.95 USA
0-88022-337-5, 520 pp.

HyperCard QuickStart

by Richard Maran

More than 100 two-page illustrations provide a detailed introduction to the HyperCard environment. Designed for quick reference, Que's award-winning visual approach helps you easily modify HyperCard stacks, enter text, and create graphics. An ideal text for beginning HyperCard users!

Order #841
$21.95 USA
0-88022-350-2, 380 pp.

Free Catalog!

Mail us this registration form today, and we'll send you a free catalog featuring Que's complete line of best-selling books.

Name of Book _____

Name _____

Title _____

Phone (___) _____

Company _____

Address _____

City _____

State _____ ZIP _____

Please check the appropriate answers:

1. Where did you buy your Que book?
   - ☐ Bookstore (name: _____)
   - ☐ Computer store (name: _____)
   - ☐ Catalog (name: _____)
   - ☐ Direct from Que
   - ☐ Other: _____

2. How many computer books do you buy a year?
   - ☐ 1 or less
   - ☐ 2-5
   - ☐ 6-10
   - ☐ More than 10

3. How many Que books do you own?
   - ☐ 1
   - ☐ 2-5
   - ☐ 6-10
   - ☐ More than 10

4. How long have you been using this software?
   - ☐ Less than 6 months
   - ☐ 6 months to 1 year
   - ☐ 1-3 years
   - ☐ More than 3 years

5. What influenced your purchase of this Que book?
   - ☐ Personal recommendation
   - ☐ Advertisement
   - ☐ In-store display
   - ☐ Price
   - ☐ Que catalog
   - ☐ Que mailing
   - ☐ Que's reputation
   - ☐ Other: _____

6. How would you rate the overall content of the book?
   - ☐ Very good
   - ☐ Good
   - ☐ Satisfactory
   - ☐ Poor

7. What do you like *best* about this Que book?
   _____
   _____

8. What do you like *least* about this Que book?
   _____
   _____

9. Did you buy this book with your personal funds?
   - ☐ Yes   ☐ No

10. Please feel free to list any other comments you may have about this Que book.
    _____
    _____
    _____

que

Order Your Que Books Today!

Name _____

Title _____

Company _____

City _____

State _____ ZIP _____

Phone No. (___) _____

Method of Payment:

Check ☐   (Please enclose in envelope.)

Charge My: VISA ☐   MasterCard ☐

American Express ☐

Charge # _____

Expiration Date _____

Order No.	Title	Qty.	Price	Total

You can **FAX** your order to **1-317-573-2583**. Or call **1-800-428-5331, ext. ORDR** to order direct. Please add $2.50 per title for shipping and handling.

Subtotal _____

Shipping & Handling _____

Total _____

que

BUSINESS REPLY MAIL

First Class Permit No. 9918   Indianapolis, IN

Postage will be paid by addressee

que®

11711 N. College
Carmel, IN 46032

BUSINESS REPLY MAIL

First Class Permit No. 9918   Indianapolis, IN

Postage will be paid by addressee

que®

11711 N. College
Carmel, IN 46032